Instructional
STORY
DESIGN

Develop Stories That Train

atd
PRESS

Rance Greene

ATD Press is an internationally renowned source of insightful and practical information on talent development, training, and professional development.

ATD Press
1640 King Street
Alexandria, VA 22314 USA

Ordering information: Books published by ATD Press can be purchased by visiting ATD's website at td.org/books or by calling 800.628.2783 or 703.683.8100.

Library of Congress Control Number: 2020932419

ISBN-10: 1-95049-659-7
ISBN-13: 978-1-95049-659-4
e-ISBN: 978-1-95049-660-0

ATD Press Editorial Staff
Director: Sarah Halgas
Manager: Melissa Jones
Community of Practice Manager, Learning and Development: Eliza Blanchard
Developmental Editor: Jack Harlow
Production Editor: Hannah Sternberg
Text Design: Michelle Jose
Cover Design: Rose Richey

Printed by Data Reproductions Corporation, Auburn Hills, MI

For Sharon and Tia

Contents

Appendices

Foreword

Sandi, a graduate student in Bloomsburg University's well-known Instructional Technology program, burst into her professor's office after her first class. "Dr. Kapp, I am very excited about using technology for learning. I think the latest and greatest technology makes learning stick. What a great time to be in the field."

"Sandi," Dr. Kapp responded, "while our program has the word 'technology' in its title, it's really the underlying instructional design that makes the difference between effective and ineffective instruction, not the technology. It's that difference that makes our students so sought after in the field of L&D."

But Sandi plowed right along, her eagerness reminding him of his own kids. "Virtual reality is just so cool; I want to create an environment where a learner wanders around a warehouse looking for safety violations or a volcano where kids explore the internal workings of the Earth. And augmented reality . . . think of the possibilities."

"Hold on a moment, Sandi, hold on. Why don't you take a seat? I think you and I need to explore what really is the heart of effective instruction. It's not technology." Dr. Kapp paused, trying to slow Sandi down. He appreciated her enthusiasm but wanted to make sure it was focused on the right area. This type of wild enthusiasm is what made his job rewarding and frustrating at the same time.

Sandi caught her breath and sat down in one of the chairs reserved for visiting students. They were not overly comfortable. She placed her backpack on the floor.

Dr. Kapp waited until she got settled. "Sandi, there are lots of methods for delivering instruction but, underneath it all, you need to have effective instructional design. You shouldn't worry about the technology until after you've created the right design for the learning. In fact, one good design method is to use stories."

Sandi shook her head. "Dr. Kapp, no offense, but I've been in undergraduate classes where the instructor tells these long, drawn-out war stories that don't make any sense. I keep wondering, 'What's the point?' I don't think stories are a good way to teach."

"Unfortunately, that's a common occurrence both in academia and in many corporate training sessions, but that's not the fault of the technique; it's the fault of the design of that particular story. The instructor in those cases hasn't used a systematic method to design the proper story. Instead, they winged it."

"Yeah, those stories didn't sound well planned at all. In fact, they were more like jumbled ramblings," Sandi replied, now nodding her head.

"Stories have been used for centuries as tools for passing on knowledge. Think of the parables used in ancient times to teach morals or how parents pass lessons to their kids through stories or organizations pass on their culture through stories. The tradition of sharing knowledge through narrative is as old as humans themselves. Stories and training go hand in hand," Dr. Kapp said, scanning his bookshelf for a certain book.

"Yes, but how do I create a story that has a point, that leads to learning? No offense again, but I don't want to be like those boring trainers or faculty members who tell stories for no apparent reason. I'm determined to do it right."

"While we are all capable of telling stories, where we need help is crafting a story to meet specific instructional goals. This is where the work of my friend and colleague Rance Greene comes into play." Dr. Kapp located the book he was seeking and handed it to Sandi. It was called *Instructional Story Design* by Rance Greene.

"Rance Greene? Does he know storytelling?" Sandi raised an eyebrow as she began thumbing through the book. After a few moments, she was impressed by what she saw.

Dr. Kapp interrupted her thoughts. "He has the perfect background to teach you, and others, about instructional story design. He seamlessly meshes training and storytelling because he has been an actor, choreographer, visual artist, playwright, teacher, and speaker. Plus, because he currently works in learning and development, he knows a great deal about the convergence of learning and storytelling. He's been doing it for years."

Sandi closed the book and looked up at Dr. Kapp. He continued, "Rance has created what is called the Story Design model, which provides a step-by-step process for creating effective instructional stories. It's a wonderful and effective methodology that can help designers of instruction like you create effective, impactful learning through stories."

"Wow, this looks like a great book and that Mr. Greene sounds awesome!" Sandi replied. "He does have a great balance of training knowledge and storytelling chops. Was he really an actor? Was he on *Game of Thrones*?"

"Ah, yes, Mr. Greene was an actor but no, he wasn't on *Game of Thrones*. But more importantly for you, he is a gifted teacher. He's conducted workshops on instructional story design, developed presentations on the topic, incorporated stories into his design of instruction, and was even named by *Training* magazine as an emerging training leader. He definitely has storytelling *and* instructional design chops, as you say. And he's boiled all that knowledge down into this great book."

Enthusiastically, Sandi asks, "Hey, Dr. Kapp, can I borrow this book? I promise to give it back when I'm done."

"Keep it. Just pay it forward."

Sandi doesn't know it yet, but her approach to instructional design is about to become more memorable, actionable, and emotional.

Instructional Story Design can do the same for you. Take the advice, guidance, and information contained in this book and use the Instructional Story Design Plan to create meaningful instruction that resonates with learners and helps change behavior. In short, this book will help you create brilliant instructional stories.

—Karl M. Kapp
Professor of Instructional Technology
Bloomsburg University

INTRODUCTION
Story Design's Story

It was a cold, wet February day. I had been asked to present examples of story-designed learning solutions at a lunch & learn for ATD Dallas, and I wasn't sure how many people would actually show up. But after a few stressful minutes, fellow talent development professionals began to arrive. The room filled to capacity. Their genuine interest in seeing how stories can work for training programs was palpable, filling the room. As I demonstrated each story, the crowd seemed to recognize the teaching opportunities in store for them. As the session concluded, one of them hit me with the question that all of them were thinking: "How do you do that? How do you create stories for talent development?" I didn't have a complete answer for the question, but it stayed with me.

How *do* I write stories that teach? Coming to instructional design from theater made writing stories second nature. I loved playwriting and I loved equipping people with new skills. It was a good match. Designing instruction with stories center stage was intuitive. I hadn't had to think much about my process—until then.

That's where the journey of Story Design began. I'd already read books and articles, attended webinars, and pored over research papers that lauded the power of stories to influence and change behaviors. The psychology, the brain science, the learning theories all aligned: Stories are great for learning! The problem was that almost none of these resources offered practical advice on how to write or produce a story that trains.

The interest in storytelling for instruction that I witnessed that day in February, many years ago, inspired a mission to equip fellow talent developers with a story-building model they could easily translate into practice. It needed to be a methodology in alignment with instructional design. It needed to be simple and flexible to meet any training need. Most of all, instructional designers needed to feel empowered to take a creative leap from a foundation of sound analysis.

With these guideposts in mind, I took a critical look at my own story-making process. Patterns emerged and formed the Story Design model I present in this book. I began sharing the model with others in the field—among my peers, through online webinars, and at learning conferences. I wanted to put the model to the test. Particularly, I wanted to know if others could take the model and use it for their own training, so I developed a live online workshop. The first of such workshops attracted 22 talent development and HR professionals. The outcome was remarkable! Not only were the stories that they created during the workshop sound material for instruction, but most participants went on to apply Story Design to their own training programs. One of these first participants later contacted me with this testimonial: "After taking the Story Design Workshop, it's become second nature to use stories in nearly everything we design." I've now delivered this workshop for several years, and the results continue to prove that Story Design can be mastered . . . and it works!

The success of the workshops convinced me that Story Design is worth sharing. In these pages, you'll encounter the methodology that has worked for many others. You'll learn from stories. You'll watch stories unfold. You'll craft stories of your own. Ultimately, I hope you'll gain a new way of connecting with your learners. Because if you connect with your learners, you can train them to do anything.

Develop Your Storytelling Capability

The goal of this book is to thoroughly equip you to design stories for any training initiative on any timeline. You'll develop an ability to take full advantage of story's power and build training that connects with your audience intellectually and emotionally. Best of all, your training will prepare and motivate your audience for action.

The book is a blend of stories, theory, and practice. Each chapter begins with a narrative that follows Dayna, a young instructional designer who is struggling to meet a challenge posed to her by a stakeholder: Tell a story for training. The second section of each chapter is devoted to learning from the story, with occasional exercises. I encourage you to take these pauses in the reading to reflect on the story and complete the activities, which will prepare you for the third section of each chapter: practice! You'll be introduced to a client for whom you will design a story, applying the principles from that chapter. By the end, you will have a fully written story ready to be produced and delivered.

Chapter 1 outlines the Story Design model and why it's effective. It illustrates how Story Design seamlessly blends with the instructional design process through discovery, design, and delivery, the three phases of Story Design and the three main parts of this book.

In Part 1, discover the story through analysis of who your audience is and what you want them to do. Chapters 2 through 4 will help you successfully engage with stakeholders and subject matter experts to unearth the best story for instruction. You'll spend some time analyzing actual stakeholder conversations. You'll work with a subject matter expert to structure an action list. And you'll learn how to use some tools and templates to master similar conversations in your own work. In my workshops, I've observed that this is the most challenging phase for most participants to complete. But it is vital to master discovery before moving on to design. The foundation you lay here will determine the success of the story you build.

Next, you'll use the information you've gathered in the discovery phase to advance to part 2, where you will develop relatable characters (chapter 5) and strong conflict (chapter 6). These two chapters culminate in a final written story in chapter 7 (Build the Story). Part 2 contains practical guideposts, simple tools, and fun exercises that, with practice, will develop your own storytelling capability. Use these resources as a reference throughout your design career when you feel stuck or need a refresher.

After you've discovered and designed the story, the next logical question is, "How do I deliver this story?" Part 3 answers this question. Chapter 8 walks you through a simple process of storyboarding and some simple ways to present the story using tools that are readily available to you. Chapter 9 offers more complex ways to produce the story with many examples. More story demonstrations, plus editable versions of the tools in the book, can be accessed at needastory.com/book-resources. Once the story is fully produced, it's important to maximize its use for training. Chapter 10 shows you how to do that with a simple, effective method that encourages your learners to self-discover. This method will also open your mind to new ways of engaging your audience that would never have been possible without the story.

The last part of the book is devoted to helping you overcome common barriers to implementing Story Design. Chapter 11 begins part 4 with some inspirational case studies from companies like Southwest Airlines, Pizza Hut, and PepsiCo, who have used stories for training. You'll learn best practices and identify the Story Design principles in each case study. What may be the most inspiring part of this chapter is how different each case study is. You'll see examples of virtual training, in-person training, e-learning, and blended learning for training initiatives from new hire onboarding to leadership development. If you face resistance to stories for training, you must read chapter 12, which provides strategies and research for winning stakeholders over. As we look toward the future of our industry and the digital disruption of business, it's important to remember that stories are still, and will always be, powerful and relevant. Chapter 13 provides best practices for integrating stories into new and current training techniques and technologies. No matter how advanced the technology is, story can make the training experience even more powerful.

Every story for training needs a good designer. That's you. This book is just the beginning. I can't wait to hear how you use it.

CHAPTER ONE

Storytelling at Warp Speed

Easy Assignment

Dayna gets a call from Fayette to meet her in her office. As Dayna enters, Fayette is looking at her phone.

"Hi Fayette." Dayna sits across the desk from her.

"Look at this, Dayna." Fayette holds up her phone to show Dayna a picture of a young woman, a little younger than Dayna, with a cap and robe. Next to her is Fayette. "My baby girl."

"That's right! Her college graduation was this weekend!" Dayna smiles.

"Time goes so fast." She puts her phone down. "How's your day going?"

"Busy." Dayna brushes a piece of hair from her face and straightens her glasses.

"I'll let you get back to work. But I wanted to let you know that I just heard from Susan Chambers, a new director over in compliance. She wants training on privacy, regulations, that sort of thing. I'd like for you to take this one."

Dayna lets out a breath. "I'm already swamped."

Fayette rests her chin on her hands. "When you came on board six months ago, I knew, 'This girl is sharp!'" Dayna smiles and looks down. Fayette continues, "You're doing a great job, Dayna, and I think you can handle this one." Fayette hands Dayna a stack of papers. "Here are the policies Susan wants training on. I know you're juggling a lot of projects right now, but compliance has always made it clear that they just need to check their boxes. It'll be a fairly easy assignment."

Dayna looks at the stack of policies. "Can't we recycle last year's course?"

"Apparently Susan wants a refresh. Don't worry, it's pretty straightforward." Fayette smiles and shrugs. "It's compliance."

Dayna doesn't know it yet, but her entire world of instructional design knowledge is about to be turned upside down. Dayna spent three years out of college teaching in a middle school. She enjoyed lesson planning but felt like she wasn't cut out for the daily disciplining of her students. Her college friend, James, who is supporting his acting career as a corporate trainer, got her interested in talent development. She took a certification course in instructional design and found her calling. Dayna felt lucky to land a corporate instructional design job during the summer, just before the new school year started. She still has much to learn in applying her instructional design education to the fast-paced world of business.

And to make things even more interesting, she's going to come face-to-face with storytelling in training, something she feels very inadequate to do. Her response to the challenge will make all the difference for those required to take the course she designs. It could be a predictable "easy" course, or it could be an action-driven learning experience that resonates emotionally.

What's Your Assignment?

You may not design training for compliance. You may design safety training or leadership development programs or new hire onboarding. No matter what the content is, you care about making people better at what they do. That's why you are in this industry. But often, you are asked to churn out courses at lightning speed to keep up with the pace of business. And you find yourself checking boxes.

Who has time to write a story that makes people stop and think and immerse themselves in learning something new? The creative process can be a long and thoughtful one for those who are sculpting a marble statue or writing a novel. That's not you, though. You're developing talent. But believe it or not, you already have everything you need to start writing the best story for your audience.

We Like Stories

Your training initiatives take many forms—instructor-led, microlearning, gamification, branching scenarios, virtual reality—and underneath all of it is a solid foundation of instructional design. So why do you need stories? There are three great answers to that question.

Stories Are Memorable

When you hear the words, "So, the other day I saw this girl . . . " or "You won't believe what just happened to me!" or "Once upon a time . . .", your mind is programed to listen for a story. It knows the patterns of conflict and resolution. It pictures the characters. It puts you right in the middle of the action, as if it were your own story. You feel what the people in the story feel when they encounter something that makes them frustrated or content. And all of this happens beginning with the very first words of a story. Then, after you've heard the story, you are able to repeat it, recalling details with accuracy. Generations of oral history, teaching, and skill building can be attributed to the tradition of repeating stories.

But there's a tendency to avoid the language of stories when it comes to training. Somewhere along the way, we strayed from the tried and true. We abandoned storytelling as an instructional design skill. One of the repercussions of moving away from stories is that people remember less of what they are trained to do. With the memorable framework of stories and the brain's recognition of story patterns, instructional designers can significantly increase immediate engagement and lasting retention.

In her book, *Design for How People Learn*, Julie Dirksen puts it succinctly: "We like stories. We learn a lot from them. A well-told story can stick with us for years, even if we've only heard it once."

Stories Are Actionable

"A story is powerful because it provides the context missing from abstract prose . . . putting knowledge into a framework that is more lifelike, more true to our day-to-day existence. More like a flight simulator. Being the audience for a story isn't so passive, after all. Inside, we're getting ready to act."

—Chip Heath and Dan Heath, *Made to Stick*

Flight simulation is among one of the most powerful training tools in existence. Simulator training qualifies a pilot to fly a new airplane for the first time on a revenue flight. Undoubtedly, it is the most affordable and effective way to train pilots without having to be in the air. Why does this work? They aren't in a real airplane that's really hurtling towards the earth in an ice storm over the ocean. So, how does sitting in a machine that simulates this situation prepare them for the real deal? The pilot is living out the situation as if it were real. All of the controls that would be in the plane are there, responding to the pilot's actions. If those actions are performed accurately in the correct order, he saves the plane. If they aren't, he crashes.

Stories have a similar effect. Studies of the brain and the body have made the connection between storytelling and the chemical phenomena happening inside of us. One of the most fascinating responses is that of mirror neurons, in which the brain activity of the story-listener begins to align with the story. These neurons fire not only when you perform an action, but when you observe someone else perform it. Fictional things in the story become real in your body. As the plot unfolds, you put yourself in the shoes of the characters, living out their experiences in your mind as if they were your own. Watching the story prepares you to act. Think of the goal of training: to take action on new skills, new knowledge, and new attitudes. Stories are the flight simulator to make this happen.

Stories Are Emotional

The reason stories are memorable and actionable is because they touch our emotions. This is also the at the root of much of the resistance against stories for training. Business stakeholders who shirk at emotional language would rather appeal to the learner's intellect.

Jonathan Haidt wrote a book called *The Happiness Hypothesis*, in which the brain is compared to a rider on an elephant. The rider is rational and the elephant is emotional. Both of them influence behavior. So, when it comes to training, the rider may say, "I really should read this screen of text so I can learn something in this course." But the elephant is saying,

"Are you kidding me? Order pizza!" If you only speak to the intellect and ignore the emotions of a person in training, you are missing an enormous opportunity to fully engage them. But when you speak to the rider and the elephant, you help both of them to stay on course, and they learn together.

Once, I was asked to design a live training experience for a group of employees who were struggling with effective teamwork. The problems this team had included an array of issues like favoritism, gossip, bickering, and withholding information, stemming from a root of misunderstanding. Individuals were becoming entrenched in their cliques. It resulted in low productivity and poor decision making. The department became a hotbed of compliance issues. Appealing to this group's intellect wasn't going to change anything. Instead, I designed a story that formed the centerpiece of the hour-long session. It was developed simply, in PowerPoint with stick figure characters. This story of four coffeeshop employees followed the repercussions of a careless remark and a misunderstanding that resulted in a fallout between the characters. It ended unresolved. But afterward, attendees were asked a series of open-ended questions to identify some solutions for the characters. Then they participated in activities that were designed to flesh out these solutions. Each activity referred back to the story. Because the training was closely tied to the story's emotional attributes, the learning objectives became memorable and actionable.

We know that the training was memorable and actionable because behaviors on the team changed drastically and productivity increased. We found out later that the team had adopted an easy way to remind one another when behaviors started to creep back to the way things had been before. They simply said, "Remember the coffeeshop!" They did not say, "Remember point number five on the list of healthy teamwork behaviors." They didn't need to do that because remembering the story was enough to recall everything they had learned. Why? The story touched them emotionally and made them think. It made their elephant *and* rider happy.

Our Common Language

Your brain is constantly making sense of the world around you, both intellectually and emotionally. It is processing life and forming stories. Think back on your week. How many times did you encounter a story? You read a news article, watched a video, saw a commercial. A co-worker told you about his harrowing commute and the lady who cut him off. Your kids told you about their day. The number of times you encounter stories throughout the week are innumerable.

Now think about the times you've created a story this week. Yes, created one. Perhaps you thought ahead to a difficult conversation you were going to have with someone and rehearsed it in your mind. You just created dialogue. What about the homeless person you saw on the street? You wondered how they got there in life. In a nanosecond, your brain created a mini backstory for that person. You just created a character. Someone you care about was supposed to meet you and they didn't arrive on time. You thought of every possible scenario that could be delaying them, including some far-fetched awful ones. You just created conflict. We are wired to the core for stories! It's our common language.

Stories in Talent Development

Here's what stories in talent development may look like for your learners. Your audience comes into the classroom, joins the virtual session, or opens the e-learning module. They are immediately engaged by a story involving characters they completely relate to. Your audience may laugh at something a character says or furrow their brow as a character takes action that seems inappropriate or out of place. But the entire time they are listening to the story, they are right there with the characters, living out their story vicariously, wading through conflict and thinking of how to solve their problems. Then the story ends. There are conflicts left unresolved. There's a feeling that change needs to take place. Each learner feels an instinctive desire to resolve and repair. They want to know how the story ends.

That's when the instruction takes the learners seamlessly into activities that give them a chance to explore possible solutions or offer their own solutions, followed by feedback that gives them clear guidance. On-the-job resources are available for them to consult as they make choices that advance the instruction and the story. When the training is done, they are still thinking about it, not because of the attractive bullet points but because of the story. And when they go to do their job and encounter a situation where they were trained to perform differently, they remember the story. They remember the consequences of doing things the wrong way. They remember how they felt. And they change.

Wouldn't you like to create an experience like that? There's good news! You aren't starting with a blank canvas. As a talent development professional, you are already collecting the right information. Think of the essentials you need to create training. Once you've determined that training is the best solution, there are two questions you need to answer:

- Who is my audience?
- What do they need to do as a result of training?

The answers to these questions provide the structure of your learning solution. This is also the heart of your story. This is Story Design.

Where Instructional Design and Story Design Meet

Before plunging into the Story Design model that will form the backbone of this book, it's important to emphasize that what you are already doing during the instructional design process directly supports Story Design. Let's continue the comparison between instructional design and Story Design using the ADDIE model as a frame of reference. The instructional design process involves analysis, design, development, implementation, and evaluation (ADDIE). Used iteratively or sequentially, ADDIE is a methodology for creating effective training. There is a mirror process of Story Design that is equally methodical and effective (Figure 1-1).

Figure 1-1. ADDIE Model and Story Design Comparison

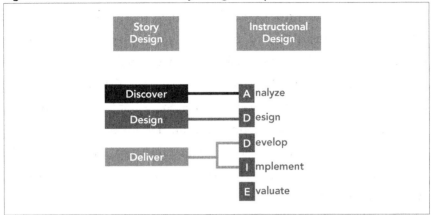

Discover

When a stakeholder comes to you or your team requesting training, you ask them questions to figure out what the root problem is and identify what the business outcome will be as a result of training. If training is the right solution, you interview subject matter experts (SMEs) to flesh out the actions learners need to take in order to meet that business outcome and alleviate the root problem. Every training initiative begins with questions, followed by analysis of the answers. Everything you design and evaluate hinges on proper analysis. You wouldn't think of designing a course if you didn't know who the audience was or what they needed to do.

As you form an audience profile and develop an action list for them, you are discovering material for characters and conflict, the essentials for story-telling and for Story Design. The intelligence you gather that is good for instruction is also good for stories.

Design

Think about how you approach the design of a course. Once you've done the analysis—you know who you are designing this course for and you know what they need to do as a result of training—what is your go-to for starting the design of instruction? Do you start a development list? Do you jump into an authoring tool? Do you storyboard? Do you write a script? Do you spend hours crafting formal learning objectives? Whether your approach to design is strictly academic, somewhat haphazard, or somewhere in between, Story Design asks you to begin your design by thinking immediately about story. In this phase, you design the characters and the conflict based on the information you've collected during the analysis and discovery phase. You write the script and determine how the story will be produced. For training, you will, of course, apply sound instructional design, including definitions, descriptions, examples, demonstrations, and practice as needed, but the story itself will set the stage for even more powerful instruction and open up innovative options for interacting with your audience.

Deliver

You've designed the course and now it's time to develop it. If you're creating training for a live audience, you may start building a slide deck based on the script and a look-and-feel you've designed. If you're developing an e-learning course, you're probably going to use an authoring tool that contains branching capabilities and built-in interactions. But hold on just a moment. You also have a story, and that needs to be developed as well. It needs to be compatible with the development and implementation of instruction. It needs to be integrated in a way that seamlessly leads the learner through the instruction. Stories are powerful no matter how they are delivered to their audience. From simple text to professional videos, a well-crafted story evokes the memorable, actionable, and emotional response you're looking for.

Evaluate

Story Design does not differ from instructional design in the realm of evaluation and, other than this paragraph, evaluating effectiveness won't be addressed in this book for the following reasons: We already know that stories have the impact we need for training. It's an established best practice, as you've read in this chapter. Implement Story Design, and skills, knowledge, and attitudes will be enhanced. Your evaluations will prove it. Business objectives will be met, and root problems conquered.

What this book will tackle is evaluating the design of the story itself. How do you know when you've got a winner? What are the red flags of ineffective stories? There are some key indicators that will help you determine the answers to these questions and ensure that your story has the maximum impact on your audience.

The Story Design Model

This book is structured to help you discover, design, and deliver stories for training, with a closing section on how to overcome common barriers to implementing Story Design. Throughout each of these sections, the Story Design model is fleshed out in detail, giving you practice with each step. To see all the parts in context, let's take a look at the Story Design model, the heart of this book. Appendix 1 contains an at-a-glance version of the Story Design model. (Visit needastory.com\book-resources to download a copy of the Story Design model and many other resources and tools used in this book.)

Figure 1-2. Story Design Model: Story > Action

Connecting Story to Action

Figure 1-2 shows where you stand right now. You know you want to include stories in training to equip and empower your audience to take action. There's a business outcome at stake and there's a root problem getting in the way. You want to fill the gap between telling a story for training that leads to action. Let's fill that gap.

Figure 1-3. Story Design Model: Story > Relatable Character + Strong Conflict > Action

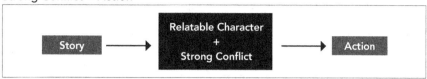

Relatable Characters in Strong Conflict

There are two essential story elements that must be present in order to tell a powerful story for training. You need characters and conflict (Figure 1-3). Not just any characters and not just any conflict. First, you need characters that your audience is going to relate to, connect with, identify with. Think of a course you recently designed. Can you think of a character that the audience of that course could relate to? If you can, you know your audience well. If you struggled to do that, you will need to collect more information on your audience. This book will show you how to do that more effectively.

The second element of the story is strong conflict. The word "strong" is used to indicate that the conflict needs to be intense enough to trigger a significant emotional response. If you think back to stories you've watched or read or listened to, the ones with the strongest conflict rise to the top as the most memorable. Think about lessons you've learned in your personal life. In which of those experiences did everything go right? Most likely, you made some mistakes when you learned those lessons. And mistakes create conflict. But where does conflict come from for stories in training? Take a look at the list of actions you're asking learners to do. Put your relatable characters in strong conflict with those actions and you have a tailormade plot for your audience.

Figure 1-4. Story Design Model: Story > Relatable Character + Strong Conflict = Desire for Resolution > Action

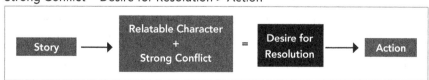

Desire for Resolution

There is a wonderful by-product of combining relatable characters with strong conflict—learners want resolution! Their natural response is to figure out how to fix the problem (Figure 1-4). Whether or not they have a solution, they are hooked. You have their full attention. And that leads to the last piece of the model that completes the gap between story and action.

Figure 1-5. Story Design Model: Story > Relatable Character + Strong Conflict = Desire for Resolution > Training > Action

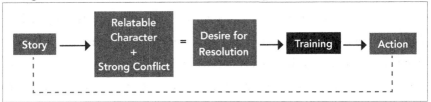

Training

Now that you have their attention and their desire to resolve, train them (Figure 1-5). The story has opened your audience up to receive new ideas, new ways of doing things, and new perspectives. Now share that new knowledge and those new skills and use the power of the story to motivate them to carry it through at work. We will spend a good deal of time in this book exploring how to integrate your story with training after you've gone through the Story Design process.

Storytelling Is a Competency

The Story Design model is simple enough to comprehend quickly because we all speak in stories. Storytelling for training has its specific challenges, but you're starting on the right foot. Like any skill, it requires the kind of in-depth study and practice you will receive in this book. Start applying the methodology for projects at work right away. Immediately, you will begin to see instructional design in a completely different light, using creative venues you've never thought of before. You'll start thinking like an Instructional Story Designer!

Training trends come and go, but storytelling has always been and will always be. Storytelling is a competency. It is foundational to the human experience and, therefore, should be a foundational skill for anyone who trains people. The more solidly you can craft a story, the better equipped you will be to adapt to the high demands placed on talent development in a world and a workforce that is constantly changing. Once you've seen Story Design's power, you'll use it everywhere. Business isn't slowing down any time soon. Don't worry, Story Design can keep up. Master the principles in this book and you'll be storytelling at warp speed.

Dayna's Story, and Yours

You'll continue to follow Dayna's journey at the top of each chapter. You'll learn from Dayna's experiences and have a chance to help her along the way. Starting with chapter 2, you will have the opportunity to put the principles you learn about to work in the closing section. In these practice sections, you are the designer. You'll meet the owner of a chiropractic clinic and use the chapter's tools and resources to discover, design, and develop a story for training his staff. The tools used in the practice sessions are compiled in a comprehensive toolkit in the appendix, including a collection of worksheets that support each stage of the Story Design process (appendix 1), an Instructional Story Design Plan Template (appendix 2), and a completed Instructional Story Design Plan with suggested outcomes for the chiropractic clinic practice sessions (appendix 3). The Instructional Story Design Plan and worksheets are also available as downloadable tools at needastory.com/book-resources; you can also view sample story solutions on the website.

PART I
Discover

Unearth potential stories through analysis of who
your audience is and what you want them to do

CHAPTER TWO

Set the Stage With Stakeholders

The First Conversation

Dayna walks out of Fayette's office with a stack of compliance policies. She skims through and reads them aloud to herself. "Cybersecurity, privacy, conflicts of interest, confidentiality of information, social media, fraud, working with government clients. I'm getting sleepy already." She schedules some time with Susan, the new compliance director, for the next day and spends a couple of hours going through each policy and writing down questions for her.

The next day, she joins Susan in her office. "Thanks for meeting with me, Susan."

Susan smiles. "It's not often someone outside of compliance wants to sit down and chat about policies."

Dayna chuckles, "Yeah, I guess it's not the most exciting topic." She catches herself. "I hope that's not rude . . . "

Now Susan laughs. "Our reputation precedes us! No offense."

Dayna fumbles with the papers in her hand. "Um, I did read through each of the policies."

Susan leans back in her chair. "Any questions?"

Dayna finds her notes. "Yes, I have a few questions. First, what outcome do you expect from this training?" She's prepared for the "check-the-box" answer, but that's not the answer she gets.

Susan doesn't hesitate. "We have a mandate to provide effective training. For what outcome?" Susan pauses. "I'd say . . . to mitigate risk."

Dayna thinks about that. "OK," she says. "Um . . . " Dayna makes a note. "What kind of issues are happening in the workplace that promote risk?"

"Good question," Susan says. "A lot of the issues we're seeing have to do with lack of awareness of the policies themselves. That's why we need training."

"So, you don't think employees know what these policies say?" asks Dayna. Susan is silent. Dayna continues, "What about employees who have been here for five or more years and have taken compliance training every year?"

"OK," Susan says, "I suppose it's not always a lack of awareness. It's . . . hm . . . lack of motivation?"

"Alright." Dayna makes another note. "They may know what to do but they lack motivation to do it. Do you feel that there are some skills that they have not mastered that could be preventing them from performing in accordance with these policies?"

Susan is quick to respond, "Yes, actually, there is a new process for encrypting email that contains sensitive information. Employees have been slow to use it."

Dayna takes a note. "So, would this be a cybersecurity issue?"

"More of a privacy issue," Susan explains. "But we also have a cybersecurity issue. We've seen a spike in cases where employees unknowingly introduce viruses to our network."

Dayna asks, "How does that happen?"

"They receive a phishing email with an attachment or link that contains malware."

Dayna makes a note to ask for examples of phishing emails and clarifies, "So employees are opening those attachments or clicking on the links?"

"Exactly," says Susan.

"Alright, those sound like some specific training needs," says Dayna. "Are there any others?"

"Not that I can think of, but those two are important. If employees could master those two things, we'd see a huge difference in the number of incidents that are taking employees away from their jobs to fix."

Dayna holds up the stack of policies. "This is a lot of policy to cover in one course. Since the privacy and cybersecurity issues rise to the top as concerns, would it be alright to design a series of shorter courses that focus on one or two topics at a time? I think it will increase retention."

"That's a great approach. I want these two issues dealt with first. Then we can move on to the other policies."

"Is there someone in cybersecurity or the privacy office who I can speak with to talk through some of the details? Some of the skills you mentioned don't appear in the policies."

"I'll introduce you to Randall. He's in compliance but communicates frequently with all of our sister departments. He's helped orient me to our procedures and policies this past month. I think he's in a meeting right now. Can you stop by this time tomorrow?" asks Susan.

"That would be great!" Dayna stands up.

"One last thing," Susan says. "I'd like to make this training . . . " She thinks for a second. " . . . engaging. It's important that employees know what to do with all of these policies and regulations, so I want it to be as practical as possible." Dayna had never heard anyone in compliance say anything close to that before.

"OK, and what does *engaging* look like to you?" she asks.

Susan looks up toward the corner of the ceiling. Dayna shifts her weight, waiting. Susan's brow furrows. Then, a small smile. She almost speaks, but instead picks up her pen and scribbles something on a sticky note in front of her and hands it to Dayna.

"That's what engages me."

Dayna looks at the yellow note and reads it out loud. "I love a good story?" It comes out as a question.

"Tell me a story and you've got me!" Susan smiles. Dayna halfway smiles back. She isn't sure what to say to that.

"Thanks for stopping by, Dayna. And let me know if I can clarify anything."

"Sure," she replies. There's a lot she wants to clarify, but before she can think, she's already on the way out the door. "Thank you," she says over her shoulder, "I'll stop by tomorrow." She walks away. There's only one thing on her mind: *I love a good story? What does she think I am, a novelist?*

Your Story on Stage

Let's pretend, for a moment, that the story you are going to design for training will be produced in a theater. Your story for instruction is like the bare stage, begging for scenery, lights, and, of course, action! You will need designers for the set, lights and costumes and skilled carpenters and costume builders. You'll want some backstage hands and a stage manager and operators to run the lights and sound. You'll need a producer to provide some financial backing and box office staff to handle customers on the front end. There are a lot of people involved in making your story come to life.

Since it's your story, you'll want to create a certain mood. You'll want all of the designers to be on the same page, so you'll have to communicate your vision for the story to them. You may want the story to take place in a certain locale and in a certain period of time, which will affect what the actors will wear and how they will talk. You want the story to have a certain pace, so you'll need to help the actors with that and tell them where and when they should enter the stage. The collaborative effort needed to create an experience that the audience will enjoy must be deliberate. Your story will not spring to life without a clear direction at every level of the design and production process. It's the role of the director—you—that influences all the key players to make the biggest impact on your audience. The director is at the heart of the story-making process.

You can imagine how the story might turn out if your set designer built a modern cityscape, the costumes were 18th-century French, and the lighting designer went with a disco theme. It'd be a disaster. But, as the director, you know who your audience is and how to best reach them with the story. As the designer of a learning program or an individual course, you are in a similar position. You're setting the stage for learning. The analysis you're already doing for instruction can work for your story too.

You are central to the process, but that process often begins with a meeting between you and the stakeholders. This is your opportunity to find out what's going on in the stakeholders' minds. Why are they asking for training? What are the expected outcomes? The result of this conversation usually initiates the eventual solution. And depending on how that conversation goes, the solution will make a business impact ... or not. There are some things you can do during this conversation to ensure a successful outcome.

The Stakeholder Conversation

You'll come back to Dayna's concerns about story writing, but first, reflect on Dayna's questions during the stakeholder interview. Dayna did a good job navigating the conversation, but were there some questions she should have asked that she didn't? And what was the purpose of the conversation? What does she know now that she didn't know before she walked into her office?

As you prepare for the stakeholder conversation, there are three questions that must be answered to set the stage for good instruction and a winning story:

1. What is the desired business outcome?
2. What is the root problem?
3. Is training the ideal solution?

Looking at her conversation with Susan, how would you answer these questions? Pause for a moment and look back at the conversation to see if the answers are there.

The Business Outcome

Dayna actually starts the conversation with a direct question regarding the desired business outcome, and Susan gives her an answer: mitigate risk. This is a good place to start. Dayna could ask a few more questions to dig a little deeper to find out how mitigating risk will affect the business. Susan later hints at another business outcome when she says, "If employees could master those two things, we'd see a huge difference in the number of incidents that are taking employees away from their jobs to fix." Ah! A quantifiable outcome. Dayna can help her stakeholder quantify the effectiveness of training or other interventions by comparing the number of incidents before and after training. To show business impact, Susan can take the number of hours it takes to correct incidents and place a monetary value to that number. The two outcomes Dayna can suggest to Susan, that training can help affect are:

- **A privacy outcome**: Reduce the number of unencrypted emails containing sensitive information to outside parties.
- **A cybersecurity outcome**: Reduce the number of incidents in which employees introduce a virus to the company system through a phishing email.

Compliance training is often a mishmash of policies owned by different departments to ensure the company is operating within the law, so there are several business outcomes to identify. Dayna's instinct to limit the course to the highest risk items was a good one. The rest of Dayna's story will focus on training for the privacy and cybersecurity outcomes. Dayna can help stakeholders think through what each business outcome may be. Assuming that most compliance training outcomes have the ultimate goal of reducing risk and, therefore, unnecessary costs, it will help to bring the outcome down to a level that the stakeholder can initially measure. More examples of business outcomes for compliance training may be:

- increase in reports to the hotline
- decrease in workplace accidents
- shortened turnaround time in reporting noncompliance.

This will not only help Dayna determine the success of the training, but it will also help the stakeholder speak to senior leadership in business value terms. The credibility of the stakeholder increases, and the training function of the organization is viewed as a business partner.

The Root Problem

How would you describe the root problem that Dayna's training solution is going to help employees overcome? What obstacle is preventing the desired business outcome? In compliance training, unless there is a new process or a new skill to learn, the answer is rarely a lack of knowledge. Dayna called this out in her conversation, and she's right. Susan suggested that the root problem may be lack of motivation to act on what employees already know how to do. Dayna would be wise to follow up on this information and find out why. She will also need to follow up with the subject matter expert on the new process of encrypting email that contains confidential information.

So far, from the conversation, you could infer that the root problem for each business outcome is:

- **A privacy problem**: Employees lack the knowledge (or motivation) to encrypt email correctly, putting the confidential information at risk.
- **A cybersecurity problem**: Employees lack the skills to detect and mitigate the risk of phishing emails that expose the company to malware and give hackers valuable confidential company information when employees click on links or open attachments.

The two skills Susan mentioned (encrypting email and properly handling phishing emails) seem to be things the employees already know how to do. But some employees aren't doing it. Who are those employees? How many of them are there? Why do they continue to fall short in performing the skills? How long has the new way of encrypting emails been in place? Has everyone been trained on it? Without a clear root cause, it's very difficult to design training that will truly enable and motivate her learners to perform in compliance. The root problem question needs an answer. Assuming that Susan is right—employees are unmotivated to encrypt emails the new way—Dayna will need to find out what is causing this underlying attitude.

One of the most important reasons to pursue an answer to the root problem question is because it will indicate whether or not training is the solution, and what kind of training solution to implement.

The Ideal Solution

Is training the ideal solution to achieve the business outcome and overcome the root problem? To answer this question, think in terms of knowledge, skills, and attitude (KSA).

Imagine the information from stakeholders coming down into a filter that separates those answers into two main categories: training solutions and other solutions. It is in the best interest of the business to make a clear distinction between these categories and tell stakeholders what the ideal solution is. When you know the business outcome and the root problem, the ideal solution is evident. Either the solution is within the scope of training to make a difference through increasing knowledge, training skills, or impacting attitudes; or the solution is outside the scope of training and would best be affected by changing something in the work environment, like processes or systems (Figure 2-1).

Figure 2-1. KSA Filter

Use the KSA Filter in Conversations

Imagine you enter the stakeholder's office. You know you need to walk out of that office with a business outcome and a root problem to determine the ideal solution. If training is the solution, these three factors combine to formulate a clear goal for training. The following series of conversations with stakeholders will give you practice thinking in this way. Conversations are shortened, but each contains what you are looking for. The conversation is followed by possible answers, but take time to see if you can identify them for yourself before reading on.

Customer Service Training

Stakeholder: We need customer service training.

You: Can you give me an example of what's happening that brought this to your attention?

Stakeholder: Well, our customer satisfaction scores are way down.

You: What's one of the stories you've heard that illustrates why customers may be unhappy?

Stakeholder: Mostly that staff is just unfriendly, inattentive.

You: Do *you* feel that the staff is unfriendly and inattentive?

Stakeholder: No, we hire good people. I think they just need better training.

You: That may be a good solution, but before we do that, is there anything else to consider? Are they distracted by anything that could prevent them from giving good customer service?

Stakeholder: With all of the new regulations, my staff has more paperwork than we can handle!

What is the business outcome, root problem, and ideal solution? Based on this limited conversation, you might say:

- **Business outcome**: Increase in customer satisfaction scores.
- **Root problem**: Paperwork is overwhelming staff.
- **Ideal solution**: Increase efficiency of paperwork so staff can focus on customer service; training is not the answer.

When Training Isn't the Solution

In the customer service stakeholder conversation, the problem with customer satisfaction scores has more to do with inefficient paperwork processes than actual customer service knowledge, skills, or attitudes (KSA). This doesn't mean, after further discussion, that KSA issues might not come up. But in this snippet of conversation, it appears that the bigger problem lies outside the realm of training. To truly affect the business outcome, the paperwork efficiency problem should be addressed. Though you may not have influence to implement those changes, you can help the stakeholder see more clearly that throwing training at the problem will not fix it. Plus, you've helped them identify the business outcome and root problem.

Some signs that you are dealing with a work environment problem include staff who cannot perform because of broken systems, inefficient processes, or negative pressures in the workplace. Negative pressures might include unreasonable production expectations, interpersonal conflicts, and stressful changes within the organization. You can consider nontraining solutions such as fixing broken systems, streamlining inefficient processes, and relieving workplace pressures.

It is worth noting that the implementation of work environment fixes may produce a true need for training, such as how to use a new system or process or training on change management or communication skills.

Sales Training

Stakeholder: My associates need sales training.

You: What brought this need to your attention?

Stakeholder: Sales numbers are awful!

You: Help me understand what's behind the numbers. Give me an example of what's driving those numbers down.

Stakeholder: They are constantly caught off guard when customers ask them tough questions.

You: What are the nature of those questions?

Stakeholder: I think they usually have to do with industry trends and how our product can help with things my associates have no idea about.

You: OK, it sounds like they are winging it and not hiding it very well.

Stakeholder: Exactly!

Early in this conversation, the business outcome, root problem, and ideal solution are beginning to show themselves. Do you see them?

- **Business outcome**: Increase sales numbers.
- **Root problem**: Lack of industry knowledge.
- **Ideal solution**: Increase business acumen.
- **Goal of training**: Increase sales numbers by 4 percent by end of Q3 by increasing the business acumen of sales associates to accurately and confidently explain industry trends and product application to clients' needs.

The root problem indicates a knowledge problem. Training can help the sales team increase their business acumen. Here's how:

- **Signs of a knowledge problem**: Simple. Learners don't have the information they need to perform. If they had the knowledge, they would be able to perform successfully.
- **Instructional design for knowledge**: Design problem-solving activities and provide job aids in a form that is easily accessible to the learner.
- **Story Design for knowledge**: Look for case studies. How are things actually playing out at work as a result of lack of knowledge? In your conversation with this stakeholder, you will want to ask for sample discussions sales people have had with clients. Talk with sales reps or their managers. Get the specifics on the flow of the conversation. This will help you instructionally as you pinpoint where the lack of knowledge kills the sale, but it will also help you construct a story that reflects real-world sales experiences that demonstrate common mistakes. Case studies are discussed in detail later.

The Goal of Training

Combining the business outcome, root problem, and ideal solution results in the ultimate goal for training, with some added details by the stakeholder. The goal should be constructed similar to this:

> Eliminate the root problem + to achieve the business outcome + by implementing the training solution.

Notice that the goal for training in the sales scenario indicates a specific percentage of increased sales by a certain time (4 percent by end of Q3). Stakeholders will help determine these details. Notice also that training for lack of knowledge results in specific actions (to accurately and confidently explain industry trends and product application to clients' needs) to achieve the goal of increasing sales. The goal of training serves as a guiding light for both the stakeholder and the instructional designer and should be agreed upon before training is designed. It also brings clear focus to the story and keeps the characters and conflict centered upon the ultimate goal.

The goal itself hints at a story. It provides the relatable characters (sales associates) and the source of conflict (they currently are not confident to explain industry trends and applications of their products to their clients' needs). Solid analysis during the stakeholder conversations will result in powerful, targeted stories.

With what Dayna knows now, an example of the training goals Dayna might construct with Susan could look like this:

- **A privacy office outcome**: Reduce the number of unencrypted emails containing sensitive information to outside parties (root problem) 15 percent by June 15 (business outcome) as employees encrypt email correctly (training solution).
- **A cybersecurity outcome**: Reduce the number of incidents in which employees introduce a virus to the company system through a phishing email (root problem) 30 percent by September 27 (business outcome) as employees detect and mitigate the risk of phishing emails (training solution).

The training solution of encrypting email correctly is specific and observable. The cybersecurity training solution of mitigating risk of phishing emails needs more, but Dayna will uncover more information about what employees need to do during her conversation with Randall. Asking stakeholders to commit to specific outcomes is important to measure the impact of training upon business. It's not always easy to gain that commitment, and sometimes it's impossible. You may be designing compliance training, like Dayna. You've been told that it's required training and that's all you're going to get. Or stakeholders haven't been tracking any numbers and have nothing measurable to compare results to. In such cases, you may be limited to measuring knowledge, skills, and attitude, but at the very least, your training goal must identify who your audience is and what they need to do as a result of training. You must push stakeholders and subject matter experts beyond awareness and give employees concrete steps to take.

New Hire Onboarding

Stakeholder: I need a better new-hire onboarding program.

You: What's wrong with your current onboarding program?

Stakeholder: It doesn't seem to resonate with employees. We lose a lot of them after the first three months!

You: What insights have you received from employees during exit interviews?

Stakeholder: Not much. Some of them complain about too much work.

You: Can we take a look at the exit interview reports?

Stakeholder: Sure.

Report: "I feel like a number." "Management is not responsive to employee needs. I waited three weeks for system access and my manager never helped me." "I work really hard, but my work is not appreciated."

You: It looks like the reason why many of these employees are leaving has more to do with management. What is your turnover rate?

Stakeholder: Thirty-one percent.

You: What kind of training do your managers receive?

Stakeholder: They learn on the job.

The stakeholder, in this conversation, comes with a solution, but after investigation, the root problem suggests a different one. What is the business outcome and root problem?

- **Business outcome**: Decrease turnover.
- **Root problem**: Management struggles to build effective teams.
- **Ideal solution**: Develop managers' team building skills.
- **Goal of training**: Decrease turnover 9 percent by Q2 as managers build more effective teams. (This is a good start. Training managers to build effective teams is complex, so you will likely create some sub-goals to this larger one.)

Here's how training can solve a skills problem:

- **Signs of a skills problem**: Is it reasonable to think that the learner can be proficient without practice? If not, you're dealing with a skill. In this case, there could be some environmental factors that prevent managers from spending as much time as they'd like with their teams, but assuming the evidence is consistent and that no manager training is offered, it's reasonable to assume a skills need.
- **Instructional design for skills**: Practice! Simulate the actual work environment and give learners hands-on practice with the skills. Think of the flight simulator. Use role play in live settings and scenario-based training for e-learning. Games are great for skill building too.
- **Story Design for skills**: The importance of designing stories that are concretely connected to the actions that learners need to take is paramount in skill-building. Stories are the core of scenario-based training and often of games. Mastering the principles of Story Design will also increase the effectiveness of these and other forms of instruction that are particularly useful in building skills. You'll learn more about how to strengthen scenarios and games with stories in chapter 13.

Systems Training

Stakeholder: My staff needs more training on our new data entry processes.

You: What brought this need to your attention?

Stakeholder: Reporting. My staff is supposed to enter data in a certain way. Reporting is messed up, so they can't be entering the data correctly.

You: It sounds like you have trained them on the new data entry process before. Is that right?

Stakeholder: Of course!

You: Is it a difficult process?

Stakeholder: Not really. They're just not willing to make the change! If you ask me, they're just being stubborn.

You: Did you tell them that the data would be used to create reports?

Stakeholder: No, they're not involved with reporting. They just need to enter the data correctly!

It sounds like the stakeholder is a bit exasperated in this conversation, for good reason. Systems training has been provided and still things aren't working as they should be. After some questioning of supervisors in the area, you confirm that everyone on the team has the knowledge and skills to enter data the new way. So what gives? Are they really being stubborn? Maybe. Read the conversation again and see if you spot the business outcome and root problem. Also see if you can determine the ideal solution.

- **Business outcome**: Increase accuracy of reporting.
- **Root problem**: Staff doesn't realize the impact of the new data entry process.
- **Ideas solution**: Give staff the full picture from data entry to reporting as part of the training.

- **Goal of training**: Increase the accuracy of reporting 50 percent by end of the month as data entry team enters data correctly using the new process. (Notice, the goal still focuses on what employees will do. You will still give employees the full picture, but it's the entering of data correctly that will fix the reporting problem.)

Keep the following in mind when designing a solution for attitude:

- **Signs of an attitude problem**: Remember, attitude refers to how important learners feel it is to change the way they do something. You caught that, right? The way they *feel* affects performance. Are learners asking, "Why are we doing this?" or "What's in this for me?" Are learners unaware of the entire process? It could be that this team took the systems training as a suggestion, not a command, so they glossed over it as unimportant. It could be that they felt the change in process was unnecessary or inefficient and therefore less important than the old way. It's not likely that they are plain stubborn.

- **Instructional design for attitude**: Every course should include its purpose, importance, and benefits to the learner, co-workers, and customers. Give the learners the big picture and show them how their piece of the process fits into that picture. Tell them how entering data correctly affects reporting.

- **Story Design for attitude**: The benefits of doing things correctly provide a treasure trove of plot lines. And since stories thrive on conflict, your plot will include negative consequences that demonstrate the opposite of those benefits. Pick up on prevailing negative attitudes and incorporate them into the story to help drive the emotional impact and ultimately empower your audience to embrace the benefits. If your audience needs to see the bigger picture or is confused by the process, use a metaphor to relate this new process to something they are already familiar with.

Training for Attitude

Importance is at the core of attitude, akin to motivation. How important is it to the learner that the knowledge or skill be implemented? If the weight of importance is low, there's an attitude problem. There are questions Dayna can ask to explore the attitudes of employees toward email encryption: Are managers telling employees to do it the old way? She may need to restrict training to managers. Is the new way more difficult? She may need to explain why the more difficult way is necessary. If the new way is a recent change, have all employees been trained yet? There may be an actual knowledge gap. Dayna will need to keep asking questions until a root problem for each business outcome is identified and agreed upon by the stakeholders. This includes root problems stemming from attitude.

It's good to identify existing attitudes in the workplace toward the new behavior you are asking learners to adopt. To counteract negative attitudes, work with stakeholders and SMEs to clearly articulate the importance of training. Designing *importance* into the training through storytelling positively affects learners' attitudes toward behavior change. Don't throw out lack of motivation as a nontraining issue. Capture those attitudes in your interviews. You will use them later in your stories to drive the emotional impact of the training.

To overcome prevailing negative attitudes, it may not be enough for learners to know why training is important. Learners also want to know the benefits. What's in it for them? Regarding the encryption problem in Dayna's story, if an employee encrypts email properly, it protects the confidentiality of information of the customer and reduces risk to the company. Their behavior benefits the customer and the company, but what's in it for the employee personally? Perhaps, in the end, they save time by encrypting it correctly. Maybe they get a boost in their quality review at the end of the month. Ask stakeholders and SMEs directly, "What's in it for the employee if they do this?" and keep a record. You'll use the benefits as you build the plot for your story later.

For both the privacy and cybersecurity issues, knowledge, skills, and attitude are factors in solving the problem. Dayna can move forward with confidence that training will positively affect the business outcome.

Designing in Reality

Though the previous examples are somewhat clear cut, you do not work in a vacuum. There will almost always be a mix of root problems that require the proper mix of solutions. The new hire onboarding example that turned into manager training is focused on skill-building. But you will also need to make a clear case for what's in it for the learners (attitude), since you will be asking managers to do something different and perhaps inconvenient and initially time consuming. Along the way, you may unearth some work environment issues, such as inefficient processes that could be streamlined to give managers more time to spend on team building.

To uncomplicate real life without over-simplifying it, put your efforts toward defining the business outcome, the root problem, and training's part in the solution. Then focus on understanding who your audience is and what they should do as a result of training.

PRIMED for Stories

You never quite know what to expect when going into stakeholder interviews. Will they be skeptical of the process? Will they cooperate? Will they answer in complete sentences? More importantly, will the stakeholder provide the insight to identify the root problem and the business outcome? Your role is to help bring focus to that conversation by asking questions that will unearth the root problem and the business outcome. You'll also be looking for possible stories for training during the stakeholder interview.

Water pumps, whether the old-fashioned hand-cranked types or modern electric pumps, rely on water pressure and suction to pull water through and get it flowing. For that to happen, the pump must already have some water in the works. If it doesn't, it means the pump has lost its prime, and water will not flow. Think of your questions as the prime that gets the information flowing out of your stakeholder. Let's use an easy-to-remember mnemonic—PRIMED—to frame each category of question.

PRIMED will help you remember the questions you need to ask to keep the information pump primed (Figure 2-2). Keep in mind that PRIMED is a framework of question types that can be asked in any order, depending on the flow of the conversation. Download the PRIMED questions and other resources at needastory.com/book-resources or refer to it in the appendix.

Figure 2-2. PRIMED Questions

Ask Stakeholders for...

Personal Opinions
Real Stories
Initial Indicators
Metrics
Examples
Distractions

Personal Opinions

"What do you feel the root problem is? What would you like to see change as a result of training?"

Asking the stakeholder's personal opinion will go a long way in building relationship and winning complete buy-in to the final solution. Asking them directly what they believe the root problem or business outcome to be could cut right to the chase, but use this option with caution and define what is meant by *business outcome* and *root problem*. Personal opinion questions work very well with stakeholders you have worked with before who are familiar with your process. Dayna used a form of this question with Susan when she asked, "What outcome do you expect from this training?"

Real Stories

"Can you share a real story that illustrates the problem? Can you provide a case study?"

Listen for root problems—behaviors or systems that can be changed or fixed—when stakeholders answer this question. Also, listen for stories that can be used in the course to provide context for the learning objectives. Real stories can be modified or they can be used as actual case studies, depending on the sensitivity of the content. Identify the characters and the conflict and build stories that mirror those real situations.

Initial Indicators

"What brought this problem to your attention? Describe how you became aware that training was needed."

This is a great opening question. It immediately turns the conversation away from assumed solutions and toward the root problem. Look for the business outcome: a measurable difference in the business, such as an increase or decrease in numbers, scores, or behaviors. If they became aware of the issue second-hand, you may need to dig a bit further or speak to someone with firsthand knowledge.

Metrics

"Can I take a look at the survey results? What are the reports indicating in regard to this problem?"

Data tells a story. If the stakeholder relies on metrics to make business decisions routinely, it will be easier to keep the conversation focused on moving those numbers. Depending on the type of data you are reviewing, you may find the business outcome in the numbers, or you may discover the root problem in qualitative feedback. If metrics are not immediately available, try an initial indicator question.

Examples

"Can you provide an example of the kinds of issues you've noticed in regard to this problem?"

This is a good warm-up question. Expect to receive general, though valuable, observations in response: "They need better people skills. Trends indicate a problem with data security. Employees are being careless." This question is often best followed by a real stories or metrics question to flesh out each of the examples provided.

Distractions

"Is there anything distracting employees from performing their jobs well? If training was not available, what would you change?"

Ask this question when you are uncertain that training will fix the problem. Look for answers that indicate work environment issues or broken processes. In the customer service example earlier, it was an overwhelming amount of paperwork that was hindering staff from performing optimally. Fixing the paperwork problem will also help fix the customer service problem.

Figure 2-3. The Combined Power of PRIMED and the KSA Filter

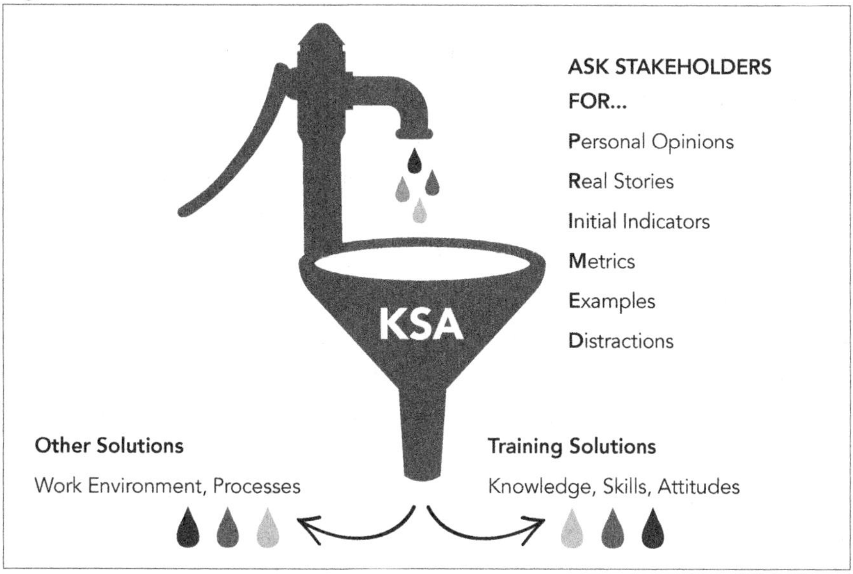

ASK STAKEHOLDERS FOR...

Personal Opinions

Real Stories

Initial Indicators

Metrics

Examples

Distractions

KSA

Other Solutions
Work Environment, Processes

Training Solutions
Knowledge, Skills, Attitudes

Armed with questions to prime stakeholders and the KSA filter, you will skillfully navigate stakeholder meetings and ultimately discover the business outcome, the root problem, the ideal solution and lots of story ideas (Figure 2-3). The stage is set!

PRACTICE STORY DESIGN:
Meet Your Client

This is the first practice session. Meet Dr. Kobal, the owner of Well Adjusted, a fictional chiropractic clinic. Dr. Kobal is having problems with his staff. You're going to design a story for instruction that will make a significant difference in the lives of his employees. Take a moment at the end of each chapter to apply the principles and get to know Dr. Kobal and the Well Adjusted staff along the way. Your first task is to ascertain the business outcome, the root problem, and the ideal solution. Read the conversation below and record your observations. Suggested answers are contained in appendix 3, but complete the exercise on your own first.

You arrive at Well Adjusted and tell the young lady at the front desk that you're there to speak with Dr. Kobal. "Are you new patient?" she asks.

"No, I'm not here for an adjustment. I have an appointment to speak with him about some business priorities."

The young lady stares back at you. She looks over her shoulder toward another woman who's taking files out of a drawer and placing them on the desk. "Um . . . Carrie?"

Carrie keeps working on the files. "Hm?"

"There's someone here to see Dr. Kobal."

Carrie looks up. "Do you have an appointment?"

"Yes," you say, then clarify, "I have an appointment to *speak* with Dr. Kobal."

"Oh, you're not here for an appointment?" Carrie walks up to the front desk and pulls out a calendar. "What's your name?"

You tell Carrie your name. Carrie shakes her head. You pull out your phone and open the email from Dr. Kobal. "He asked me to meet him here in the waiting room at 8:30 a.m. I'm a little early, so maybe I should just wait over here?"

Carrie picks up the phone and quickly dials. "Sure, have a seat. I'll see if I can . . . " She speaks into the phone. "Hey, Breanne, have you seen Dr. Kobal? There's someone . . . " She looks up at you. "Sorry, what did you say your name was again?"

At that moment, the door to the back office opens and a tall man strides into the room, open and smiling. "I'm glad you made it!" His voice is booming and happy. He shakes your hand. "I'm Dr. Kobal. Come on back to my office." As you walk with him, he calls over his shoulder, "Thanks, Carrie! Thanks, Janine!" He turns back to you. "Janine just started yesterday." He shows you to a large leather chair. His office is big. Pictures of his grandchildren line the wall. His desk and bookshelves are peppered with mementos from his trips abroad. Massive amounts of paper are stacked on every surface. "Can I get you a drink?" He's already opening a mini fridge.

"Sure, water would be nice. Thanks, Dr. Kobal," you say.

"That's actually one of the problems," Dr. Kobal says as he sits down. His broad frame dwarfs the desk chair.

You take out a notebook. "I'm sorry, what's one of the problems?"

Dr. Kobal cracks opens a seltzer and leans back in the chair. "Turnover." He motions toward the wall in the general direction of the front desk.

"Oh, the front desk?" you ask.

"Front desk, therapists, back office." He takes a gulp of seltzer. "Even the doctors! Turnover is bad. We're constantly training new staff."

"Why do you think that is?"

"I'm not sure. We have competitive pay. It's just . . . I don't know. We hire a lot of young people? Some of our doctors go on to start their own practice after a couple of years."

"When did you first notice this problem?"

Dr. Kobal laughs. "I can't remember . . . well, in my younger days, I was a lot more involved with the employees than I am now. But I have a good office manager: Brandi. She keeps things running for me. And my sister stops by every once in a while to help me manage . . . " He motions to the stacks of paperwork. " . . . this!" He chuckles and looks over his glasses at you. "I do actually know where to find things, believe it or not."

You smile. "Would you say that during the days when you were more involved with employees that turnover was less?"

"Absolutely! For 20 years, I practically had the same staff."

"Sounds like you already know how to run a successful office," you say.

"Well"—Dr. Kobal raises his eyebrows—"Yes, I do."

"When you passed responsibilities over to your office manager, did you coach them on how to do what you did to keep people engaged?"

"Hm. Yes, at first I did, but that was three office managers ago. I think I see where you're coming from. I should spend time with Brandi." He furrows his brow. "I can do that. But I feel like there's some other issues in the office that need to be fixed. I can't put my finger on it, but it's affecting our clients."

"In what way?" you ask.

"Well, see, a lot of people come in because they have injuries. They come for the first visit, then many of them don't ever come again to finish their therapy plan. Plus, our steady clients who come in for maintenance check-ups have steadily decreased."

"Why do you think there's been a decrease in customer loyalty?"

He puts his hand to his chin. "What do you think?"

You pause. "The high staff turnover could have something to do with the high client turnover. Maybe there's a common root problem?"

Dr. Kobal nods slowly. "Loyalty. You know, I had a mentor in college who told me trust was the foundation of every successful business."

You prompt him, saying, "And you feel like there's a connection between loyalty and trust?"

Dr. Kobal continues your thought. "Our clients aren't loyal. My own staff isn't loyal!"

"Do you see signs of lack of trust among your staff?" you ask.

"I'm not around them as much anymore. I'm not sure."

"What if I spend some time observing how your staff interacts with one another and with clients. Would that be OK?"

"Of course!" He stands. "You can start right now!"

"Good. I'll come by again this time next week to share my observations with you. Then we can work on building loyalty among your staff and your clients."

Dr. Kobal walks you to the back office and introduces you to the staff. He takes you through the open waiting room and front desk area and down the hallway to the examination rooms where patients are being adjusted. You meet a couple of the doctors. They smile and nod politely. In the therapy bay, you meet two ladies and a high-school-aged boy dressed in scrubs chatting in a small huddle. A few patients are doing exercises or lying down for electrostimulation treatments. They break from their conversation long enough to greet you. Dr. Kobal sees one of the patients wincing as they perform a shoulder exercise. He goes to them and gives them some pointers. They thank him. He walks back over to you. "If you need anything, please let me know. Feel free to stop by anytime this week." In three long steps, he exits the therapy bay.

You settle down and spend time observing the staff in the therapy bay. You come back two more times to observe each of the four main areas of the practice. These are your observations:

- Key information about patients, such as appointments, ailments, prescribed therapy, and financial matters, are not effectively communicated between the four areas of the practice.
- Staff often gossips about other staff members within earshot of their clients.
- During treatment and in the waiting room, staff members will talk loudly about their personal business with other staff members.
- Staff members will discuss clients' conditions in the presence of other clients, especially during therapy.

At the end of the week, you look over your notes on your conversation with Dr. Kobal and the list of observations. Answer the questions below to formulate your suggestions to Dr. Kobal next week.

What are the measurable business outcomes?

What's the root problem?

What are the ideal solutions?

After you've recorded your thoughts, you may compare your conclusions with the completed Instructional Story Design Plan in appendix 3. When you return to the story in chapter 3, you'll formulate the goal for training and begin the process of getting to know the staff at the clinic.

CHAPTER THREE
Your Audience

The Question Mark Grill

That evening, Dayna meets some of her college friends at the Question Mark Grill. James, a theater major turned corporate trainer and the person responsible for introducing her to talent development, is there.

"Hey Dayna! How's the job going?" asks James.

"Full of surprises lately," she says.

"How so?" James and Dayna find a vacant table near the bar.

Dayan slides into her seat. "Well, I had a meeting with a compliance director today and something she said is bugging me. She wants compliance training."

James sits across from her. "And that's bugging you? Come on, compliance is a blast!" he teases.

Dayna shakes her head. "This should have been an easy project. Just a bunch of boring policies that people need to know about. Awareness stuff, you know."

"Hm," he says thoughtfully. "Awareness . . . I don't know. Wouldn't you put awareness into the same category as marketing or communications? Is that really the realm of training?"

"What?"

James eats a chip, then continues, "Think about it. What should you actually do if you are aware of something? Shouldn't you focus on that?"

Dayna looks at James sideways. "Focus on what?"

"Focus on the action. Like theater. When you read the policy, what are you supposed to do with it? It's like an actor reading a script and just . . . you know, you can't just read it. You've got to act!"

"That's what Susan said."

"Who?"

"Susan, the compliance director. She said that too."

"She talked about theater? I like this lady!"

"No, she said it was important for employees to know what to do with the policies. And of course, I agree, but . . . "

"Did she give you some examples?"

"Yeah, she gave a couple of ideas. I meet with the subject matter expert tomorrow. I'll ask him."

"Well, what do the polices say? You read them, right?"

"Yeah."

"What do they say you're supposed to do?"

"Have you read a corporate policy lately? They don't tell you to do anything. They tell you not to do things."

"Good point," he says, but he's still thinking. "But what if during one of my sales training classes, all I did was teach sales people what not to do. How is that going to help them?"

"That's an interesting way to put it." Dayna thinks a minute. "But compliance is different."

"How?" he asks. "If you aren't training people to do something, how can you call it training?"

"Yeah," she concedes. "But seriously, the policies are basically a list of 'do nots.' To your point, they're more like, what would you call it? Nonperformance?"

James laughs, "I can just see the looks I'd get if I started my class with: 'Ladies and gentlemen, let's review the non-learning objectives before we get started.'"

Dayna smiles. "Anyway, that wasn't the surprise."

"OK." James is still laughing. "What was the surprise?"

"So Susan—she's the compliance director—is going through her list of compliance topics, right? Everything is boring and fine, and then she asks me if I can make the course engaging!"

"Really? That's great! I knew I liked her!" James looks at Dayna, prompting her to go on. "What did she mean by that?"

"That's exactly what I asked her!"

"And what did she say?"

"She didn't say. She wrote. On a sticky note! I'll tell you her words exactly—I'm not kidding—this is what she wrote." Dayna pauses, "'I love a good story.'" She leans back in her chair. "That's what she said: 'I love a good story.' That's it!"

James puts both hands on the table. "Brilliant! That's some good drama right there. How did she give you the note? Did she slide it over to you? Did she slap it on the desk?"

Dayna can see her actor friend imagining a staged production of compliance-on-Broadway. She isn't having it and tries to bring him back to reality. "Isn't that crazy?" she asks, looking for a little bit of empathy.

"You know, I think she's on to something," says James.

"Come on!" says Dayna, "You're siding with the compliance director?"

"Listen, I tell stories all the time when I'm facilitating training."

"Yeah, but that's with sales people in a classroom! We're talking about e-learning for thousands of employees. The entire company. And it's compliance training!"

"So?" he challenges her.

"There's a huge difference!"

"How is it different?" He goes on, "I tell success stories. I tell stories about sales people who make missteps. We do role play. You could do something like that in e-learning, right? Maybe not role play, per se, but what about writing some scenarios?"

Dayna didn't like the direction of the conversation, but James made some sense. "OK, maybe I could see where scenarios would be helpful. Maybe."

"Look, it's not that complex," he says. "You have some fictitious employees in some sort of an ethical dilemma. True?"

"OK," Dayna relents. "You're the actor. Any tips?"

"Well, a scenario needs characters, right?" Dayna barely nods. "So, in order to write a relatable character your audience . . . "

Dayna interrupts. "I am not a playwright."

"Not yet." James smiles. "But you've got to know who you're training before you can train them."

"Sure," Dayna concedes.

"When I first started corporate training in sales, I did a lot of research to find out who my audience was."

"Wasn't it pretty obvious? I mean, it was sales people, right?" asks Dayna.

"Yes, but I wanted to know things like what motivated them, and what their fears were, and how far out of their comfort zone I was asking them to go."

"OK." Dayna still isn't sure what this has to do with her story assignment.

"So," James explains, "If I know that the group I'm about to train is motivated by recognition, I'm going to give them a lot of it in the class. If they're biggest fear is speaking in front of a group, I will limit activities to one-on-one."

"Yeah, I get it," Dayna says. "But what has that got to do with stories?"

"Doesn't it stand to reason that the more you know your audience, the more believable of a character you can create for your story?" Dayna can't argue with that. "Find out who your learners are, so you can create a character they can relate to."

Dayna is getting it but still has objections. "It's a big company. How do I get to know them? Do you mean like demographics?"

"Demographics can help. But what's going on with them? What are their values. What do they do for pleasure? What's happening in the company that affects everybody?"

Dayna shakes her head. "I don't know how to find out all that stuff!"

"I didn't know either when I first started. But I found people who did! I talked with managers in sales, I visited with sales account managers and asked them a lot of questions about my audience."

Dayna is impressed. "You did all of that?"

"Yes, unfortunately none of that work was done by the instructional designer. I had to do it myself. Frankly, I don't do a lot of the activities that are designed for the class because they just don't make sense for my audience. I've come up with my own based on what I know about them."

"Ouch," says Dayna.

"But you are no ordinary instructional designer!" He points at Dayna, smiling. "You are an instructional designer who knows her audience!"

"I guess I could ask my manager if she knows some of the answers to these questions."

"And once you have those answers, you'll be able to create characters!"

"Kind of a tall order, James."

"Dayna . . . " James stops. "Do you have a pen?" Dayna raises her eyebrows. She takes a pen out of her purse and hands it to him. James scribbles on a napkin and slaps the napkin face down on the table in front of Dayna. He grins and walks over to the bar.

Dayna sighs. "Always the actor," she says as she turns the napkin over. There's James's dramatic flourish:

"You are a storyteller."

Dayna has a meeting with Randall tomorrow. She's not feeling quite up to the task of designing a story for training. And as of yet, she doesn't have what she needs to write one. She will need to find out more about who the audience is and what the course will train that audience to do. This will benefit both the design of the instruction and the design of the story.

As she rightly points out, the course will be assigned to the entire company. That's a large audience. She decides to speak with Fayette and some other managers to create an audience profile of the company. She will use this company audience profile later to create individual characters that they can relate to.

Audience Data

If developing an audience profile is already part of your instructional design process, good! If not, it will be soon.

Not surprisingly, the information you collect about your audience to design good instruction for them is nearly the same information you will need to create relatable characters. Pick a selection of questions below from each category to develop a profile that will help you make the best design decisions for instruction and for relatable characters. Dayna uses these categories of questions to build a profile of her own audience:

- personal information
- what they already know
- values and motivation
- circumstances at work and reactions to circumstances at work
- fears, risk, comfort zone, and commitment

- benefits
- technology and logistics.

At the end of each category, note the information Dayna has collected about her own audience. Remember, her audience, as far as she knows right now, is the entire company. In the next chapter, she will learn more about her audience during her conversation with the subject matter expert, Randall.

Personal Information

The answers to personal questions will inform language, writing style, visual style, audio choices, references to popular culture, level of education, and company position. Look for character backstories and ideas for the type of story this audience would appreciate.

Here are some example personal information questions:

- What is their primary language?
- What is their education or background?
- What is their job or role?
- How long have they been with the company?
- What industry is the company in?
- How long have they been in this field of work?
- Where does the learner live?
- Are they remote employees? In office?
- What types of music do they listen to?
- What types of games do they like to play?
- What types of movies do they like to see?
- What type of humor do they appreciate?
- What types of sports do they like?
- What forms of entertainment do they enjoy?
- What are the demographics of the company?

Dayna's audience profile: Headquarters is in a thriving mid-sized city with a few regional locations across the country and about 90 employees who work remotely. The four main departments are engineering, IT, customer service, and sales. High school football is a big deal in the headquarters location. They also have a local minor league baseball team. The company offers discounted tickets to those games and many employees go with their families. Seventy percent of the employee population is male.

What They Already Know

What is the learner's pre-existing knowledge of the material being presented? The answer to this one question will give you a solid place to begin designing instruction—see the design continuum in Figure 3-1. The less learners know about the performance, the further down on the continuum you can begin to design. For instance, if Dayna's audience doesn't know what a phishing email is, she should start with a definition. But she can't stay in definition-land forever or her learners will go to sleep. She needs to provide activities that will increase their proficiency, moving up the continuum until finally, they are able to put the new knowledge into practice.

Though the design continuum is helpful, don't think of the learners' experience in the course quite so linearly. Starting with a story puts the audience in the situation and opens opportunities for them to practice up front and discover definitions, descriptions, and examples along the way. In a sense, you are throwing them into the deep end of the pool to teach them to swim and tossing in the necessary life preservers along the way.

Figure 3-1. Design Continuum

		DESIGN CONTINUUM
Practice		Today, you're going to encrypt an email.
Demonstration		I'm going to show you how to encrypt an email.
Examples		Here are a few examples of emails that have been encrypted correctly.
Description		Encryption is like a secret code that can't be deciphered by hackers.
Definition		Email encryption: "Encryption of messages to protect the content from being read by entities other than the intended recipients."

**Design Continuum,
Using Email Encryption As an Example**

Stories cover a large part of the design continuum, making storytelling an appealing design choice for instruction. Notice that although stories can include definitions and descriptions of performances, where they really shine is in examples and demonstrations. Add in some realistic choices along the way and put decisions in the learners' court and you've reached all the way up to practice!

Dayna's audience profile: Dayna doesn't have the time or resources to do a formal learner analysis, but she does a high-level assessment of what the entire company has been trained on before. Employees have had training on phishing and privacy, but the courses are essentially the policy on PowerPoint slides with no examples of phishing emails or practice encrypting emails successfully. The policies do not tell employees what to do if they do click on a link or open an attachment containing malware or how to handle the situation if they've sent an unencrypted email.

Values and Motivation

Identifying values and motivation clearly falls into the category of attitude. Content should make the connection between the performance and the company's values, and appeal to employees' personal values. Look for opportunities to set up the training for success with pre-course communications, or course descriptions that are motivating for your audience.

You've already read how stories are like a flight simulator, preparing your audience for action. If your characters value the same things your audience values, you will form a quicker connection between the audience and your characters. Motivation to change will increase.

Here are some example values and motivation questions:
- What do they value most about their job?
- What do they value most in life?
- What motivates them at work?

- What do they do in their spare time?
- What will motivate them to take the training?
- What will motivate them to act on the training?

Dayna's audience profile: In addition to asking managers, Dayna asks co-workers what they value about their work. She puts together a short list of the most common answers: innovation, quality, customer service, hard work, and celebrating accomplishments.

Circumstances at Work and Reactions to Circumstances

Is training part of a larger change management project? Should it be? Are there things in the work environment that could be enhanced or changed to help learning be more successful? Knowing what's actually happening in the workplace will only serve to make your stories more real to life. Answers to these questions may reveal powerful emotions that you can tap into for the story. Integrate these circumstances, like deadlines or production quotas, into the story as external pressures that intensify the conflict.

Here are some example work circumstances questions:

- What are their current circumstances at work? Describe.
- How are they currently reacting to circumstances at work?
- What challenges them most at work?
- Has anything happened recently in the organization that may make them feel vulnerable?
- Who or what has influence over them?
- Who do they have influence over?
- Will this training or message create a shift in power?
- How are they likely to respond to this training in light of their circumstances at work?

Dayna's audience profile: Dayna records some of the current circumstances at her company: A new product release has had a ripple effect of change within the organization, including restructuring two of its divisions. IT has recently outsourced its help desk to a vendor. The transition has been bumpy.

The company has a strong financial standing and rewards its employees well for strong performance.

She also records how employees are reacting to those circumstances: Employees in the affected divisions are adjusting to the new reporting structure well. They are used to organizational changes that facilitate more innovation. However, because of the frequent team changes, effective communication regarding new policies and expectations sometimes suffers. There is general distrust of the vendor who has taken the help desk function. Many employees avoid calling the help desk. Employees are motivated to bring innovative products to the market and rally behind new products.

Fears, Risk, Comfort Zone, and Commitment

High levels of discomfort, noncommitment, perceived risks, and fears pose a challenge for instruction. Learners may not act on what they are being trained for due to any one of these factors. They may need a firmer grasp of the purpose, importance, and benefits of training to ease into the new reality. Use the next category of questions (benefits) to help solve for negative situations in this category.

Fears, risk, comfort zone, and commitment are sources of internal or external conflict that can be demonstrated through story. Most of the time, when these situations exist in the workplace, it's best to include them as part of the story's conflict, either head-on or subtly as secondary sources of conflict. Many times, you will find relevant emotional content in this category.

Here are some example fear, risk, comfort zone, and commitment questions:

- What keeps them up at night?
- What fears will keep them from taking action?
- What other mental or practical barriers will prevent them from taking action?
- Can these fears or other barriers be dispelled? How?
- What might they misunderstand about the message?

- Why might they believe the change doesn't make sense for them or their organization?
- What would they sacrifice if they acted upon the training?
- What is the perceived risk of changing the way they do things?
- What are the physical or emotional risks they will need to take?
- How will this stretch them?
- Who or what might they have to confront as a result of this training?
- What is their tolerance level for change?
- How far out of their comfort zone are you asking them to go?
- Are you asking them to unlearn something? What?
- Are they willing to commit time to take the training?
- Are they willing to commit to acting upon the training?
- What preconceptions do they have regarding the training?

Dayna's audience profile: Dayna asks one question from this category: "What keeps you up at night?" or "What are your work-related fears?" Some managers qualify their answers to this question with preambles like, "Well, I wouldn't say I stay up at night thinking about it . . . " or "I'd call it more *concerned* rather than *feared*." But their answers are exactly what she is looking for. She summarizes their answers like this: They fear that their new product will fail. They are concerned about being sidetracked from their focus on innovation and customer service.

She also finds out that compliance is sometimes perceived as a hinderance to innovation and that employees struggle to complete compliance training on time.

Benefits

Showing learners what's in it for them provides motivation to complete training and act on it. Make the benefit clear, compelling, and personal. You'll learn more about how benefits fit into the instructional design plan in the following chapter.

The fallout of conflict results in consequences, which your stories will clearly demonstrate. But how many times have you heard the phrase, "I learned more from my successes than I did from my mistakes"? Never. Let the characters make mistakes and let learners learn from them. The benefits will be implied.

Here are some example benefits questions:

- How will they personally benefit from the training and taking action? What's in it for them?
- How will training help their sphere of influence?
- How will the company benefit?
- How will clients benefit?

Dayna's audience profile: The answers she receives from managers regarding the benefits of detecting phishing and encrypting emails revolve around the company's reputation and protecting member data. Both of these benefits make sense. The company values customer service, which aligns with why employees may fear a compromise of the customer-company trust. She does not receive responses that shed light upon why employees may personally benefit from the training. She will learn more about what's in it for the employee during her conversation with Randall in the next chapter.

Technology and Logistics

Technology and logistics questions are great for external consultants who need to have a better lay of the land. Technology often defines constraints for you that affect how you develop the training solution. Similarly, the technology available will be a factor in how you deliver the story you create for training. Embrace constraints as opportunities to explore creative ways to deliver the story.

Here are some example technology and logistics questions:

- What is their experience with e-learning? Mobile learning? Gamification? Social media?
- Where will they take the training?
- Describe the environment where they will take this training.

- Will the learner be able to hear or play audio when taking the training?
- What types of mobile devices do they own?

Dayna's audience profile: Dayna's company already uses e-learning extensively. Their learning management system (LMS) is not particularly user-friendly, but employees have no issue accessing courses that have been assigned to them. The LMS does not support mobile. Most employees will take this course in the office on their work computer or connected remotely to the company's system through VDI.

Summarize the Profile

When you are preparing to design training for a new audience, select questions that will paint the most accurate picture of them. You will not use all these questions for each new audience. You can select those questions that you feel will give you the best insights into who your audience is. At the minimum, collect enough information on your audience to describe the following:

- a brief personal description unique to that audience with select demographics
- their pre-existing knowledge of the performance you are training on
- what they value
- their current circumstances at work
- their reactions to current circumstances at work
- their fears and preconceptions of training
- the benefits to the company and to the learner
- their technology options for training delivery.

If you can describe your audience using these eight attributes, you have a good grasp on who they are, what they know, how they feel, and what brings them pain and pleasure. You also know how training should be delivered. All of this is good for both instruction and stories! The Audience Profile Questionnaire is located in appendix 1. Download the editable version at www.needastory.com/book-resources.

Figure 3-2 shows Dayna's final audience profile of the company.

Figure 3-2. Audience Profile for Entire Company

- **Personal information:** Most employees work at headquarters and live in a thriving mid-sized city. Ten percent work in smaller regional locations across the country and about 90 employees work remotely. The four largest departments are engineering, IT, customer service, and sales. High school football is a big deal in the headquarters location. They also have a local minor league baseball team. The company offers discounted tickets to those games, and many employees go with their families. Seventy percent of the employee population is male.
- **Their pre-existing knowledge of the performance you are training on:** Employees have had training on both phishing and privacy, but the courses are essentially the policy on PowerPoint slides with no examples of phishing emails or practice encrypting emails successfully. The policies do not tell employees what to do if they do click on a link or open an attachment containing malware or how to handle the situation if they've sent an unencrypted email.
- **What they value:** Innovation, quality, customer service, hard work, and celebrating accomplishments.
- **Their current circumstances at work:** A new product release has had a ripple effect of change within the organization, including restructuring two of its divisions. IT has recently outsourced its help desk to a vendor. The transition has been bumpy. The company has a strong financial standing and rewards its employees well for strong performance.
- **Their reactions to current circumstances at work:** Employees in the affected divisions are adjusting to the new reporting structure well. They are used to organizational changes that facilitate more innovation. However, because of the frequent team changes, effective communication regarding new policies and expectations sometimes suffers. There is general distrust of the vendor who has taken the help desk function. Many employees avoid calling the help desk. Employees are motivated to bring innovative products to the market and rally behind new products.
- **Their fears and preconceptions of training:** They fear that their new product will fail. They are concerned about being sidetracked from their focus on innovation and customer service. Compliance is sometimes perceived as a hinderance to innovation. Employees struggle to complete compliance training on time.
- **Benefits of training:** Protect the company's reputation as innovative and trustworthy.
- **Their technology options for training delivery:** They use primarily e-learning for corporate-wide training. Employees have no issue accessing courses that have been assigned to them. The LMS does not support mobile. Most employees will take this course in the office on their work computer or connected remotely to the company's system through VDI.

Getting the Answers

You know the questions to ask, but how do you get the answers? There's really only three ways to find out who your audience is: get out and meet them, ask someone who knows them, or Google them! All three are suitable, depending on who your audience is.

Small Targeted Audience

If the group of people to be trained is accessible, go out and spend some time with the team. Observe and take notes of their behaviors. Ask them questions from the audience profile questionnaire. Gather inspiration from their side conversations about what they did over the weekend. If you can't do that, ask these questions of someone who knows the group well.

Large Corporate Audience

Some general demographics will get you started on this audience. Interview several people from across the company and look for commonalities. Ask questions from the circumstances at work category to unearth these commonalities, like shared challenges and reactions to the company's situation.

Untouchable Audience

There are occasions when even those who know your audience either don't know them well enough to answer the questions or simply won't do it. I experienced this when training the members of a company's board of directors. Employees in the legal department were vague in their answers to the questions I asked. Fortunately, the members of this board were accomplished businesspeople who had run successful companies, written books, done public interviews, and had a long list of accomplishments available on the Internet. So, I researched online until I had enough information to create an audience profile that yielded relatable characters.

When you know your audience, creating relatable characters and making plot choices becomes infinitely easier. The time you spend getting to know them on the front end will reap great benefits when it's time to design instruction and write the story.

PRACTICE STORY DESIGN:
Get to Know Your Audience

It's 8:25 AM. You've been in the waiting room for about five minutes. No one is at the front desk yet. Finally, Janine, the new young lady comes down the hall and sits behind the desk. She looks a little bit worried. She doesn't see you. After a minute, you approach the front desk.

"Hi."

Janine is startled. "Oh! I didn't see you in here! I'm sorry. Are you here for an appointment?"

"I'm here to speak with Dr. Kobal."

"Oh." Janine fumbles with some of the papers in front of her.

You ask her, "Is everything OK?"

"Yes, I'm new and . . . " She stops and looks up at you. "I recognize you. You were in here last week taking notes and stuff."

You laugh. "Yes, that's me! I'm helping Dr. Kobal out. You'll probably see me a few more times."

Janine seems to relax a little. "Okay. Sorry, yeah, he's in a staff meeting. He might be a little late. We had somebody . . . well, Carrie quit. I don't feel like I know enough to run the front desk by myself. It's—it's a little overwhelming."

"I'm not in a rush," you say. "It's OK."

"Thanks. I'm not sure who to ask now about how to get stuff done."

"What about Brandi? Isn't she the office manager?" you offer.

Janine shrugs. "Yeah, I guess I could ask her. It's just, we're supposed to make sure people get into the doctor's office as quick as possible. And there's so much paperwork they have to fill out each time they come in that . . . " She shakes her head. "It's hard to keep track of it all. And then, we're supposed to be nice to everybody, but it's hard when you've got so much to do. I'm sorry, this isn't your problem."

After a moment, you ask, "What excited you about getting this job?"

The question takes Janine off guard. You let her think for a minute. "Well, I was looking forward to getting some job experience. I graduated from high school last spring. I'm taking some night classes and working on a degree."

"That's great!" you say. "What are you studying?"

"I'm just getting core classes out of the way at the community college. I'm not sure what I want to major in. Maybe nursing. I've been helping my mom out at home. She's got MS. Sometimes she needs me to get her dressed. I do most of the cooking for her."

You nod. "That's extremely responsible of you to do that for your mom."

Janine smiles.

"Was there anything else that excited you about working here?"

"Well, I thought I'd get to know my co-workers and have kind of a little family here."

You think you know the answer already, but you ask anyway. "Has that happened?"

"Not really. I mean, everybody's nice, but . . . it's not a family."

You hear voices coming down the hall. "Thanks for your honesty, Janine," you say. "Good luck on your studies!"

"Thanks!" Janine swivels around in her chair and begins pulling files out of the drawer behind her.

Brandi, a short, energetic woman enters the waiting room area. "How are you doing, Janine? Everything under control?"

"I'm good," she says, continuing to pull files.

Brandi looks at you. "Hey, I've seen you around, but we haven't met officially. I'm Brandi." You exchange greetings. "Come on back. Dr. Kobal would like to talk with you in the consultation room." You follow her down the hall, past the examination rooms and into the small consultation room. A stark room, except for two chairs, and a table with a computer. But the adjacent wall is dominated by an aquarium. You smile. *"Funny guy,"* you think.

Shortly, Dr. Kobal strides in. "Morning! Enjoying the fish? Sorry I'm late this morning. More turnover problems."

"I heard," you say.

"Thanks for meeting here. My sister is in my office taking care of HR stuff. I hate it when people leave a voicemail over the weekend to let you know they've quit." He gets right to the heart of the matter. "I've been thinking about our last conversation. I think trust is the problem." He looks at you. You nod. "No trust, no business. What do you think?"

"I agree. I think that's part of the problem," you say.

"OK, how do we fix it?"

You take out your notes. "It seems like what you want most for the business is an increase in loyalty, both from your clients and from your staff."

"Yep, I'm with you there!"

You continue, "If loyalty springs from trusting relationships as you mentioned, and I believe it does, then we need to find out where the breakdown of trust lies."

He leans forward in his chair and nods. "Where is trust breaking down?"

"Communication." You hand Dr. Kobal the list of observations.

He reads the list under his breath. "Key information . . . not effectively communicated . . . Gossiping? Really?" He looks up at you. He reads on. "Talking loudly about personal business . . . mm . . . Talking about clients in front of other clients! Are you serious?" He shakes his head. "I guess I've been out of touch. No wonder we're losing so many clients!" He looks back at the list. "Yeah, I guess all of these things are communications-related."

You clarify, "These forms of communication undermine trust."

"Why are they doing this? I mean, this is all commonsense stuff!"

"But if no one corrects them and trains them how to communicate in a way that builds trust, how will they know?" you ask.

"Is it the doctors too?"

"From what I've observed, there's very little guidance from doctors when a patient moves from the examination room to therapy, other than the prescribed exercise regimen." You add, "And they don't seem too open to the therapists asking them questions."

He looks at the fish tank. "Yeah, I can see that."

"Training can help with a lot of this, but there's another problem."

He looks at you. "What?"

"Paperwork."

He groans and leans back in his chair. "You have no idea! Regulations are so hard to keep up with! There's a form for everything!"

"I noticed that a lot of documentation is manual. Have you considered automating some of it?"

"I've never been that good with technology but . . . yeah, I should look into it. What else do I need to do?"

"Have you met with Brandi yet?"

"No, but I'll set up a meeting with her."

"Good, you pass along your wisdom of team-building to Brandi and look into automating some of the paperwork. I'll work on a plan for training the staff how to communicate with one another in a way that builds trust among one another and your clients."

He stands. "OK. Let's do this!"

As you stand you ask Dr. Kobal. "By the way, do you know what Janine does when she's not at work?"

He shrugs. "Shop, go to movies, go to the gym, like the other staffers?"

You smile. "You should ask her. You've got a real gem there."

Based on your observations and the conversation with Dr. Kobal, adjust the root problem, business outcome, and recommended training from the last chapter, if necessary. Then, write a goal for training using the format below.

Eliminate root problem	To achieve the business outcome	By implementing training on . . . .

Now, create an audience profile based on what you know about the staff at Well Adjusted Chiropractic, using the following eight categories as a guide. Once you've completed the exercise, you can compare your answers to those on the completed Instructional Story Design Plan in appendix 3.

A brief personal description unique to that audience with select demographics

Their pre-existing knowledge of the performance you are training on

What they value

Their current circumstances at work

Their reactions to current circumstances at work

Their fears and preconceptions of training

The benefits to the company and to the learner

Their technology options for training delivery (keep in mind their access to computers)

CHAPTER FOUR

Analyze What You Want the Audience to Do

A Talk With Randall

The next day, Dayna goes to Susan's office for her meeting with Randall, the subject matter expert for compliance training. Dayna has brought a task list of performance objectives that she wants to verify with Randall. She also feels that there are some missing steps that the policy doesn't address.

Susan escorts Dayna to a nearby cubicle. She waves at Randall. Randall takes off his earphones and raises his eyebrows. "Randall, I'd like for you to meet Dayna. She's from learning and development." Randall nods at Dayna. Dayna smiles. "Randall is in touch with the owners of all of the policies we're training on, so he's your point person."

"Thanks, Susan," says Dayna. Susan walks back to her office. Dayna turns to Randall. "Mind if I sit?"

"Nope." Randall removes a stack of papers from the chair by his cubicle.

"Well, as Susan said, I'm the instructional designer for the compliance course." Randall nods again. "I'd like to take a look at the performance objectives with you and see if we can identify gaps." Randall looks at her but says nothing. Dayna tries again. "Susan mentioned some new privacy procedures? Maybe we can start there?"

"Sure," says Randall.

"Um, maybe you could describe the new process of encrypting email," suggests Dayna.

Randall inhales and glances at his screen. "Yep. When you send an email containing sensitive information, you need to *encrypt* it."

Dayna waits for more information. Randall's done. "Alright, what performance expectations do you . . . " Dayna rephrases the question. "What are the steps for encrypting an email?"

Randall demonstrates on his computer how to encrypt the email while Dayna takes notes. "That seems fairly simple," says Dayna. "Type the word encrypt in the subject line of the email and send it." Randall shrugs and nods. "So, why do you think employees aren't doing it?" asks Dayna.

"They are," says Randall matter-of-factly.

"So . . . why do we need to train them?" asks Dayna. "What's the problem?"

"Attachments," Randall says. "The problem is really the attachments."

"What's wrong with the attachments?" she asks.

"They have confidential information in them," says Randall.

"Right." Dayna still doesn't get it. "But isn't that normal? Isn't that part of what we do as a business?"

"Yeah." Randall takes another deep breath. Dayna makes a mental note not to ask yes-or-no questions going forward. This time Randall offers more information. "But they're hiding rows."

"Rows?" asks Dayna. "So are we talking about a spreadsheet here?" Remembering her mental note about yes-or-no questions, she adds, "What file types are being sent as attachments?"

"Yeah, that's it. Excel spreadsheets. They hide rows that have information that doesn't belong to the person they're sending it to. That's an unauthorized disclosure," explains Randall.

Dayna takes some notes and recaps, "So, the recipient gets access to sensitive information that they are unauthorized to see. Because the sender hid rows?"

"Sometimes a report will bring in more information than what's needed . . . you know, more than the minimum necessary." Randall turns to his computer and scrolls through his email.

Dayna is starting to understand. "OK, so when that happens, the employee is just hiding the rows with the extra information that the recipient shouldn't see. But what they should do instead is . . . "

"Delete the rows," says Randall, still scrolling through his email.

"They should delete the rows," Dayna says aloud as she writes it down. "Because the recipient could unhide the rows in the spreadsheet to view sensitive information they are not authorized to see. And that's what you called more than the minimum necessary?"

"Mm-hm."

"OK, what happens if they don't do that?" asks Dayna.

Randall spins around toward Dayna and sits up in his chair. "Let me tell you. Privacy had this one case where the sensitive information of over 12,000 people was disclosed to an unauthorized party in one email. What a headache! Took us over a month to get all of that settled. If people only knew!"

Dayna leans back, surprised at Randall's sudden animation. "If people only knew . . . ?"

Randall continues, " . . . . how much time it takes for disclosure tracking and reporting and the time crunch! We've got to notify people that their information has been sent to the wrong person within 60 days!"

"Yeah, that sounds like a lot of work for one misstep," Dayna empathizes. "This, uh, disclosure tracking. Is this something the employee is responsible for doing?"

"Maybe," says Randall, suddenly sedate. He turns back to his email.

Dayna kicks herself for asking another yes-or-no question. "What should the employee do if they have done something like this—an unauthorized disclosure?

"They should contact the privacy office, I wouldn't worry about putting all of the disclosure tracking stuff in training, just tell them to call the privacy office and they will take it from there."

"But employees may be responsible for doing some of this disclosure tracking—I mean, what are their responsibilities?"

"First, let their supervisor know, then contact the privacy office. They will give further instructions. And yeah, sometimes the supervisor and the employee have to do some of the grunt work, and believe me, it's not fun."

"Thanks, Randall," says Dayna, "That's really helpful." She jots a note on her audience profile: WIIFM—Save time! As she writes, she asks Randall, "If you could tell employees one thing about this issue, what would it be?"

"Use your head! Think before your send an email!"

"Good advice," says Dayna. "OK, so it sounds like what the privacy office is asking them to do is check the spreadsheet for hidden rows, minimum necessary, and accuracy?"

"And the email address!" Randall puts his head in his hand, "You'd think people could remember who needed the information. I can't tell you how many cases we've had where people encrypt everything and quality check the spreadsheet attachment but send it to the wrong person!"

"Wow, yeah." Dayna takes some notes. "Is there any other reason why you think people are doing this?"

"None that I know," says Randall, "Except maybe that they are slammed and just want to get it out the door."

"Who?" asks Dayna.

"Well, 95 percent of the time it's customer service," explains Randall.

Dayna makes another note on her audience profile: *customer service.* "That's interesting." Dayna feels an urge to question further about this piece of information but isn't sure what to ask. "What about the cybersecurity issue? The phishing email?"

Randall nods. "Yeah, it's a problem."

Dayna asks, "Why do you think people are still clicking on links that contain malware?"

Randall shakes his head, "I have no idea. Cybersecurity has sent out the policy, like, a hundred times!"

"Wait," says Dayna. "So have employees ever received training on how to handle phishing emails?"

"Well, basically, it's a PowerPoint with the policy on it and a quiz at the end," he answers.

Dayna vaguely remembers taking that course. It was the text of the policy on the screen with an occasional unrelated stock photo. One of those "can't-click-Next-until-the-narration-is-finished" courses. She pulls out the cybersecurity policy from her stack and holds it out to Randall. "But the policy doesn't have anything in here about what to do with phishing emails. Or how to detect them. How are employees supposed to know what to do if the policy doesn't tell them?"

Randall takes the policy and scans through it. Then he points to the page and says, "See, it's right here."

Dayna looks at where Randall is pointing and reads aloud, "Also, employees should always be vigilant to catch emails that carry malware or phishing attempts." Dayna looks at Randall. She looks back at the page. "That's it? This is all the guidance employees are receiving?"

"It's common sense!" says Randall, a little defensively.

Dayna realizes that she could put minimal effort into making this course engaging and probably make Susan and cybersecurity pretty happy. Anything would be better than the death-by-narrated-text course they are used to. But then she thinks of every employee in the company enduring 30 minutes of nonsense and still leaving the course without knowing what to do. And there's Susan's request for a story. She can't think about that right now. The very least she can do is train employees on what they can act on.

"Maybe it's common sense," says Dayna. "But it's not common knowledge. I think with your help we can make detection and prevention steps a little clearer. Let's review these performance objectives . . . " She doesn't want to use instructional design jargon with Randall. How can she describe it succinctly? Finally she says, "Let's build an action list."

Talk Straight

Though many instructional design certification programs have a deep focus on writing learning objectives, a highly academic approach does not always adequately prepare professionals and students to enter the warp-speed world of business. The theory is solid and mastering it is helpful, but when it comes down to communication with stakeholders, SMEs, and learners, it's best to talk straight: "What actions need to be done to achieve the business outcome?" Dayna caught on to this by the end of her conversation with Randall.

You will find success in speaking the language of your subject matter experts and making it easy for them to speak yours. Calling the task list of performance objectives an action list is one of the ways you can bridge that gap. It keeps you and your subject matter experts focused on what's most important: action! Check appendix 1 for an action list template in the Instructional Story Design Plan. Download an editable version of the action list template and an example of a completed action list at needastory.com/book-resources.

Figure 4-1. Action List Template

Action List Template

Use the reminders at the bottom of the template to structure the action list. Record your final action list in the Instructional Story Design Plan in Appendix 2.

Main action	
Sub-action 1	
Sub-sub action A	
Sub-sub action B	
Sub-sub action C	
Sub-action 2	
Sub-sub action A	
Sub-sub action B	
Sub-sub action C	
Sub-action 3	
Sub-sub action A	
Sub-sub action B	
Sub-sub action C	
Sub-action 4	
Sub-sub action A	
Sub-sub action B	
Sub-sub action C	

Observable Action

Let's work on identifying observable actions. Look at the following example of a training goal and its matching actions. Which ones rise to the top as something the learner would be able to do?

> **Goal of training**: Increase sales numbers by 4 percent by end of Q3 by increasing the business acumen of sales associates to accurately and confidently explain product application to clients' needs.
>
> - Understand why clients need to know how products work.
> - Show how the product may meet the client's future need by comparing industry trends to the client's situation.
> - Avoid putting off client questions about how products work.
> - Use the product sheet to show clients product features that will meet their needs.

- Explain how the client's needs will be met by the product.
- Be aware of product applications.
- Share testimonials of how the product has worked for other clients in similar situations.

If you are struggling with this, think of the above list as actions you should be able to observe someone doing. Now, it should be clearer. You can't watch someone *understand* or *be aware*. Both of these verbs must manifest themselves through an observable action. It doesn't mean that learners don't need to understand why clients need to know how products work, but this new knowledge must be acted upon. Those are the actions that need to be included on the action list. *Be aware of* is a commonly used objective. Awareness is a good thing for marketing and communications and can be coupled with training for a powerful experience, but instructional designers need to press beyond this and get to the actions learners will have to perform. Ask the subject matter expert, "If the sales associate understands and is aware of why clients need to know how a product works, what will they do to demonstrate that?"

This holds true even if you may be tasked with designing *core values* training. It is only logical, if *respect* is a core value, that the main action may be "Respect your co-workers." But it can't stop there. The same principle of observable action applies. If employees respect their co-workers, what will they do to demonstrate it? They may "Communicate with co-workers in a way that values their contributions" or even more specifically, "Stop typing, put away your phone, and give your undivided attention during conversations with co-workers."

There's another item on this list that should also be struck. It's a non-action. Remember James's joke in the last chapter about non-learning objectives? That's exactly what *avoid* is telling us: something they shouldn't do, rather than something they can do. If an action list contains words like *avoid* or *do not* or *refrain from*, there is either a positive action hidden somewhere in the negative, or it belongs in the content as part of the purpose, importance or benefits of the course.

In this case, the nonaction, "Avoid putting off client questions about how products work" could have a positive hidden in it, such as "Explain how the client's needs will be met by the product," but that's already on this list. More likely, it would be more powerful to use this information not as a nonaction on the action list, but as part of the content describing the course's importance, such as, "An important step in making the sale is answering clients' questions regarding the application of the product to their needs. Avoiding this step is a mistake that will most likely end in losing the client." Or, even better, imagine a story about a sales person who puts off questions from the client about how products work. Show the fallout of that action and you won't even need to say anything about the importance. They will experience the importance for themselves through the story.

When you scan your initial action list, first look for ones that should be eliminated. Can I observe someone doing this? Is there a nonaction represented? When removing those items from the action list above, this is what's left:

> **Goal of training**: Increase sales numbers by 4 percent by end of Q3 by increasing the business acumen of sales associates to accurately and confidently explain product application to clients' needs.
>
> - ~~Understand why clients need to know how products work.~~
> - Show how the product may meet the client's future need by comparing industry trends to the client's situation.
> - ~~Avoid putting off client questions about how products work.~~
> - Use the product sheet to show clients product features that will meet their needs.
> - Explain how the client's needs will be met by the product.
> - ~~Be aware of product applications.~~
> - Share testimonials of how the product has worked for other clients in similar situations.

Organized Action

Using the pared down version of the sales action list as an example; there's another step that needs to be taken to shape it into an action list with a logical sequence. Right now, the action list is flat. Nothing is more important than anything else. There is no obvious sequence of steps. To make this a more usable action list, let's put the actions in a logical order.

First, take a look at the goal of training. What is the main action sales people will need to do? It's the last phrase of the goal: "Explain product application to clients' needs." Is this represented in the action list? Yes, it's part of all of the actions. The third action, "Explain how the client's needs will be met by the product," is almost identical to the goal of training, so let's move that to the top as our main action. You may call it a terminal performance objective. Since all of the others are parts of this main action, indent them underneath. Now the list looks like this:

- Explain how the client's needs will be met by the product.
  - Show how the product may meet the client's future need by comparing industry trends to the client's situation.
  - Use the product sheet to show clients product features that will meet their needs.
  - Share testimonials of how the product has worked for other clients in similar situations.

After showing this to the subject matter expert, they might agree that all the steps are represented, but in the wrong order. They want sales associates to first use the product sheet to show clients product features that will meet their needs, and they want to bring in testimonials earlier in the process (because success stories are also powerful). Showing how the product may meet the client's future needs by comparing industry trends to the client's situation is last and optional, if the first two steps haven't worked. You modify the action list:

- Explain how the client's needs will be met by the product, using these three steps:
  - Use the product sheet to show clients product features that will meet their needs.
  - Share testimonials of how the product has worked for other clients in similar situations.
  - Show how the product may meet the client's future need by comparing industry trends to the client's situation (if steps 1 and 2 haven't convinced the client).

Now the action list makes a lot of sense. If sales people do steps 1-3, they will accomplish the main action above it. It's easy to digest at a glance and sales associates will be able to use this process on the job. Look back to the first list. It contained all of the right things, plus some extras, but it wasn't organized in a way that was easy to grasp. Though you will have to ask more questions about the sub-actions for steps 1-3, you have a solid framework for designing the instruction and the story.

You might be wondering, *Don't subject matter experts already know these steps? Shouldn't they be able to just hand you a list of steps?* On rare occasion, subject matter experts will have an organized sequence of actions they expect learners to take, but more often, you will help them discover their own process.

Dayna's Action List

Let's refer back to Dayna's conversation with Randall. Before that conversation, Dayna's action list for the privacy training looked like this (Figure 4-2).

Figure 4-2. Dayna's Pre-SME Action List for Privacy

Mitigate risk! ⟶ What should employees do?

Be aware of policies

Increase motivation to act upon policies

    Encrypt email with sensitive info to outside parties (ask for steps)

Even before she goes into the conversation, she's already thinking about how to get past awareness. She wants to identify the actions employees need to take. You read about her conversation regarding the action list for encrypting emails. Before reading on, go back to the conversation and jot down the actions that employees should do for the privacy action list. Did you come up with something that looked like this?

Figure 4-3. Dayna's Post-SME Action List for Privacy

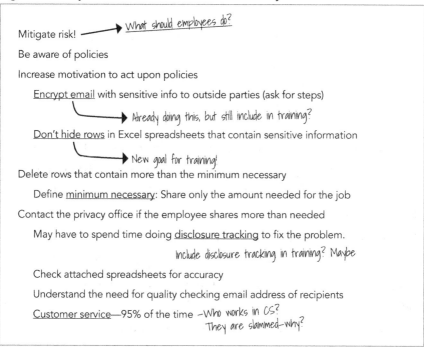

Note that Dayna picked up from Randall that the bigger problem was not encryption but hiding rows on spreadsheets instead of deleting them. Most likely, you will walk away from stakeholder conversations with a list that looks similarly unorganized. That's OK. You've got all of the information you need. Now take a stab at organizing this list in a logical sequence. Does anything need to be eliminated or re-written? Cross it out or rewrite it. Can you place these actions in a hierarchy that makes sense? In what order should they be listed? Number them in a logical sequence. After you've done these things, come back to see how Dayna organized her list.

Figure 4-4. Dayna's Revised, Organized Action List

Mitigate risk

Main action: Protect the company's confidential information

1. Emails—mainly customer service issue (95% of the time)

2. Share only the minimum necessary in emails

    a. Employees should type the word *encrypt* in the subject line of the email if it contains confidential information

    b. Verify the email address is for the intended recipient

    c. Don't hide rows in attached spreadsheets that contain more than the minimum necessary

    d. Define minimum necessary

3. Understand the importance of reporting unauthorized disclosures of confidential information

    a. Notify your supervisor

    b. Call the privacy office

    c. Disclosure tracking can take a lot of time

Dayna's first pass at organizing the action list is good. This list contains some common red flags, though. Let's refine the action list even more.

Read through Dayna's final action list in Figure 4-6. Are the actions observable? For the most part, yes. Though you couldn't necessarily observe someone verifying an email address outright, the action is written as strong as it can be. Are they organized logically? Notice that everything under number 1 relates to sending email securely and everything under number 2 relates to reporting. And, at a glance, one can easily identify the two main actions that will help mitigate risk concerning privacy: Send emails securely and report unauthorized disclosures.

Action lists help stakeholders confirm their own process and make it easier for them to spot if something is out of place or missing.

Figure 4-5. Action List Red Flags

Action List	Red Flags

Mitigate risk
Main action: Protect the company's confidential information
1. ~~Emails—mainly customer service issue (95% of the time)~~
2. ~~Share only the minimum necessary in emails~~ **Send emails containing confidential information securely**
   a. ~~Employees should~~ type the word encrypt in the subject line of the email if it contains confidential information
   b. Verify the email address is for the intended recipient
   c. ~~Don't hide~~ **Delete** rows, instead of hiding them, in attached spreadsheets that contain more than the minimum necessary
   d. ~~Define minimum necessary~~
3. ~~Understand the importance of reporting~~ **Report** unauthorized disclosures of confidential information
   a. Notify your supervisor
   b. Call the privacy office
   c. ~~Disclosure tracking can take a lot of time~~ *(move to PIBS)*
	#1 describes the audience—this belongs in the audience profile; delete this one.
	
	#2 is repeated in 2c and 2d; should be more overarching (i.e. an action that includes all the ones below it); delete and replace with "Send emails containing confidential information securely"
	
	#2a should speak directly to the employee; begin with the word "Type" and this action is good to go.
	
	#2c should be converted to a positive statement; give the learner something to do, like "Delete rows, instead of hiding them."
	
	#2d is a note for Dayna, not the learner. She can define minimum necessary as part of the content, but this is not something the learner will do. Delete this one.
	
	#3 can go deeper than "understand." In fact, this action could start with the word "Report."
	
	#3c is not part of this training, but a mention of it could be used as a benefit to the learner. If the learner does a quality check, they prevent using a lot of time on disclosure tracking. Move this one to the PIBS list (see the following sidebar).

Figure 4-6. Dayna's Final Action List

1. Send emails containing confidential information securely
   a. Type the word encrypt in the subject line of the email if it contains confidential information
   b. Verify the email address is for the intended recipient
   c. Delete rows, instead of hiding them, in attached spreadsheets that contain more than the minimum necessary
2. Report unauthorized disclosures of confidential information
   a. Notify your supervisor
   b. Call the Privacy Office

PIBS

As you compile and organize the actions for your action list, items like Dayna's listed below may end up on yours:

- Understand the importance to protect our clients' trust in the company.
- Comply with company policies regarding the protection of our information.
- Reduce time spent on restoring affected systems.

While not observable actions, they are important and should be recorded, but not on the action list. They represent another kind of content that will prove useful, especially for your story. It's called PIBS, which stands for purpose, importance, benefits and similar to:

- **Purpose**: The stakeholder will help define the purpose of the instruction. Usually the purpose statement is woven into the course's description or pre-course communications.
- **Importance**: The importance is derived from the purpose. Think of the purpose as the surface-level "why" (to comply with laws, to build an effective team, or to implement a new system) and the importance as the second-level "why" (because we want to keep our clients, because employees on effective teams are more efficient, because the new system will help streamline our processes). Expressing the importance in the story in instruction helps motivate employees to take action.
- **Benefits**: The results of adopting the new behaviors should have an outcome that positively impacts the company, the team, and the individual. There may be more benefits for her to discover. In the story, since characters are in conflict with the actions from the action list, they will naturally reap consequences that are in conflict with the benefits. Benefits also help with motivation.
- **Similar to**: This is particularly helpful when the content is somewhat foreign to the learner and they need something familiar to explain the unfamiliar. When your story solution is a metaphor, go to your *similar to* for inspiration.

There is a PIBS for each item on the action list, but that can get a little overwhelming. PIBS for Dayna's cybersecurity and privacy course may look similar to this:

- **Purpose**: To comply with company policies regarding the protection of our clients' information.
- **Importance**: Because we want our clients to keep trusting us with their information and do business with us.
- **Benefits**: Our company's brand reputation increases and reduce time spent on restoring affected systems. Individuals benefit from encrypting emails successfully by saving them time on the back end, when they might have to spend hours assisting with disclosure tracking.
- **Similar to**: The trust you place in a credit card company to guard your information.

Training and Stories Are All About Action

Dayna has extracted, from her conversation with Randall, the things that employees should be able to do. She's placed them in a logical order. She will need to go back to Randall to confirm with him that the action list is accurate and complete and that there is nothing extraneous on it.

The action list is essential for instruction and for storytelling. Learner actions must align with the business outcome, which is why they must be observable. Could you take a video of someone doing it? Great! You've got an observable action that you can teach.

This is also important for storytelling, because stories are all about observable action. Earlier in the book, you were asked to imagine your training story as a staged play. Go through your action list and imagine yourself as a director telling the actor to do the things on that list. "Bonnie, I'd like you to cross stage left and be aware of product applications." Sounds ridiculous, right? But if you told Bonnie to cross stage left and use the product sheet to show the client product features that will meet their needs, she can actually do something. There's even a prop she can use to do it!

Characters do things, and in Story Design, they are doing things that conflict with the action list. Get the action list right and the conflict of your story will be spot on.

The End of Analysis

You leave the Discover phase with two things in hand: an audience profile and an action list. Along the way, you've made note of case studies and other possible stories. You've also got a handle on the training's purpose, importance, benefits, and similarities (PIBS). Now it's time to turn to the Design phase. We'll leave instructional design for now and focus exclusively on designing the story, but we'll come back to it in the Deliver phase of the book, where we'll explore the application of storytelling to training delivery.

PRACTICE STORY DESIGN:
Structure an Action List

You gather all of the notes from your conversations with Dr. Kobal and his staff and make a list of the actions that will need to be taken in order for Well Adjusted Chiropractic to retain its customers and staff members.

All of these actions funnel up to the main objective of building strong client loyalty. You've divided your list into three main categories that focus on communication as a foundation of trust building: manager-to-staff communication, staff-to-client communication, and staff-to-staff communication. Dr. Kobal is coaching Carrie on how to communicate with the staff more effectively. For the most part, the staff is cordial to clients when speaking to them directly. You decide to focus training on the last category: staff-to-staff communication.

First, narrow this list down to observable actions. You may need to convert some of them into strong positive actions. Then organize them in a logical sequence. It may not be chronological, but put them in an order that makes sense. Try to narrow the actions down to one main action and four sub-actions that are written as statements directly to the learner. After you've completed the exercise, you can compare your answers to the completed Instructional Story Design Plan in appendix 3.

- Respect other staff members as you want to be respected in the presence of clients.

- Don't talk about personal issues in front of the client.
- Understand the importance of respectful communication.
- Don't withhold information; let staff members in other areas know about important information concerning clients.
- Be aware of clients in the room when speaking to fellow staff members; keep their personal information private.
- Explain the difference between respectful and disrespectful communication.
- Openly communicate with your fellow-staff members.

Write your revised action list below:

PART II
Design

Create characters, conflict, and action

CHAPTER FIVE
Develop Relatable Characters

First Attempt

Dayna reads through the short paragraph she has typed and retyped a dozen times. She mumbles the words audibly: "This is a story about phishing and how to respond to an email containing attachments or links. An employee of our company received an email from a friend—or at least it appeared to be from a friend. In the email, the friend asked the employee to click on a link in the email that would take them to a webpage containing some great store coupons. The employee is about to click the link when the employee realized that the email might not be from a friend after all. It could be from a scammer. Our policy regarding protection of our company systems states, 'Be aware that emails containing malware pose a threat to our company systems.'"

"OK," Dayna nods, "Not bad. Let's see what Susan thinks about it." She composes an email to the director of compliance and attaches her first—actually her thirteenth—attempt at writing a cybersecurity story for the compliance course.

At the end of the day, she receives a response.

"Dayna, thank you for giving the story a try. It's heading in the right direction. Maybe give the employee a name? Let's talk tomorrow."

"That's it? Nice try? I give up! What does she expect? *War and Peace*?" Dayna says to herself. She grabs a copy of her story and heads out. It's Question Mark Grill night.

"So how's the story coming?" James asks.

"I knew you were going to ask me that." Dayna slumps into the booth seat across from him. "I brought it with me."

"Oh, good. Let me see!" Dayna takes a folded piece of paper out of her tote bag and hands it to James. "My masterpiece," she mutters. She feels intimidated putting her scrap of a story into the hands of someone who acts out stories on the stage almost every weekend. But with a meeting with Susan the next day, she needs some perspective.

James reads it silently. Dayna searched his face for a clue. Does he think it's good? He looks up and asks, "Has the compliance director read this yet?"

Dayna looks away, "Yeah."

"And? What did she say?"

Dayna rolls her eyes. "Basically she said, 'Nice try, don't call us, we'll call you.'"

James chuckles. "No, really, what did she say?"

"She wants to meet tomorrow and talk about it. What do you think about it? The story."

"That's all she said?"

"Pretty much, so what do you think?"

James looks down at the creased paper. "Well, you might start by giving the employee a name."

"That's exactly what Susan said!"

"I thought you said . . . " James starts.

Dayna interrupts, "I was trying to make it like, you know, like a character that could be anybody!"

"Anybody has a name," says James.

"I know that! But, OK, if I give this person a name, it might be too . . . " Dayna isn't sure what she wants to say. "I really don't think I'm cut out for this. I'm not a novelist."

"I doubt the compliance director is expecting the course to win a Pulitzer Prize. Giving the character a name will just make them more real," he suggests.

Dayna knows he's right. "Alright, what do I name her? Mary? Beth? . . . Jamie?"

James swoons. "Would you really name your leading woman after me?"

"If you're not nice to me, I will," she says.

"Oh, come on, Dayna, it's not that bad! It just needs action."

Dayna is a little more defensive than she means to be. "You don't think my story has action? What about when she's about to click the link? That was kind of scary." Dayna looks at James.

James grins. "Yeah, I was on the edge of my seat when the employee realized it was a scammer!" He fakes screams, "No! Not the store coupons trick!"

They both laugh. James tilts his head. "How many women work for your company?"

Dayna is still smiling. "What?"

"Well you keep calling this character a woman. I was curious why."

"Not many, actually."

"Not many women work at your company?"

"I actually know the percentage." She smiles. "I did my homework. Our company is 70 percent men."

"Look at you! So, maybe the character's name should be Eric, instead of Mary . . . or Jamie."

"Eric? No way!" James isn't following. "I knew an Eric once." Dayna pauses. "Nevermind. Eric isn't right."

James smiles, "Alright, what would you name him?"

"I don't know."

"Josh?" he asks.

"No."

"Ricardo?"

"No."

"Archibald?"

"No!"

"Why not?" asks James.

"Too uppity. The guys in this company are straightforward. Analytical, you know?"

"OK, so what's a straightforward analytical name?"

Dayna thinks a minute, then nods. "Steve."

"Steve." James smiles. "Nice! What else about these guys do you know?"

"Well, I did make this audience profile thing, at your suggestion. They value innovation, for sure. They're pretty good at navigating change, 'cause it's happening all the time. The company got this third-party vendor that's handling the help desk, which nobody is thrilled with. People avoid calling the help desk at all costs . . . including me," she interjects. "I'm not sure what this has to do with training, but I also made a note that they like football and baseball . . . "

"That is so impressive, Dayna! Do you know what you're doing?" Dayna shakes her head. "Character analysis!" He throws up his arms. "In reverse! This is exactly what I was talking about. You can use this audience profile to write characters!"

"I can't write characters that look like everybody!"

"But you can write characters that everybody can relate to! Right? Characters aren't look-alikes, they're people we understand. I mean if 70 percent of the company fits your description, then everybody knows someone like that! And maybe there's more characters that reach the rest of your audience!" James was half standing, leaning over the table towards Dayna. "Get it?"

Dayna laughs at her friend. "Yes, I get it."

"So, what kind of character would your audience relate to?" He sits down. "Who is Steve, besides straightforward and analytical?"

Dayna thinks. She really thinks about it. "I'm not sure. I haven't been with the company very long and I don't interact with employees in operational areas that much." She looks at James. "I don't know."

"OK, let's start with this: Is Steve a coupon collector?" asks James.

"Hm?" Dayna doesn't catch what James is getting at.

"Your character, Steve? Would he really be tempted by a link to store coupons?"

"Oh, yeah . . . no. OK, I think I see where you're going."

"What does your audience profile say about him?" he presses.

Dayna looks up. "Um, I guess something about engineering might be better?" Dayna is prepared to talk more, but James is looking past her. He's thinking. Of something, probably devious. Then he looks at Dayna.

"I'm teaching an acting class at the Boys and Girls Club this Saturday at two. Can you come?"

That's the last thing Dayna expects James to say. "What? What's that got to do . . . "

"Tell me you'll come!" James interrupts.

"OK, sure," Dayna stumbles, "But . . . "

"Great! You work on Steve and I'll see you Saturday!" James gets up.

Dayna has to smile at her friend's dramatic departure. Never a dull moment. Her mind drifts back to her pending meeting with Susan the next day. What is she going to say?

Jumping-Off Point

Coming out of the Discover phase you will have a long list of actions that need to be trained. If you feel like Dayna, staring at your analysis wondering how to make a story out of it, you are not alone. But by now, you know that you are not starting with an empty stage. The Discover chapters helped you identify your audience and what you need them to do. This is your jumping off point. Let's take that information and translate it into the two essential story elements: relatable characters in strong conflict. In this chapter, we begin with relatable characters (Figure 5-1).

Figure 5-1. Relatable Characters in the Story Design Model

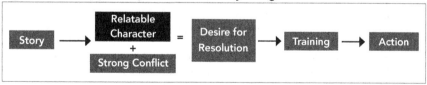

Start With Discovery

No matter what size audience, you have to choose the characters in your story based on the audience profile. There are some guideposts in designing characters for your story that will help keep you on track. Dayna has already started creating a character—Steve—for the cybersecurity story. At this point, though, Steve is just a name. Dayna uses the audience profile of the company to create an individual character that employees can relate to (Figure 5-2).

Figure 5-2. Dayna's Audience Profile and Action List for Cybersecurity

Company Audience Profile

- **Personal information**: Most employees work at headquarters and live in a thriving mid-sized city. Ten percent work in smaller regional locations across the country and a about 90 employees work remotely. The four main departments are engineering, IT, customer service, and sales. Engineers and sales staff stay with the company for decades. IT and customer service have a decent turnover rate. High school football is a big deal in the headquarters location. They also have a local minor league baseball team. The company offers discounted tickets to those games and many employees go with their families. Seventy percent of the employee population is male.
- **Their pre-existing knowledge of the performance they are training on**: Employees have had training on both phishing and privacy, but the courses are essentially the policy on PowerPoint slides with no examples of phishing emails or practice encrypting emails successfully. The policies do not tell employees what to do if they do click on a link or open an attachment containing malware or how to handle the situation if they've sent an unencrypted email.
- **What they value**: Innovation, quality, customer service, hard work, and celebrating accomplishments.
- **Their current circumstances at work**: A new product release has had a ripple effect of change within the organization, including restructuring two of its divisions. IT has recently outsourced its Help Desk to a vendor. The transition has been bumpy. The company has a strong financial standing and rewards its employees well for strong performance.
- **Their reactions to current circumstances at work**: Employees in the affected divisions are adjusting to the new reporting structure well. They are used to organizational changes that facilitate more innovation. However, because of the frequent team changes, effective communication regarding new policies and expectations sometimes suffers. There is general distrust of the vendor who has taken the help desk function. Many employees avoid calling the help desk. Employees are motivated to bring innovative products to the market and rally behind new products.
- **Their fears and preconceptions of training**: They fear that their new product will fail. They are concerned about being sidetracked from their focus on innovation and customer service. Compliance is sometimes perceived as a hinderance to innovation and employees struggle to complete compliance training on time.
- **Benefits of training**: Protect the company's reputation as innovative and trustworthy. Unhindered use of tools to do job as employees prevent viruses.
- **Their technology options for training delivery**: They use primarily e-learning for corporate-wide training. Employees have no issue accessing courses that have been assigned to them. The LMS does not support mobile. Most employees will take this course in the office on their work computer or connected remotely to the company's system through VDI.

Training Goal for Cybersecurity
Reduce the number of phishing email incidents 90 percent by end of the quarter as employees detect phishing attempts and take appropriate action.

Action List
Main action: Protect the company's information from scammers
1. Scan emails for common phishing clues using the Phishing Clues job aid
2. Report suspected breaches in security
   a. Call cybersecurity office
   b. Notify your supervisor
3. Forward suspicious emails to the help desk without clicking links or opening attachments

---

Guideposts for Character Descriptions

Your goal is to describe characters your audience can relate to. After reading through Dayna's case study, characters and plot lines may already be formulating in your mind. That's great! Act on those instincts and use the following guideposts to help shape them into characters that best contribute to the goal of training this audience: *Detect phishing attempts and take appropriate action.*

Their Position

Dayna chooses to set the story in her company's office. Since one of the largest departments in the company is engineering, she chooses to make her character an engineer.

Naming the person's position in the story is not always necessary, but it's a good place to begin a character description. If your audience is an enterprise-wide audience, choose a position that many in the company will either occupy themselves or know someone who does.

Their Conflict

This is the most useful of the guideposts. Look back at the action list. The main action is to *Protect the company's information from scammers*. Underneath it are three sub-actions. Imagine the character (the engineer) in conflict with one of those three actions. For instance, Dayna could pair her engineer with action 1:

Scan emails for common phishing clues using the Phishing Clues job aid

Building strong conflict will be addressed in detail in the next chapter, but already you can see how matching up your characters to be in conflict with one (or more) of the actions on your action list helps define who they are.

Take a moment and think about the engineer. He struggles to scan emails for common phishing clues. Write a short list of adjectives or nouns that describe the engineer based on this new information.

Dayna may describe him as:

- busy
- an innovator
- preoccupied
- a workaholic
- impetuous
- a go-getter.

The engineer in this story could be a busy innovator, a preoccupied work-aholic, or an impetuous go-getter. You can imagine any of these characters struggling to take time to scan emails for phishing clues. The stories would be very different, but the character of the engineer is in alignment with the action list and, therefore, reinforces the outcome of training.

Dayna chooses to be conservative and make her character a busy inno-vator, which seems to capture the spirit of the problem. It's not that this audience is intentionally disregarding compliance. They're just busy with other things and scanning emails for phishing clues is not at the top of their minds.

By simply putting the character in conflict with an action on the list, describing the character becomes easier. In her final story about the engineer, Dayna will strive to put him in conflict with all three sub-actions. For now, though, the conflict with action 1 has helped shape the character.

Their Peers

Dayna starts with a simple story that involves only one character, the engi-neer. In a moment, we'll look at her characters for the privacy story, which will involve two people. In the practice session, you'll also create two characters.

When you have two or more characters, view them as a cast of peers, with contrasting personalities. There may be occasions where two toxic people need to battle it out in your story, but not usually. You want to aim for balance in your stories. Rely on your experience as a daily consumer and teller of stories to guide you toward that right balance and contrast in your cast of characters.

Demographics should also play a role in balance. Depending on your audience profile, you will want to cast characters with the appropriate ratio of women and men, young and old and in-between, and the spectrum of cultural backgrounds. Dayna already has a man in mind for this character, which seems appropriate, given that 70 percent of the company is male.

Their Appearance and Mannerisms

Brief physical descriptions can be helpful, especially if you plan to develop the story using pictures, video, or animation. Dayna describes her engineer as:

- broad-shouldered and tall
- high energy.

Dayna doesn't need much in this category to picture in her mind who the engineer is. Even if these physical attributes don't make it into the story exactly as she initially imagines it, it will help her to connect with the character more concretely as she writes the story.

So far, Dayna can describe her character as:

An engineer, a busy innovator, tall with broad shoulders, high energy.

She's getting there.

Build in More Detail Using the Audience Profile

In chapter 3, you narrowed the audience profile down to eight key pieces of information. Five of these attributes will act as further guideposts to help describe the character:

1. personal information
2. values
3. current circumstances at work

4. reaction to current circumstances at work
5. fears.

Personal Information

The character's personal history with the company may be helpful and relevant to the story's action. Are they a new hire? Have they been with the company for 20 years? Did they leave the organization for a few years and have recently come back? Mentioning a personal outside activity in the story can be a point of connection with your audience, as long as it's related to the conflict of the story.

Dayna looks at the personal information of her audience profile to gain inspiration for her character's description:

- He loves sports, and is a former football player at a local high school.
- He's high energy.
- He's married and has a seven-year-old son.

Knowing that Dayna's character loves sports, has high energy, and is married and has a seven-year-old son may help move the plot forward. For instance, it may help Dayna narrow in on what kind of phishing email would be a temptation. Since he loves sports, perhaps the lure to make him click the link is free tickets to a game or coupons for sports equipment. Including personal information in the character description is not always necessary, but it is helpful when the story involves outside influences.

Values

You don't need to dive deeply into the psyche of your characters, but it's helpful to know how their values affect their behaviors. Behaviors equal action. Dayna looks at the values of her audience and feels that her character's values would likely align with innovation. This is how she describes it:

- values fast innovation
- works hard and plays hard.

Imagine this character coming into contact with a phishing email. He's got email pouring in and a phishing email advertising something he loves comes across his desk. He's going to make decisions based on his values. For instance, if he's a fast innovator, he may make hasty decisions, which is great for some things, but not when it comes to scanning emails for phishing clues. Someone who values detailed accuracy is probably not going to be tempted to click a link in a phishing email in the same way as this character who values fast innovation. Remember, values show themselves through action. So, if you have the opportunity to observe the audience you're designing for, write down their actions. Their actions should reveal their true values regardless of the words painted on the corporate wall.

Let's add personal information and values to the character description.

> An engineer, a busy innovator, tall with broad shoulders, high energy, **married and has a seven-year-old son. He's been with the company for five years, loves sports, former football player at a local high school. Values fast innovation, works hard and plays hard.**

Are you beginning to know who this man is? Is the character description sparking ideas for action?

Their Current Circumstances and Reactions to Current Circumstances at Work

These two items from the audience profile work in tandem. Each of your characters is immersed in the same work environment, producing different reactions. Draw from the audience profile to define those circumstances for the story. In the audience profile, Dayna notes the following circumstances and the employees' reactions to them (Figure 5-3).

Figure 5-3. Circumstances and Employee Reactions

Circumstance	Reaction to Circumstance
A new product release has had a ripple effect of change within the organization, including restructuring two of its divisions.	Employees in the affected divisions are adjusting to the new reporting structure well. They are used to organizational changes that facilitate more innovation. However, because of the frequent team changes, effective communication regarding new policies and expectations sometimes suffers. Employees are motivated to bring innovative products to the market and rally behind new products.

Figure 5-3. Circumstances and Employee Reactions (cont.)

Circumstance	Reaction to Circumstance
IT has recently outsourced its help desk to a vendor. The transition has been bumpy.	There is general distrust of the vendor who has taken the help desk function. Many employees avoid calling the help desk.
The company has a strong financial standing and rewards its employees well for strong performance.	The drive for innovation is also fueled by recognition and rewards. Employees are resourceful and try to solve problems on their own before reaching out for help.

The reactions your audience has on the job hint at plot lines, but they can also inform your character descriptions. For instance, Dayna can assign a couple of these actions to her character:

- has only met with his manager once since the reorg three months ago
- never calls the help desk for computer problems; tries to fix things himself.

Now Dayna's character is even more connected with the audience profile. His reactions to circumstances in the story will seem familiar and real to life.

Their Fears

If you are able to pinpoint the fears of your audience, it can also help define the characters. Dayna's audience fears that their new product will fail. For Dayna's character, this fear is in direct opposition to what he values most—innovation. This fear may be felt more by some in the organization than others, but as a result, they are concerned about being sidetracked from their focus on innovation and customer service. Compliance is sometimes perceived as a hindrance to innovation and they struggle to complete compliance training on time. Fear is a powerful motivation for taking action—or not taking action. For Dayna's character, if the fear of a product failing trumps taking time away from innovation to scan an email for phishing clues, it's going to affect the decisions he makes. Also, because compliance training is not a priority for this group, it's likely that when they finally do take the course, they are rushing through it at the last minute.

Let's add the character's reaction to current circumstances and his fears to the character's description:

> An engineer, a busy innovator, tall with broad shoulders, high energy, married and has a seven-year-old son. He's been with the company for five years, loves sports, former football player at a local high school. Values fast innovation, works hard and plays hard. **He's only met with his manager once since the reorg three months ago. Never calls the help desk for computer problems; tries to fix things himself. Fears being delayed or distracted from his work.**

Fears provide an excellent source of internal conflict, which you'll learn more about in the next chapter.

Their Backstory

This is not a novel. Let me repeat that. This is not a novel. You do not need to create a long, detailed history for your characters. Unless you are creating a series of stories that follows a character through their life and career, keep the backstory for your characters limited to the following details:

- education
- social interactions
- relevant family details.

Keep these questions in mind as you consider backstory details:

- Does it relate to the action of the story and contribute to the conflict?
- Is it reflective of the audience profile?

If so, it may be worthy of including in your character description. Take a look at some of the backstory descriptions below. Which ones seem extraneous for Dayna's character and which ones seem possibly relevant?

- Finished his four-year engineering degree in two and a half years.
- Loves coaching his son's Little League baseball team.
- Plays pool with his former college friends every second Tuesday of the month.
- Fourth-born of five children (all boys).

That he plays pool with his former college friends and is the fourth-born in his family are interesting facts that may ultimately have influenced who he has become, but these have little to do with the action of the story. If it helps you to know these details, go for it, but they aren't necessary for designing a story for training. Your audience certainly doesn't need to know this information to benefit from the story. Knowing that he finished his four-year engineering degree in two and a half years sheds light on this man's drive to get things done and may be useful to you as you write the plot. His love for coaching his son's Little League baseball team seems like it could be extraneous, but Dayna includes it anyway.

Backstory is generally for your own benefit as you describe your characters. Usually this information will not make it into the story, though occasionally it will. Dayna will draw upon this category for her final story.

Their Name

Often, people who are designing stories for training will ask this question: "How do you come up with a name?" To answer this, go back to the character description. If you've used the guideposts for describing your character, you have a nice description of who your character is. Take a look at the description of Dayna's character:

> An engineer, a busy innovator, tall with broad shoulders, high energy, married and has a seven-year-old son. He's been with the company for five years, loves sports, former football player at a local high school. Values fast innovation, works hard and plays hard. He's only met with his manager once since the reorg three months ago. Never calls the help desk for computer problems; tries to fix things himself. Fears being delayed or distracted from his work. Finished his four-year degree in two and a half years, loves coaching his son's Little League baseball team.

Without thinking too hard, what would you name this character? Seriously, stop and think about it before reading on. What would you name him?

What did you come up with? Chad? Michael "The Truck" Thornton? Livingston? You likely came up with something completely different but it felt right to you. Why? What inspired that name? Sometimes, it's because the description reminds you of a certain person in your life. If your inspiration is running low, read the description to someone else and ask them to offer a name suggestion. Visit a baby names site and read through until you land on the right one.

Let the character description determine the name. Don't force it. Just let the name happen. As crazy as it sounds, you instinctively know when someone has slapped a name on a character that doesn't fit. It's contrived, and you feel it.

Dayna adds a name to the character description:

> **Steve,** an engineer, a busy innovator, tall with broad shoulders, high energy, married and has a seven-year-old son. He's been with the company for five years, loves sports, former football player at a local high school. Values fast innovation, works hard and plays hard. He's only met with his manager once since the reorg three months ago. Never calls the help desk for computer problems; tries to fix things himself. Fears being delayed or distracted from his work. Finished his four-year degree in two and a half years, loves coaching his son's Little League baseball team.

That wasn't so bad, right? The guideposts for character descriptions are there for you to use as you need them. It maximizes the use of the audience profile to create characters that your audience will truly relate to. Dayna's Steve character is fully fleshed out and ready to be cast in the story. That takes care of the character for the cybersecurity story, but Dayna has more characters to create for the privacy story.

In her conversation with Randall, Dayna discovered that 95 percent of the privacy issues were happening in customer service. So Dayna creates a separate audience profile that captures unique information about that department. Figure 5-4 is her audience profile, training goal, and action list for the privacy training.

Figure 5-4. Customer Service Audience Profile

Personal information	Even split between male and female; overall younger ages than the rest of the company.
Their pre-existing knowledge of the performance you are training on	They've been trained on the new way of encrypting email. They have not received training on quality-checking emails or spreadsheets.
What they value	Production and quality of service; their performance is rated on both.
Their current circumstances at work	A recent change in the company's product has increased customer calls by 20 percent. They've attended two hours of online training to learn about the new product. Recently a group of 12 of their best advocates left to go to a competitor. They are training more customer advocates with a mentoring approach.
Their reactions to current circumstances at work	Customer advocates are challenged to keep up with the high call volume and the added responsibility of training more new employees than they are used to. They also struggle to keep up with the number of requests for forms and information. They are stressed out, but they try to encourage and help one another. They are doing well with the new product knowledge. Morale is low after losing 12 of their best advocates. Mentors are compensated for their extra effort in training the new employees, for which they are grateful but still stressed by the workload.
Their fears	That they will lose more co-workers and their performance will suffer.
Benefits of training	Protect the company's customer service reputation, unhindered productivity as advocates protect against privacy incidents.
Their technology options for training delivery	They use primarily e-learning for corporate-wide training. Employees have no issue accessing courses that have been assigned to them. The LMS does not support mobile. Most employees will take this course in the office on their work computer or connected remotely to the company's system through VDI.

Training Goal for Privacy
Reduce the number of unencrypted emails containing sensitive information to outside parties 15 percent by end of quarter as employees encrypt email correctly.

Action List for Privacy
Main action: Protect the company's confidential information.
1. Send emails containing confidential information securely.
   a. Type the word *encrypt* in the subject line of the email if it contains confidential information.
   b. Verify the email address is for the intended recipient.
   c. Delete rows, instead of hiding them, in attached spreadsheets that contain more than the minimum necessary.
2. Report unauthorized disclosures of confidential information.
   a. Notify your supervisor.
   b. Call the privacy office.

Dayna uses the guideposts to create two characters for the privacy story (Figure 5-5).

Figure 5-5. Dayna's Characters for Privacy Story

Guidepost	Character 1	Character 2
Position	Customer advocate	Customer advocate new hire
Conflict	#1 Send emails containing confidential information securely **Instinctual caretaker**	#1 Send emails containing confidential information securely **Conscientious learner**
Peers	Female, mentor, kind and encouraging to Character 2	Male mentee, anxious to learn from Character 1
Appearance	Long hair, eclectic style, bouncy	Thin, concentrated, put together, serious
Personal information	One of the few remaining long-timers. Has been with the company 10 years. Enjoys shopping online and reality shows.	Brand new to the company. Likes playing chess and Risk.
Values	Customer care	Accuracy and thoroughness
Reaction to current circumstances	Takes the departure of her former colleagues in stride; copes with the pressure of being short-staffed by focusing on one call at a time and taking care of customer needs.	Feels an obligation to get trained quickly and help out with the work. Puts a lot of pressure on himself.
Fears	That a customer won't be taken care of properly.	Letting down Character 1 and doing things incorrectly.

Figure 5-5. Dayna's Characters for Privacy Story (cont.)

Guidepost	Character 1	Character 2
Backstory	Single. Loves getting a manicure with her best friend every weekend.	Newly married. First child is on the way.
Name	Jasmine	Andrew

Dayna's characters for the privacy story have taken shape. Notice the contrast between the two character descriptions. Some of the contrasts pair well together for a positive outcome: caretaker and learner, mentor and mentee, Jasmine fears letting the customer down while Andrew fears letting Jasmine down. Other contrasts form natural conflict: bouncy versus serious, customer care versus thoroughness, focuses on one call at a time versus puts lots of pressure on himself. Dayna has a nice balance between her two characters. And both descriptions were inspired by one audience profile.

Characters Are Real People

The above cast of characters are based on an audience profile of real people. Your characters need to be real too with real personalities, strengths, weaknesses, and life experiences. Characters are not mirror images of your audience, but they must be relatable, especially at an emotional level. Your audience needs to connect with your characters.

Periodically, during a workshop, someone may give their characters names like Chatty Patty, Kyle Klutz, or Gary Go-Getter. Inevitably, these humorous names end up diluting the power of the story. The rest of the story is usually convincing. The names just get in the way. As soon as they become Patty, Kyle, and Gary, they're more relatable.

That doesn't mean that larger-than-life characters and character types don't have a place in stories for training. Television sitcoms are known for a cast of stock characters who are always the same in every episode. They are fairly two-dimensional. And it works! This can work in training as well. I created a comic series for a compliance course that involved a cast of stick figures. They were constantly causing compliance havoc. In every episode, employees who took the training knew how each character was going to behave. The trick, however, is that the stick figure characters were acting out actual case studies that had been reported through the compliance hotline. So their antics were founded upon reality, not outlandish, unrealistic imaginations. They became so popular among employees that compliance training found a fresh, positive identity. It actually changed the way people approached compliance training—with anticipation, rather than dread. So if you choose to use stock characters, be sure to ground their conflict in the action list and steer clear of stereotypes that may offend your learners.

The purpose of creating relatable characters is so that your audience connects with them, cares about them, identifies with them. Use these guideposts to write your character descriptions. You'll hit the mark with your audience and immediately engage them with the story. Use the Character Description Worksheet in the appendix 1 for your next project.

Figure 5-6. Character Description Worksheet From Instructional Story Design Plan

Character Description Worksheet

Use the guideposts to compile the final character description, which you can record on the Instructional Story Design Plan in Appendix 2.

Guidepost	Character Description
Position At work, in life	
Conflict Which action are they in conflict with? What nouns and adjectives come to mind?	
Peers How does their personality contrast with other characters in the story?	
Appearance Physical attributes can be helpful in creating the story, even if the final portrayal isn't an exact match.	
Personal information Look to the audience profile for this information.	
Values Look to the audience profile for this information.	
Reaction to current circumstances Look to the audience profile for this information.	
Fears Look to the audience profile for this information.	
Backstory Details about their history that may affect the action of the story, true to audience profile.	
Name Read through the above description. What name comes to mind?	

The editable Character Description Worksheet is available at needastory. com/book-resources.

Create Relatable Characters

You know the staff at Well Adjusted pretty well by now. You've spent a good amount of time with the owner. You've settled on a training goal. You've collected data about your audience and structured an action list. Now it's time to use your analysis to create some relatable characters!

Use the training goal and audience profile from the work you did in chapter 3 and the action list you structured in chapter 4 to create characters for your training story. Write this information in the space below before continuing.

Since there are four main areas in the clinic—front desk, back office, examination rooms, and therapy bay—you'll have four basic staff positions to choose from: front desk staff, back office staff, doctors, and therapists. Create two characters from two different areas of the clinic. Use the guideposts to help walk you through the process of creating two relatable characters based on your audience profile. Put each of the characters in conflict with a different action from the action list and develop their descriptions in contrast to one another.

In appendix 3, you'll find the completed Instructional Story Design Plan, which may help if you need inspiration. Enjoy this fun step.

When you're finished, read through the descriptions and do a gut check. Do they feel like real people? Do you see potential for conflict by putting these two people in the same room together? If not, where does it feel contrived or out of alignment with the audience profile? Also, note which guideposts gave you the most insight into the characters. You will continue writing the story using these characters. For fun, you may want to check out the completed Instructional Story Design Plan to see some other character options. Next, you'll put these characters into action!

Guidepost	Character 1	Character 2
Position		
Conflict		
Peers		
Appearance		
Personal information		
Values		
Reaction to current circumstances		
Fears		
Backstory		
Name		

CHAPTER SIX

Create Action and Conflict

The Boys and Girls Club

Dayna arrives at the Boys and Girls Club on Saturday. There's a classroom where James and several high schoolers are gathered in a circle in the middle of a raised platform. Dayna enters quietly and sits in the back row. James hears her, turns around, and introduces Dayna to the group.

"Hey, this is my friend, Dayna, everybody!" Dayna gives the group a small wave. "She's an instructional designer. I asked her to come watch our scenes today. You need an audience and"—he smiles at Dayna—"she could use some help with story writing." The kids greet her and smile.

So that's why he invited me, thinks Dayna. *Well, these kids probably know a lot more about how to tell a good story than I do.* She settles back in her seat. The high schoolers perform scenes in pairs. Dayna is sure that most of these kids have never performed in their lives. She's surprised when the first pair, Jamal and Katrina, begin to act out a scene from Romeo and Juliet. *Wow,* she thinks, *James is really stretching these kids . . . Shakespeare!*

They are performing the famous scene where Romeo comes to Juliet's house by night. "O Romeo, Romeo! wherefore art thou Romeo?" Juliet calls out.

When Katrina gets to the line, "What's in a name? That which we call a rose, by any other name would smell as sweet," James stops the scene and asks, "OK, Katrina, that's good. But what is the action here?"

Katrina looks down at her script, "Um, Juliet wants to be with Romeo." She looks back up at James. "Right?"

James stands up and walks over to Katrina, "Yes, of course. That's good. You're right. She does want to be with Romeo. But what's the action? Look at the whole line. What is Juliet doing here?" He gives Katrina time to think it over.

"I guess she's saying that she doesn't care that Romeo is a Montague and she's a Capulet?" James smiles and nods, encouraging Katrina to keep going. "And . . . she just wants to be with him?"

"Good!" James affirms her. "So what do you think the action is behind what she's saying?"

"Oh!" Jamal starts to say something. "Sorry, I just had an idea." Katrina doesn't mind being off the hot seat.

"Go ahead, Jamal," says James.

Jamal continues, thinking out loud, "Isn't she kind of denying her family? Well, really, Romeo's doing that too, right? Aren't they both, like, deciding to leave their families so they can be with one another, even though their families hate each other?"

"Yes!" James is excited. "What's the action in what you just said, Jamal?"

"Uh . . . " Jamal isn't certain.

Katrina helps him, "Leaving her family?"

"Good," says James. "But Jamal used a more powerful word to say that."

"Denying her family!" Jamal says, smiling.

"Yeah, denying, that was it!" Katrina laughs.

"OK," says James, walking back to his seat, "Deliver that line again, but this time say it like you are denying your family. Show me the action!"

"Whoa," Katrina says under her breath. She thinks for a minute and begins at the top of the line. She sounds completely different.

"'Tis but thy name that is my enemy;

Thou art thyself, though not a Montague.

What's Montague? It is nor hand, nor foot,

Nor arm, nor face, nor any other part

Belonging to a man. O, be some other name!"

Dayna leans forward in her seat. Katrina's voice rises in pitch and intensity.

"What's in a name? That which we call a rose

By any other name would smell as sweet."

Katrina stops, a little shaken by the emotional power in her voice. Everyone is stunned. Then she shakes her head and says, in a total break of character, "I'm not leaving my mama and daddy for some teenage chump!" Everybody busts out laughing.

"That was amazing, Katrina!" Jamal says between laughing. "You're an actor!"

Katrina flips her hair. "You can call me Diva, Romeo!" Everybody laughs again.

James brings the group back together to focus on their work. Scene after scene, James drives home the same question, "What's the action?" The class ends and the kids give James high fives and thank Dayna for being their audience before leaving.

Dayna walks up to James. "That was impressive. How do you do that?"

James smiles as he packs his backpack, "Thanks, how do I do what?"

"Those kids came to life for you," she says.

"I love 'em," says James, "and they are amazing kids. They work hard."

"I could never engage my students like that when I was teaching middle school. I can't believe you have them doing Shakespeare!"

"Speaking of Shakespeare, how's your story coming?" he asks.

"Well, I'm no playwright, but I've done a little more homework. I just don't know where to start with the story."

"Yeah? What kind of homework?" he asks.

Dayna fishes out two pieces of paper from her tote and hands one of them to James. "Well, I actually made up some characters. Do you think it's alright to make characters up for training?"

"Whoa!" says James, reading over the character descriptions. "I like Steve a lot more now! Of course it's OK! Fiction is great! Besides they're based on your employee profile. And who's this Jasmine lady?"

"Actually," says Dayna, "it turns out that our customer service area is not mostly men—it's more of an even split—and that's who's sending the spreadsheets with sensitive information . . . Jasmine."

"You lost me with the spreadsheet thing," says James. "But this is great! You actually know who your audience is!"

"You keep using that word, *audience*," Dayna laughs. "You make it sound like a performance."

"Um, you're an instructional designer." James teases. "What are you training people on?"

Dayna looks up, then nods. "Performance. OK, I think I get it."

"You have a lot of good material here for characters who are ready to perform for your audience. What's on the other paper?"

Dayna hands him the other piece of paper. "It's the task list for the course."

"You just happened to have all of this stuff with you on a Saturday?" James laughs. He looks at the paper. "Hey, it says up here at the top that this is an action list?"

"Oh yeah," says Dayna, "It made it easier to talk with the subject matter expert when I called it a list of actions."

James gasps. "You are a genius!"

"Not really," says Dayna.

"No, seriously!" He holds up the two pieces of paper. "You've written your story!"

Dayna is confused. "Yeah, but the coupon thing wasn't really that good."

"Not that story!" says James. "Look!" He holds up the character descriptions. "Here are your characters." He holds up the action list. "And here is your action! Boom!"

Dayna isn't sure she follows. "OK, but a story about Jasmine encrypting an email doesn't sound like a page-turner."

James asks, "What have I been asking the kids about their scenes today?"

Dayna didn't have to think, "What's the action?"

"Right! What's the action? Otherwise we're just hearing words. Remember Katrina? The first time she just quoted the words."

"Of course!" interrupts Dayna. "It was night and day. She was . . . denying her family the second time. That was really powerful."

"It was powerful because she was *acting* the second time." James pauses. "I know that the story you are writing is not classic literature. It's for training. But I think the principle is the same. You've got to have action with a purpose."

"Agreed," says Dayna, "So, what is the purpose?"

"Well, think about Romeo and Juliet. What if, after Romeo and Juliet get married, their families decide to work things out. Their parents take turns spending holidays with the grandchildren. And everything's great!?" Dayna laughs. "See!" he says, "There's plenty of action, but what do you think is missing in that version?"

"Friction?"

"Good word," says James. "There's no friction, or conflict."

"OK," says Dayna. "So my story needs action *and* it needs conflict."

"Right, but they aren't separate things. They need to be the same. The action is the conflict. Juliet denying her family is the conflict in that scene." He goes on, "It's nice if Steve doesn't click the phishing link or Jasmine sends an email properly, but that's not the kind of action you want. There's no conflict. People are going to forget those stories."

"So, why tell them if they're going to be forgotten?" reasons Dayna.

"Right. But if Jasmine is swamped at work and mistakenly sends the email with private stuff . . . I don't know, what happens after that?"

"There's this complicated disclosure tracking they have to do that can take weeks," explains Dayna.

James interjects, ". . . which is a stressor, right? So there's some conflict."

Dayna sees where James is heading and is about to ask him how he would describe the conflict in Steve's situation, but James interrupts.

"I'm starved," he says, lifting his backpack onto his shoulder and heading out the door. "Wanna grab a bite? I've got an hour before my rehearsal."

"You're coming back here?" asks Dayna.

"No, I'm in a local production of *Mary Poppins* and we open next weekend."

"*Mary Poppins*? What's your role?" asks Dayna.

But James is out the door, whistling "A Spoon Full of Sugar." Dayna follows, shaking her head. Hanging out with James is never boring.

What's Wrong With This Picture?

Remember Dayna's first attempt at a story in chapter 5? She showed it to James and got some good feedback. Take a moment and read through her short story again and apply what you've learned so far about good storytelling for training (Figure 6-1).

Figure 6-1. Dayna's First Cybersecurity Story

"This is a story about phishing and how to respond to an email containing attachments or links: An employee of our company received an email from a friend, or at least it appeared to be from a friend. In the email, the friend asked the employee to click on a link in the email that would take them to a webpage containing some great store coupons. The employee is about to click the link when the employee realizes that the email might not be from a friend after all. It could be from a scammer. Our policy regarding protection of our company systems states, 'Be aware that emails containing malware pose a threat to our company systems.'"

What advice would you give Dayna to make her story better? After you've given it some thought, take a look at the following suggestions as a review of the Story Design principles you've gained so far (Figure 6-2).

Figure 6-2. Evaluating Dayna's Story

Create a Relatable Character
In this story, we have no idea who the main character is. And since we don't know, we don't really care about them. The generic use of the word "employee" is almost comical, and definitely does not help create a relatable character. Since writing this story, Dayna has not only drafted an audience profile, but character descriptions she believes the audience will relate to.

Put the Character in Strong Conflict
In Dayna's first story, what is the action? More specifically, what is the employee's action in the story? Look at the verbs. What does the employee actually do? He *received* and *realizes*. Received an email. Realizes it could be sent from a scammer. With these two verbs, any conflict has been neatly resolved. The tension between receiving the email and realizing it is a scam is minimal, at best, but quickly dissipates within the space of two sentences. You don't see the employee doing very much in this story. Dayna now has an action list and can make the action much stronger.

Training
The story is followed by an equally lackluster statement: "Be aware . . . " If employees all over the company are "aware," will that fix things? Of course not! Employees need to actually do something, like delete the email or forward it to their cybersecurity team. Employees who take this course will click *Next* and remember the awareness message long enough to take the knowledge check at the end. Fortunately, Dayna has made strides in this area too.

Let's make the connection between that action and the story more concrete. This will lay the groundwork for the next chapter, where you will write the story's plotline and dialogue.

Show the Action

Dayna's story begins with a telling phrase, "This is a story about . . . " Dayna then proceeds to give away the story by telling us what it's all about instead of letting the learner discover it by observing the action. She tells us about an employee. She tells us about a phishing email. She tells us about what not to do. But what if she showed us the action instead of telling us about it? Dayna can use these three questions to create meaningful action for her story.

- Is the character doing realistic things?
- Is the action conflict?
- Is the character motivated to do these actions?

Use these questions to begin the process of writing the story. When you've completed the story, you may also ask these questions as an evaluation.

Is the Character Doing Realistic Things?

In Dayna's original story, the employee, whom Dayna has named Steve, passively *receives* an email and internally *realizes* that it is a scam. Also, that Steve would be lured to click on a link containing store coupons seems unrealistic now given his character description. Or, at least, too general to be believable. What are some things that you could realistically imagine Steve doing in this scene that fit his character? Review his character description and the actions below. Which ones strike you as observable and realistic?

Figure 6-3. Steve's Character Description and Actions

Steve's character description: Steve, an engineer, a busy innovator, tall with broad shoulders, high energy, married and has a seven-year-old son. He's been with the company for five years, loves sports, former football player at a local high school. Values fast innovation, works hard and plays hard. He's only met with his manager once since the reorg three months ago. Never calls the help desk for computer problems; tries to fix things himself. Fears being delayed or distracted from his work. Finished his four-year degree in two and a half years, loves coaching his son's Little League baseball team.

Which of these actions is observable and realistic (something Steve would do, given his character description)?
1. Ignores common phishing clues
2. Takes a gulp of his coffee
3. Says, "Hm, that seems odd."
4. Asks a co-worker if they can reschedule a meeting
5. Doesn't consult the Phishing Clues job aid
6. Fails to forward suspicious emails to the Help Desk
7. Clips his nails
8. Clicks a link in the email
9. Turns off the computer and hopes for the best
10. Keeps the issue to himself
11. Purchases a ball return for his son online

Just as the action list must be observable action, the action in your story must also be observable. The character must be doing things. You can delete numbers 1, 5, 6, 10, and "hopes for the best" from number 9. You're left with the following observable actions:

- takes a gulp of his coffee
- says, "Hm, that seems odd."
- asks a co-worker if they can reschedule a meeting
- clips his nails
- clicks a link in the email
- turns off the computer
- purchases a ball return for his son online.

Though clipping his nails is an observable action, it seems out of character for Steve as something we would see him do in a story. That reduces the list to the following:

- takes a gulp of his coffee
- says, "Hm, that seems odd."
- asks a co-worker if they can reschedule a meeting

- clicks a link in the email
- turns off the computer
- purchases a ball return for his son online.

Any of these actions could be performed in the scene, but not all of them directly contribute to the conflict.

Figure 6-4. Strong Conflict and Desire for Resolution in the Story Design Model

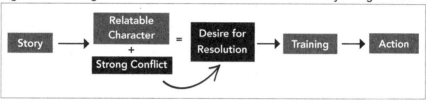

Is the Action Conflict?

The purpose for showing the conflict through action is to produce a desire for resolution within the learner. Dayna needs to put Steve in more direct conflict with the action list. Review Dayna's action list below and think of some things that Steve could actively do that are in conflict with the three sub-actions.

Main action: Protect the company's information from scammers.

1. Scan emails for common phishing clues using the Phishing Clues job aid.
2. Forward suspicious emails to the help desk without clicking links or opening attachments.
3. Report suspected breaches in security.
   a. Call cybersecurity office.
   b. Notify your supervisor.

Is it difficult? Yes, sometimes it is challenging to identify an observable action that is in conflict with the action list. From Dayna's list of actions that follow, mark the ones that directly conflict with the action list.

- takes a gulp of his coffee
- says, "Hm, that seems odd."
- asks a co-worker if they can reschedule a meeting
- clicks a link in the email

- turns off the computer
- purchases a ball return for his son.

Below are the three actions that Dayna has identified as something that is in conflict with the action list and some tips on how to do this for yourself in the practice section of this chapter.

- *Says, "Hm, that seems odd."* This action is not necessarily in direct conflict with the first sub-action on the action list, "Scan emails for common phishing clues using the Phishing Clues job aid," but it clues the listener of the story in on the fact that Steve recognizes that there is something wrong with the email and does nothing about it. You may think the verb, *says,* is not the most powerful verb in the world. But think about it. The character is actually talking. That's observable and realistic, so don't rule out speaking as an action. You'll learn more about speaking and dialogue in the next chapter.

- *Clicks a link in the email.* This one is an easy contrast to "Forward suspicious emails to the help desk without clicking links or opening attachment." This action is clearly in direct conflict with the action list. He doesn't forward the email and he clicks the link. When actions from the action list have an obvious conflict associated with them, make it easy on yourself and seize it an action for your story.

- *Turns off the computer.* He does this instead of "Report suspected breaches in security." There could be several conflicts with this action, but we know from the character description that Steve tries to fix his own computer problems instead of calling the help desk. It's plausible that turning off his computer could be his attempt at a quick fix for stopping a computer virus. Think of how your character might react if the consequences were severe.

Read through the three actions above. Steve says, "Hm, that seems odd." Then he clicks a link. Then he turns off his computer. With these three actions, which are in contrast to the actions on the action list, we see the beginnings of a plot unfolding.

Is the Character Motivated to Do These Actions?

Our behaviors in everyday life don't happen in a vacuum and neither should your characters' actions. Look at your character descriptions—their values, their reactions to current circumstances, their fears, and their personal information—to find valuable material for why they may do the things they do in the story. Dayna has an idea of the actions Steve needs to take in the story, but why would Steve do these things? Dayna can use the three actions as a place to start and cross-check them with the character description to make sure there is a viable reason for Steve to do them. Look at the table below and complete the second column (Figure 6-5).

Figure 6-5. Motivation Chart for Steve

Steve's action	Why Steve does this
Says, "Hm, that seems odd."	
Clicks a link in the email.	
Turns off the computer.	

After you've thought it through, take a look at Dayna's reasons (Figure 6-6). Are they similar?

Figure 6-6. Dayna's Motivation Chart for Steve

Steve's action	Why Steve does this
Says, "Hm, that seems odd."	Steve's busy and has a lot on his mind. It doesn't occur to him to take time to scan for phishing clues when he notes something odd about it. The email must be something that catches his attention enough to make him stop and read it.
Clicks a link in the email.	The message in the email must be pretty compelling to make Steve actually fall for the scam. Maybe something to do with engineering or sports or family?
Turns off the computer.	Clicking the link must trigger a visible response that clues Steve to the fact that a virus has been introduced to the computer. Maybe Steve panics? Maybe he gets angry because he's wasted time?

In the next chapter, as you build the story, you will look for opportunities to bring the motivations from the second column into the plot. You want to intensify the conflict to the strongest level possible. Outward and inward pressures on the characters push the action of the story to strong, believable conflict.

Nobody Should End Up Dead . . . Usually

Can conflict be intensified too much? It's rare that I've had to pull a workshop participant back from making their conflict too strong. But on occasion, it has happened. Once, someone wrote a story in which the conflict revolved around two front desk staff members talking about the personal information of a client loudly while the patient was in earshot of the conversation. The client was none too happy about it and by the end of the scene, there was a dead body on the floor! Unless you're doing training for emergency personnel or staging a Shakespearean tragedy, nobody should end up dead. If the conflict deviates from the action list or is so intense that it causes something to happen in the scene that distracts from the training, pull it back a notch and let your characters live.

Jasmine and Andrew Take Action

Dayna repeats the Show the Action process with a story for the privacy training. Review how Dayna uses the action list and character descriptions to show the action (Figure 6-7).

Figure 6-7. Dayna's Action List and Character Descriptions for Privacy Story

---

Action List for Privacy

Main action: Protect the company's confidential information.

1. Send emails containing confidential information securely.
   a. Type the word encrypt in the subject line of the email if it contains confidential information.
   b. Verify the email address is for the intended recipient.
   c. Delete rows, instead of hiding them, in attached spreadsheets that contain more than the minimum necessary.
2. Report unauthorized disclosures of confidential information.
   a. Notify your supervisor.
   b. Call the privacy office.

Character Descriptions for Privacy Story

Jasmine, a customer advocate (CA), instinctual caretaker, mentor to Andrew, long hair, eclectic style, bouncy. She is one of the few remaining long-timers, has been with the company 10 years, enjoys shopping online and watching reality shows. She values customer care, takes the departure of her former colleagues in stride by focusing on one call at a time and taking care of customer needs. She fears that a customer won't be taken care of properly. She's single and loves getting a manicure with her best friend every weekend.

Andrew, a CA new hire, conscientious learner, thin, concentrated, put together, serious, likes playing chess and Risk. He values accuracy and thoroughness, feels an obligation to get trained quickly and help out with the work, puts a lot of pressure on himself. He fears letting down Jasmine and doing things incorrectly. He's newly married, and his first child is on the way.

Dayna decides to focus the story on the major problem that exists in the company: 1(c), "Delete rows, instead of hiding them, in attached spreadsheets that contain more than the minimum necessary." The action of the story will be mostly in conflict with this one action. Dayna's job is a little more complex. She's writing action for two characters instead of one. But she can use two characters to her advantage by placing one of the characters in direct conflict with the action and the other as a foil. Dayna walks through the three steps for showing the action for the Jasmine and Andrew story.

- Is the character doing realistic things?
- Is the action conflict?
- Is the character motivated to do these actions?

Is the Character Doing Realistic Things?

Read through the character descriptions and imagine what they might be doing. At this point, don't worry if it's directly related to the action list. Picture them sitting at Andrew's desk with Jasmine listening in on the call he's taking. Picture them talking with one another. What things are they doing? Also, how might those things contrast one another? Can you see them doing these things?

Figure 6-8. Dayna's Characters' Actions

Jasmine's actions	Andrew's actions
Leans back in her chair	Sits upright in his seat
Eats a sucker	Fidgets with the mouse
Listens to Andrew talk with the customer	Talks with the customer
Answers Andrew's questions	Asks Jasmine if he's doing things correctly
Tells Andrew to hide rows in a spreadsheet	Hides rows in the spreadsheet
Congratulates Andrew	Sends the email to the customer

Is the Action Conflict?

Though all these actions may advance the story's plot in some way, there is only one action that must remain intact: "Tells Andrew to hide rows in a spreadsheet" (Jasmine) and "Hides rows in the spreadsheet" (Andrew). This aligns directly with the action list. The other actions provide insights into their character and make the story more believable. Don't get married to Jasmine eating a sucker or Andrew sitting upright in his seat, but don't throw them out completely either. If you were able to see the characters doing these things in your mind, you may be able to design a story that helps learners see them doing these things as well.

Is the Character Motivated to Do These Actions?

Let's focus on the undisputed action that must remain in the story for each of these characters. Why do Jasmine and Andrew take this action?

Figure 6-9. Dayna's Character Motivations

Action	Why does Jasmine do this?	Why does Andrew do this?
Tells Andrew to/Hides rows in a spreadsheet	She's done it this way for the past 10 years. They are under a time constraint. She may think it's the same as deleting the rows.	Jasmine tells him to do it and he doesn't want to let her down. He also feels that time is ticking. Maybe he questions her before doing it?

Notice that Dayna's reasons for her characters hiding rows in a spreadsheet are aligned with their character descriptions. Notice also that other than Andrew possibly questioning Jasmine about hiding rows in the spreadsheet, there is little interpersonal conflict, which is appropriate as the action list and the audience profile do not indicate that interpersonal conflicts are a major issue. You will note, however, that in the practice session, you will have ample opportunity to introduce interpersonal conflict in the story you are creating for the Well Adjusted clinic.

Conflict Is Real

You saw in chapter 5 how to use guideposts to make your characters real. Use the principles of Show the Action to make your conflict just as real. Once you kindle that desire, they are ready to learn. In appendix 1, use the Show the Action as your guide.

Figure 6-10. Show the Action Worksheet

Show the Action Worksheet

This worksheet will help with the completion of the next worksheet, Build the Story.

Identify the actions and the conflict for your story. Each of the characters for the story you are creating is in conflict with one or more of the actions from the action list. To begin thinking in terms of action and conflict, ask yourself these three questions and complete the worksheet.

1. Is the character doing realistic things?

First, imagine the character in conflict with their corresponding action. What are they doing in the scene? Describe some of the actions you might see them do.

Are these actions observable? Are they in keeping with the character description? Weed out any that don't fit these two requirements.

2. Is the action conflict?

Next, narrow the actions down to the ones that are in direct conflict with their corresponding action from the action list and write that action in the second column next to their name. Is the conflicting action directly related to the action from the action list?

Character name	Conflicting action	Why the character does this

3. Is the character motivated to do these actions?

Complete the table by writing some reasons in the last column of why the character might take the conflicting action. Consult their character descriptions and look for external and internal pressures that influence their decisions.

You may download an editable version of the worksheet at needastory .com/book-resources.

PRACTICE STORY DESIGN:
Show the Action

Using the character descriptions you created from chapter 5 and the action list from chapter 4, identify the action and the conflict for your story. Each of the characters for the story you are creating for Well Adjusted is in conflict with one of the actions from the action list.

Is the character doing realistic things?

First, imagine Character 1 in conflict with their corresponding action. What are they doing in the scene? Are they with Character 2? Are they with a patient? Are they with other staff members? Describe some of the actions you might see them do in the space below, then do the same for Character 2.

Are the above actions observable? Are they in keeping with the character description? Weed out any that don't fit these two requirements.

Is the action conflict?

Next, narrow the actions down to the one that is in direct conflict with their corresponding action from the action list and write that action in the second column next to their name.

Character name	Conflicting action	Why the character does this

Is the conflicting action directly related to the action from the action list? Is it a positive action that can be observed? If you're getting stuck, remember, your character can speak. Also, think of how your character might react if the consequences are severe, like in Dayna's story. Steve shuts off his computer in response to the virus. Think it through. Picture it. Write it down.

Is the character motivated to do these actions?

Complete the preceding table by writing some reasons in the last column of why the character might take the conflicting action. Consult their character descriptions and look for external and internal pressures that influence their decisions. You will use this column to heighten the conflict in the story.

For your first Story Design projects, complete the Show the Action table for each character and each of their conflicting actions. Over time, this discipline will become ingrained and you may choose to skip to the next step of building the story, keeping these principles in mind. When you've completed the table, read through each character's action and reasons for doing so. Does a plot come to mind? Conversations? Consult the completed Instructional Story Design Plan for further understanding after you've completed this exercise.

You're well on your way to realizing a fully designed story.

CHAPTER SEVEN
Build the Story

An Immediate Response

Dayna holds a paper with two paragraphs on it. Each paragraph is a story that she hopes Susan will approve. After writing an audience profile and an action list, composing characters in conflict isn't as difficult as she thought it would be. Still, she has her doubts. She reads through the Steve story one more time before going to Susan's office.

"Steve opened an email from Bryan, a fellow engineer and friend. They used to work together at another company. It'd been years since they had spoken. When he opened the email, he saw an invite to join Bryan at an engineer's convention in the spring with an attached flyer. 'Hm, that seems odd,' he says. He wondered why Bryan would send him an invitation. He knew conventions weren't his thing, but he clicked the attachment anyway. Steve's computer freezes. He tried the ESC key, Ctrl+Alt+Delete. Nothing responds. Steve turned off the computer. He'd just been scammed."

Dayna sighs and shakes her head. She's not sure this is the right story, but it's better than the store coupons. She doesn't have time to read through the privacy story. It's time to meet with Susan.

Susan welcomes Dayna into her office.

"I just want to say first that I like the action list. Randall told me how you put this together and the steps are clear. I'm on board with this."

Dayna smiles. "Thank you. Did you have time to read through the, um, stories?"

"Yes." She picks up a paper. "I printed them out. They're good."

Dayna feels like there is probably a caveat to that statement. There is.

"Steve seems like somebody who would work here. We have a lot of engineers. The email is good, but it seems odd that Steve would click on the attachment if he didn't like conventions."

Dayna nods. "Yeah, that makes sense. I can tweak that." Dayna looks down at Steve's character description. "Maybe something sports related?"

"Maybe. I'm thinking of something personal. Scammers often look at people's social posts to craft personal scams that sound legitimate."

"OK, what about his son's Little League team? That would tap into his love for sports and his family."

"I like that," Susan says.

"Anything else?"

Susan looks at her copy of the story. "Yes, it's the tenses. Sometimes it's past tense, sometimes it's present tense."

Dayna scans through the story. "Oh yeah, you're right. I can change it all to past tense."

Susan is skeptical. "Not sure about that. It strikes me as more powerful in the present tense."

Dayna nods. "Yeah, I see your point. It sounds more . . . immediate?"

"Yes, immediate," she agrees.

"Great," says Dayna, "Anything else for Steve's story?"

"Where will the training come in?" asks Susan.

"Um, I haven't really thought it through completely, but I think the training will come after the story. You know, lead the employees through the story right up to the point where they need training to fix the problem? Does that make sense?"

"I'm sure you'll figure it out," says Susan.

"Did you want to review the second story too? About Jasmine?"

Susan's phone rings. She looks down at it. "It's my boss, I better get this. I'm sorry."

"No problem," she says. "I'll work on it and send you a revised version."

Susan picks up the phone as Dayna leaves and shuts the door behind her. *Immediacy.* She reads the privacy story silently as she slowly walks to the elevator.

"Jasmine was mentoring Andrew and showing him how to take calls and send requested information. She had four minutes between calls to run a report and send it to the customer with the information attached in a spreadsheet. She showed Andrew how to pull the information into the spreadsheet but noticed that the report included confidential information about another client. She hid the rows regarding the other client and attached the spreadsheet to the email. She told Andrew it was as easy as that, then sent the email. When the client received the spreadsheet, they unhid the rows and saw all of the confidential information about the other client. They called to let Jasmine know. Now Jasmine has to go through the long process of disclosure tracking with her supervisor and the privacy office."

Dayna is proud of this story. She incorporates the long process of disclosure tracking as a piece of motivation for the employees to follow through with deleting rows instead of hiding them. But what about immediacy?

Well, I could use present tense in Jasmine's story. That would help, she thinks. Still it feels like something is missing.

Start With the Story Premise

You'll come back to immediacy later in the chapter. Dayna has done a lot of work to write character descriptions and connect the action list to the conflict of the story by showing the action. But how do those stories begin? Is it as easy as James makes it out to be? Pair the character with an action on the action list to create a plot? Actually, yes.

Dayna's Steve and Jasmine stories are a good start. All of the right information is there, but the plot and the writing need refining. They contain common mistakes, like mixing tenses and telling about the action rather than showing it. Remember in chapter 5, Dayna developed relatable characters by pairing them with one or more of the actions from the action list and putting them into conflict with it. Steve struggles with the three sub-actions of protecting the company from phishing attacks. Jasmine's conflict is with sharing more than the minimum necessary by hiding rows on a spreadsheet. This simple pairing of character and conflict inspired descriptive adjectives and nouns for these two characters. This method is just as effective for character descriptions as it is for developing a meaningful plot. It begins with a story premise.

The story premise is the most basic of story ideas. Think of it as a Mad Libs, the popular children's game of filling in blanks with appropriate parts of speech to create wacky stories. Only the blanks in your story premises are based on well-researched and analyzed content. This is the story premise form (Figure 7-1).

Figure 7-1. The Story Premise

A story about _____
                        [character name and position]

who struggles to _____
                        [an action from the action list]

Dayna's story premises look like this (Figure 7-2).

Figure 7-2. Dayna's Story Premises

A story about Steve, an engineer, who struggles to protect the company's information from scammers.

A story about Jasmine, a seasoned customer advocate, who struggles to delete rows, instead of hiding them, in attached spreadsheets that contain more than the minimum necessary.

From this story premise, Dayna is able to create a plausible plot. It helps boost her into creative writing with more confidence. The story premise is a simple and powerful way to start writing a story.

The Character of Your Audience

It's not uncommon to confuse audiences in the story premise. For example, during a Story Design workshop a participant used the audience profile of the chiropractic clinic and the action of "protect the client's privacy in the presence of other clients." They wrote the following story premise:

A story about Nadine, a client at the chiropractic clinic, who overhears two employees talking loudly about her health information in front of everyone in the waiting room.

The story was then told from Nadine's point of view. Though there is definitely conflict in this story premise regarding the action of protecting the client's privacy, the story is about the wrong character. Nadine is not the main relatable character. She's a client. Clients will not be taking the training, the staff will be. Nadine can definitely be in the story, and we can observe how the actions of the staff affect her, but the story should remain focused on the two employees talking loudly about Nadine. This story premise would be best written like this:

> A story about Ed and Francis, front desk staff at the clinic, who struggle to protect the client's privacy in the presence of other clients.

How Many Actions Can One Character Do?

You may notice a difference between Steve and Jasmine's stories. Look at the action lists and story premises for both (Figure 7-3).

Figure 7-3. Action Lists and Story Premises for Steve and Jasmine

Action list for cybersecurity (Steve's story)	Action list for privacy (Jasmine and Andrew's story)

Main action: **Protect the company's information from scammers**
 1. **Scan emails for common phishing clues using the Phishing Clues job aid**
 2. **Forward suspicious emails to the help desk without clicking links or opening attachments**
 3. **Report suspected breaches in security**
   a. Call cybersecurity office
   b. Notify your supervisor
	Main action: Protect the company's confidential information
	 1. Send emails containing confidential information securely
	   a. Type the word *encrypt* in the subject line of the email if it contains confidential information
	   b. Verify the email address is for the intended recipient
	   c. **Delete rows, instead of hiding them, in attached spreadsheets that contain more than the minimum necessary**
	 2. Report unauthorized disclosures of confidential information
	   a. Notify your supervisor
	   b. Call the privacy office

A story about Steve, an engineer, who struggles to **protect the company's information from scammers.**	A story about Jasmine, a seasoned customer advocate, who struggles to **delete rows, instead of hiding them, in attached spreadsheets that contain more than the minimum necessary.**

Jasmine's story premise puts her in conflict with only one action on the list. Steve's, however, puts him in conflict with the main action, which means, he will be in conflict with all of the actions (1-3) underneath it. That's OK. In fact, putting a character in conflict with more than one (or all) of the actions on the list is usually more efficient than using a large cast of characters to cover all the actions. It's possible, but it will take more time for your audience to get to know all of those characters.

Three Story Seeds

You've seen how a story premise functions. Simply by putting a relatable character in strong conflict with an action from the action list, you have the beginnings of a story. It is a form that sparks story ideas and implies plot. A story premise can manifest itself in three story types I call story seeds:

- nonfiction
- fiction
- metaphor.

These story seeds are written in the form of a story premise and contain all of the characteristics of the Story Design model. In general, nonfiction is the simplest story to construct, because it's a story that already exists. Metaphors are the most complex, because they must have integrity as a standalone parallel story to reality. The complexity of writing a fictional story is somewhere in between. Each story seed has its own strengths and pitfalls.

Nonfiction

The term *nonfiction* refers simply to stories that are happening in the workplace that match your action list. If the action is, "Inform staff members in other areas of important information concerning clients," collect stories of instances where people didn't inform staff members in other areas of important information concerning clients and the fallout of that action. The reason the action is on your list to begin with is because there is a problem with that in reality. Find those problem areas and gather those case studies.

Where to find a nonfiction story: If you don't have direct access to your audience to observe their behaviors in person, you may get those real stories (the *R* in PRIMED) from the subject matter experts or the stakeholder during your interviews with them. Get a hold of safety reports, hotline call reports, quality audits, exit interviews. Behind all of those incidents is a story. You may also find nonfiction stories that apply to the training in the news or online. Leadership failures, fraud scams, human interest stories, scientific breakthroughs. Often these stories have the relatable characters and strong conflict baked into them.

Why a nonfiction story is great: Nonfiction has the emotional advantage of reality on its side. Think of a story that you heard or saw, where someone overcame incredible odds and made it through successfully. At first you think it's just a cool story. Then you find out it's actually a true story. Suddenly, it changes your perspective. What was first just a cool story is now amazing because it's nonfiction. I've created countless compliance stories, but it never fails: whenever a nonfiction compliance story is published, the online views spike. It's juicy because it's real.

When to use a nonfiction story: When your audience views the content as unimportant or needs to be convinced that there is a problem that must be fixed, share a nonfiction story with them. Show them the problem that's happening in the workplace. Pair a nonfiction story with statistics and you have a very convincing case for training. For instance, Dayna could share a case study of an employee who actually clicked on a link that introduced a virus to the company's system, and couple that story with a statistic like this: "Think it couldn't happen to you? Last year alone, our cybersecurity team handled 50 security breaches. That's almost one a week!" A nonfiction story can win over skeptics and tantalize the audience with the makings of a good piece of gossip.

The pitfalls of a nonfiction story: Sometimes, it's tempting to focus on the outcomes of a nonfiction story instead of the story itself. During a Story Design workshop, a participant who designed training for people in the agriculture industry described an incident in which a silo burned to the ground because a certain piece of machinery was left running and became extremely hot. She wanted to include this as a story in her training. Watching a silo burn to the ground definitely packs an emotional punch. But the machinery heating up and burning down the silo is not really the story. It's the outcome of the story. The story happened just before the silo burst into flames. For training, the real story premise is:

> A story about Jeff, a machinist at the agriculture company, who struggled to follow protocol and shut off the heating element on a piece of machinery in the silo.

We need to see what Jeff does before the fire. He walks into the silo. He shuts things down. His boss calls him to help on another project. He skips through some of the steps of protocol. He runs out to help his boss. This is the real story. Train them on this. The inferno is important, because it shows the outcome of Jeff's behavior, but it isn't the whole story.

Sometimes, nonfiction can be absolutely boring. Think of a sales case study that blandly describes who the client is, what they bought, and how much. But there was emotion involved with that sale—a lot of it. Where did it go? If you're designing training for sales enablement, work with stakeholders and sales staff to identify that emotional content and put it into the story.

Another example of when a nonfiction story can become drab is when you tell a nonfiction story that happened internally and are required to de-identify it to death. When taken to the extreme, the story can turn almost comical. "An employee at our company received a phishing email. He/she clicked a link that downloaded malware onto his/her computer. He/she reported the incident to his/her manager." And so forth. After a while, even though it is a nonfiction story, de-identifying takes center stage instead of the action of the story. The emotional impact is lost. If legal refuses to budge, it's better to design a parallel story that mirrors what happened in reality than to use the nonfiction story. Sometimes, telling the parallel fiction story with the emotional content intact, then following it up with a very brief description of the nonfiction story, can be effective.

How a nonfiction story fits into a story premise: Use the story premise form to identify the relatable character and the action from the action list they are in conflict with, and it turns out looking like this (Figure 7-4).

Figure 7-4. Nonfiction Story Premise

A story about _____
[a real person your audience can relate to]

who struggles (in real life) to _____
[an action from the action list]

Fiction

Fiction is a versatile story type. The characters and their actions are based in reality, but the plot is not dictated by an actual event that happened in a certain place at a certain time. Unlike nonfiction, you are also free to set a relatable character in conflict with as many actions from the action list as you wish.

Where to find a fiction story: When interviewing stakeholders and subject matter experts, listen for examples (the E in PRIMED). Examples are different from case studies. Many times they are hypothetical, based in actual events, but just shy of nonfiction. Often these statements are preceded by "if" or "sometimes":

- "*If* a sales rep doesn't know how to respond to that kind of objection, they're sunk."
- "*If* this information isn't recorded properly, we could be sued."
- "*Sometimes* employees get distracted from the process of shutting down the machine, which could have some very negative impacts on the system."
- "*Sometimes* customers complain about our reps being too abrupt."

They may also use phrases like "We've seen a trend" or "In the past." Sometimes their statement is cautionary: "They should never do this or something bad will happen." Stakeholders or subject matter experts may not have actual stories top of mind when they make statements like this. You should pursue the real stories, but even if they cannot provide them, these are not wasted moments. If SMEs present a hypothetical or cautionary situation, ask them hypothetical questions.

- "If a sales rep were to receive an objection like that, what are some common responses sales reps might use that sink the sale?"
- "Tell me how misrecorded information could turn into a law suit."
- "How might an employee get distracted from shutting down the machine? What are those negative impacts to the system?"
- "What might a representative of the company say that customers consider abrupt?"

Essentially, by asking questions about their initial statements, you involve the stakeholders and subject matter experts as storytellers. Regardless of whether these stories are actual, hypothetical or cautionary, you are building a strong library of plot lines to choose from.

Why a fiction story is great: Fiction stories in training are rarely completely fictional. They are based in truth but offer more choices. The characters, created from the audience profile, are still moldable. The sequence of events can be shaped in a way that make the most impact on the learner. For instance, I mentioned earlier about designing characters for training a board of directors. They were, for the most part, untouchable. So, I searched for information about them on the Internet. I found out where they lived. I learned about their education, work experience, and political involvement. I read articles and excerpts from books they had written. I even stumbled across hobbies and favorite foods. It didn't take a long time to compose a short profile of each board member. Characters for the story borrowed from different board member profiles, creating an entirely fictional character with strikingly familiar similarities with the audience. No character was an exact copy of a board member. They were unique but inherently relatable. Fiction made that possible.

The library of plot lines gathered by asking stakeholders and subject matter experts questions, mentioned above, are great for fiction. You can pick and choose from this library to support the strongest story. Fiction gives you this freedom.

When to use a fiction story: Almost any time. Though nonfiction may seem easier because it's the retelling of an existing story, it's limited to what actually happened. Once you've mastered Story Design principles, creating fiction will become second nature and quick. Fiction puts you, the designer, in control of the characters' destinies. Fictional stories are fantastic for scenarios and games where learners are given the opportunity to make meaningful choices down a selection of guided pathways. Augmented or virtual reality are perfect for immersive fiction that puts the learner in the middle of the action. Role play provides the setting for a fictional story invented by the players. The uses of a fiction story are limitless. I've used fiction stories throughout this book, including Dayna's. Though Dayna isn't a real person, she's a relatable character in conflict with the principles of Story Design.

The pitfalls of a fiction story: During a Story Design class, where most of the participants were librarians, I was asked several times, "So, we're just making these characters up?" At first, they had a difficult time with the fictional aspect of storytelling (a bit of irony there) for the purpose of communicating with their audience. Several of them felt like they should only use real stories. But once they saw that the fictional characters were based in an audience profile, they created some great characters and powerful stories.

The pitfall for fiction is when it strays from the audience profile and the action list. Creativity loves constraints. Effective fiction stories in training can be wildly imaginative within those constraints. Embrace constraints and design within them. Use the guideposts for creating a relatable character and put them into conflict with an action from the action list. Anything more or less can lead you, and your learners, astray.

How a fiction story fits into a story premise: The story premise for fiction is similar to nonfiction (Figure 7-5).

Figure 7-5. Fiction Story Premise

A story about _____

[a fictional relatable character]

who struggles to _____

[action from the action list]

Metaphor

A metaphor is a representation of something else. For training purposes, a metaphor is something that is familiar to the learner that gives context to something unfamiliar, particularly an abstract concept. This is helpful, since most of the time training is designed to help learners take action on new knowledge, skills, and attitudes. A metaphor can be fiction or nonfiction, but it deserves its own category. It has a unique purpose in training.

Where to find a metaphor: Metaphorical stories are not always easy to find. And they are tricky to design. Stakeholders are the best source for metaphors. And, believe it or not, there is a magic question to ask them if you're looking for one: "What do you want to say to your audience?" You can expect abstract responses like:

- "Competitive intelligence is powerful."
- "Stand by our customers."
- "Engage your team."

In chapter 4, Dayna asked Randall, "If you could tell employees one thing about this issue, what would it be?" Randall responded, "Use your head! Think before you send an email!" None of these statements, by themselves, are metaphors, but they are the beginnings of potentially powerful ones. When a possible metaphor reveals itself, ask more questions. A conversation with the stakeholder may unfold like this:

You: What do you want to say to your audience?

Stakeholder: Competitive intelligence is powerful.

You: OK, in what way is it powerful?

Stakeholder: It's powerful because, when it's gathered correctly, it helps our company win.

You: What do you mean by gathering it correctly?

Stakeholder: We have to play by the rules. We can't just do anything to get the information.

You: But when you have it, it helps the company win. How does it do that?

Stakeholder: We study our competitors and know how to best position ourselves for the best market share.

Do you see a possible metaphor here? Winning. Play by the rules. Competitors. The stakeholder is providing clues about a sports metaphor. This is a conversation I actually had with a stakeholder, who agreed to let me explore some metaphorical story options in the training.

Why a metaphor is great: Of the knowledge, skills, and attitude trifecta, metaphors have the most impact on attitude. Metaphors help learners step outside of their current reality and provide an alternate perspective on why action needs to be taken. They make abstract ideas more concrete and big ideas more attainable. The sports metaphor I would develop for training on competitive intelligence would help employees experience the benefits and consequences in a football setting, using terminology they already understood so they could apply it to the more abstract idea of competitive intelligence, which they weren't familiar with.

When to use a metaphor: Since the department wanted their entire company to take action on competitive intelligence best practices, and since this was a new concept for so many of them, metaphor was an appropriate solution. Since sports references kept coming up during the conversation, the story centered around the coach of a losing football team. Suddenly, though, the team starts to win, primarily because of the coach's ability to predict the opposing team's next play almost every time. He knows something about the opponent that gives his team a competitive edge. How did the coach get this intelligence? Did he obtain it legally? The leap to apply the concept "competitive intelligence is powerful" to the workplace became much easier. What a company knows about their competitors gives them a competitive edge. But, of course, that intelligence must be gathered legally.

Metaphor can also be used as a motivator. As part of a campaign to encourage employees to take four steps to speak up when they had an ethical concern in the workplace, I worked with a team to create a metaphor that was designed to help employees overcome some common barriers to speaking up: fear of retaliation or not wanting to get a friend in trouble. These were barriers stakeholders knew their audience faced. The metaphorical story we created takes place in the neighborhood of a small town. One of the neighbors starts letting their grass grow longer than the city allows. Then they start leaving trash in their yard. Each neighbor has a reason why they don't report the issue to the city—the same reasons why people don't want to report an ethical concern in the workplace—and the junk keeps piling up. It affects the neighborhood's morale and relationships. The learner observes the consequences of not speaking up in the metaphor and recognizes that something similar could happen in real life if they don't speak up about ethical concerns at work.

Metaphors are also effective to train on sensitive issues where the learner needs some distance from what's happening in the workplace—essentially changing the setting from where the audience works to something different. In chapter 1, I mentioned The Coffeeshop, a story that made an incredible impact on a team's trust and communication skills. A big reason why this training was so successful is that the story was set not in an office, but in a coffeeshop, which gave employees the space and respect they needed to change things in the office. The Coffeeshop is metaphorical in the sense that it gives employees a different view of their own reality.

The pitfalls of a metaphor: Use metaphors selectively and for the purposes listed above. If there isn't a good case for using a metaphor, go with a fiction or nonfiction story. A metaphor can fall apart if there aren't enough equivalents to tie the metaphorical story to the real world. Read the sidebar on the importance of equivalents to ensure your metaphorical story avoids this pitfall.

How a metaphor fits into a story premise: Metaphor story premises follow the same guidelines with slight variation (Figure 7-6).

Figure 7-6. Metaphor Story Premise

A story about _____
[an equivalent relatable character in a different setting than the learner]

who struggles to _____
[action from the action list]

A story about the coach of a football team who struggles to gather competitive intelligence according to the rules.

A story about neighbors who struggle to report their neighbor for violating city ordinances.

Metaphors and the Importance of Equivalents

Metaphors rely on strong equivalents. The characters and conflict that takes place in a metaphorical story must be anchored in the audience profile and the action. The setting also must have equivalents. This is why the neighborhood story worked so well for helping employees overcome barriers for speaking up. It has many strong equivalents:

- Neighborhood = Workplace
- Neighbors = Employees
- City ordinance = Company's code
- Tall grass and junk in the yard = An employee concern about a compromise of the company's code
- Reasons for not reporting the neighbor = Reasons for not reporting a fellow employee
- Taking the steps for reporting to the city = Taking the steps to report a concern at work

The Competitive Intelligence story also has strong equivalents:

- Football = Business
- Coach and team = Managers and employees
- Opposing team = Competitor
- Opposing team's plays = Competitor's strategy and plans
- Rules of the football game = Rules for collecting competitive information

In both stories, the characters struggled with the actions on the action list. It takes place in a different setting but a similar context, where the characters interact with one another in a way that the learner readily recognizes in their own work environment. If you're struggling to find equivalents in a metaphor, it's best not to force it. Look for a metaphor that has many strong equivalents.

Map the Plot With Core Actions

Once you've planted to the story seed in the form of a story premise, begin writing the story by mapping out the plot. After Dayna takes another look at her stories, she decides to rebuild them. She begins with Steve's fictional story premise:

> A story about Steve, an engineer, who struggles to protect the company's information from scammers.

If you need help jump-starting your own story, begin by answering these four questions to identify the core actions.

1. Where is he in this story?
2. What is he doing?
3. What does he encounter that gives him opportunity to do the action?
4. What does he do that's in conflict with that action?

Using what you already know about Steve's character from chapter 5 and the action from chapter 6, Dayna may answer these questions like this:

1. Steve is at his desk.
2. He's checking email.
3. He says, "Hm, that seems odd," when he reads a phishing email.
4. He clicks a link in the email, then turns off the computer.

Now she writes these in paragraph form.

> Steve is at his desk checking email. He says, "Hm, that seems odd," when he reads a phishing email. He clicks a link in the email, then turns off the computer when he realizes the link contains a virus.

The action is clear. This is a good start. You can picture Steve doing the core actions that make this story a story. Using the Show the Action worksheet from chapter 6, you can ask:

- **Is the character doing realistic things?** Yes, but not in the last phrase. He needs to show that the computer contains a virus. Realizing is not observable.
- **Is the action conflict?** Yes, the action is conflict, specific to an action from the action list. These are the actions Dayna identified in the Show the Action exercise.
- **Is the character motivated to do these actions?** No, we don't see much motivation in the story yet, but she will get to that soon.

From there two things need to be revised. *Realizes* needs to be shown, rather than told, and we need to see Steve's motivation for doing these actions. Dayna fixes the first problem:

> Steve is at his desk checking email. He says, "Hm, that seems odd," when he reads a phishing email. He clicks a link in the email. **His computer screen freezes. Steve frantically presses ESC. Nothing happens. Finally, in a moment of desperation, he turns off the computer.**

Now we see the computer freezing and Steve reacting to it. This may not be the best story solution, but now, instead of the internal act of *realizing*, the action is observable. This is a step in the right direction.

Connect With the Character

The core actions make up the bones of the story. They're like a Cliff's Notes version of Romeo and Juliet. You understand what's happening, but there's not a strong connection with the characters or their situation. Though a bare bones story may be all you need for certain scenes, to help your audience connect with the characters, consult the motivations you created in chapter 6. As a reminder, here are the motivations Dayna created for Steve (Figure 7-7).

Figure 7-7. Motivation Chart for Steve

Steve's action	Why Steve does this
Says, "Hm, that seems odd."	Steve's busy and has a lot on his mind, doesn't occur to him to take time to scan for phishing clues when he notes something odd about it. The email must be something that catches his attention enough to make him stop and read it.
Clicks a link in the email.	The message in the email must be pretty compelling to make Steve actually fall for the scam. Maybe something to do with engineering, sports, or family?
Turns off the computer.	Clicking the link must trigger a visible response that clues Steve to the fact that a virus has been introduced to the computer. Maybe Steve panics? Maybe he gets angry because he's wasted time?

Gleaning at least one motivation from each action, Dayna re-writes the story:

> Steve is at his desk checking email. **An email from his friend, Bryan, catches his eye. He hasn't spoken with Bryan in years. He reads it aloud. "'Hey Steven! came across this incredible sale on sports equipment. Thought you might be interested with your son's little league. The link is below. Take care!'**. . . Hm, that seems odd." Bryan never called him *Steven*. ~~He says, "Hm, that seems odd," when he reads a phishing email.~~ **Steve had been thinking of purchasing a ball return for his son's birthday. Couldn't hurt to check it out.** He clicks ~~a~~ the link. ~~in the email~~. His computer screen freezes. Steve frantically presses ESC. Nothing happens. Finally, in a moment of desperation, he turns off the computer.

Now Steve seems genuinely motivated to read the email. He notices something odd, clicks the link, and turns off the computer. See how Dayna draws upon some of Steve's personal information—his love for sports and his son's birthday—in the character description to give him motivation to do the action in the story.

Refine the Verbs

Let's work on the verbs in this story. First, notice that all of the verbs, with the exception of "had been thinking," which refers to an action that has been ongoing, is in present tense.

Dayna's first story was in past tense (mostly), telling what happened in retrospect. But then it lapses into present tense when "the employee *realizes* that the email might not be from a friend after all." Why the tense switch? This is not an uncommon mistake. When writing one part of the story, it sounds right to use the past tense, but in another part, the present tense sounds correct. It's easy to mix the two tenses. But it's also easy to fix. It's OK to use past tense, but consider the two sentences below and honestly gauge your interest level.

- He clicked a link in the email. His computer screen froze.
- He clicks a link in the email. His computer screen freezes.

Both are action-driven. But the first one is action that took place in the past. The second is happening right now. For training stories, you want to use every technique possible to engage as quickly as possible. Setting your stories in present tense helps to immerse the learner in the here and now and get their attention right away. Even case studies can be written in present tense, even though they are an event that has already happened.

Next, think about how some verbs feel more powerful than others. Below is a list of the actions Steve does in the story in the here and now:

- checking
- reads
- clicks
- presses
- turns.

Let's explore each of these verbs. There may be opportunities to strengthen them.

- *Checking* is a potential problem. It requires the helping verb is, which is a weaker way of showing the action. In cases such as this one, opt for the more direct version: *Steve sits at his desk. He checks his email.* Or, to make it even more like Steve may be busy, *He scans his inbox.*
- *Reads* is straightforward and appropriate in context. He *reads* the email aloud. No changes needed.
- *Clicks* is specific to a mouse click. This shouldn't be changed.

Think of three synonyms for the last two verbs that could heighten the
action and emotional intensity of the scene. What are some possible alterna-
tives? You might swap them out for:

- *Presses* ESC—bangs, slams, hits
- *Turns* off the computer—switches, unplugs, yanks the cord out of
  the wall.

Focusing on the verbs, Dayna makes revisions. Now the story reads:

> **Steve sits at his desk. He scans his inbox.** An email from his
> friend, Bryan, catches his eye. He hasn't spoken with Bryan in
> years. He reads it aloud. "'Hey Steven! Came across this incred-
> ible sale on sports equipment. Thought you might be interest-
> ed with your son's little league. Take care!' . . . Hm, that seems
> odd." Bryan never called him *Steven*. Steve had been thinking
> of purchasing a ball return for his son's birthday. Couldn't hurt
> to check it out. He clicks the link. His computer screen freez-
> es. Steve frantically **hits** ESC. Nothing happens. Finally, in a
> moment of desperation, he **yanks the cord out of the wall**.

The ending of the story is a little more intense. Dayna has more opportunities to increase the heat on her character, though.

Escalate the Conflict With Dialogue

Nothing brings immediacy to a scene quicker than hearing characters speak.
Steve doesn't share this scene with anyone, but already Dayna has introduced speech as Steve reads the email aloud. Are there other opportunities
for Steve to speak? Reread the story and see if you can identify at least two
more opportunities for Steve to speak, then continue reading and compare
your answers to Dayna's.

> Steve sits at his desk. He scans his inbox. **"An email from
> Bryan?! I haven't heard from him in forever!"** He reads it
> aloud. "'Hey Steven! Came across this incredible sale on sports
> equipment. Thought you might be interested with your son's
> little league. The link is below. Take care!' . . . Hm, that seems
> odd. **Bryan never calls me Steven."** Steve had been thinking
> of purchasing a ball return for his son's birthday. **He says, "Can't**

hurt to check it out." He clicks the link. His computer screen freezes. Steve frantically hits ESC. Nothing happens. Finally, in a moment of desperation, he yanks the cord out of the wall. **Steve groans miserably. "I shouldn't have clicked that link!"**

As you read through the story, it seems more alive. Steve seems more real. We're getting a closer look at who he is when we hear him speak.

In narrative, like the Steve story, dialogue tags are used to indicate who is speaking. There are three dialogue tags in Dayna's story:

- He reads it aloud.
- He says.
- Steve groans miserably.

The third tag gives us much more information than just who says it. It tells us how he says it. He groans miserably. How could the other two dialogue tags be altered to show how Steve says the quote? Start with *He reads it aloud*. How does Steve feel about Brian? We're not sure from the way it is written. But if it were someone he didn't care for, he would probably delete the email without opening it. Dayna has some choices.

- He reads it happily out loud.
- He gladly reads it out loud.
- He reads it out loud with gusto.

Nope, nope, and nope. There is a better way to show the emotion Steve is feeling without using adverbs; do it through his actions! Look at the options below:

- He reads it aloud, smiling.
- He laughs as he reads it aloud.
- He chuckles quietly, then reads it aloud.

All three of these options show us the action, but which ones seems most appropriate for Steve? Dayna chooses the last one. She can picture Steve chuckling quietly, then reading the email aloud. What about the other dialogue tag, *He says*, "Can't hurt to check it out"? Picture what Steve might be doing at this point to show how he feels. Would you choose one of the options below? Something different?

- He raises his eyebrows.
- He shrugs.
- He sighs.
- He looks away.

Dayna replaces the two dialogue tags. Now her story looks like this:

> Steve sits at his desk. He scans his inbox. "An email from Bryan?! I haven't heard from him in forever!" **He chuckles quietly, then reads it aloud**. "'Hey Steven! Came across this incredible sale on sports equipment. Thought you might be interested with your son's little league. The link is below. Take care!' . . . Hm, that seems odd. Bryan never calls me *Steven*." Steve had been thinking of purchasing a ball return for his son's birthday. **He shrugs his shoulders**. "Can't hurt to check it out." He clicks the link. His computer screen freezes. Steve frantically hits ESC. Nothing happens. Finally, in a moment of desperation, he yanks the cord out of the wall. Steve groans miserably. "I shouldn't have clicked that link!"

Her story is shaping up nicely. There's more action, more emotion. No matter what the format of your story is—narrative or dialogue—look for opportunities to give your characters a voice. Let your audience hear them. Use descriptive dialogue tags to show your audience more of the action and emotion. You'll see examples of how to develop a dialogue-driven story later in the book. Now that flesh has been added to the core actions, she will take it another step further and ground her story in reality. But let's take a break from Steve's story and explore how Dayna might increase immediacy with dialogue in the Jasmine and Andrew story.

Increase Immediacy With Dialogue

One of the best ways to bring your audience into the here-and-now is through dialogue. Dayna questioned how to make the Jasmine story more immediate. Her narrative version looks like this:

> "We'll get that to you right away! Thanks for calling! Bye" Andrew runs his hands through his hair. He shakes his head and turns to Jasmine. "I don't know if I'm ever going to be ready to fly solo."

Jasmine smiles and pops a lollipop in her mouth. "You'll be ready. You're great on the phone!"

Andrew takes a breath. "I'm OK with the phone stuff. It's the documentation and things in between each call that are so hard!" Jasmine agrees. It's tough to fit it all in under four minutes between calls, but she assures Andrew that he'll get it. She asks Andrew what the last customer needed. He checks his notes. "A spreadsheet with the customer's billing information for the past six months."

Jasmine prompts, "You remember how to pull up the information, right?" Andrew pulls up the information. He notices that there's more information in the spreadsheet than just the customer's.

"Do I need to start over? What's the procedure for this?" Andrew asks. Time is ticking. Jasmine shows Andrew how to hide rows containing the information from the other customer. Andrew questions her. "Are you sure that's it?"

Jasmine responds, "Yep!" Andrew attaches the spreadsheet and send the email. "See?" Jasmine points at Andrew with her lollipop. "You've got this! Easy!"

The client receives the spreadsheet, unhides the rows, and sees all of the confidential information about the other client. They call to let Andrew know. Now Jasmine has to go through the long process of disclosure tracking with her supervisor and the privacy office.

Dayna has done a good job of showing a lot of the action. You have probably noticed some ways Dayna could improve her story by showing more of the action, connecting with the character's motivations, refining the verbs, and replacing dialogue tags. Converting this story to pure dialogue will help with some of these things. First, let's simplify the task by eliminating the second scene where the client receives the spreadsheet and the scene where the client calls Andrew to let him know. Keep the scene contained to one time and place: Andrew's desk. If Dayna decides to develop the second and third scenes, she will need to show the action rather than tell about what happened.

Take a moment and convert the narrative version into pure dialogue, ending with Jasmine's last line, "You've got this! Easy!"

Andrew	
Jasmine	
Andrew	
Jasmine	
Andrew	
Jasmine	
Andrew	
Jasmine	
Andrew	
Jasmine	
Andrew	
Jasmine	
Andrew	
Jasmine	
Andrew	
Jasmine	
Andrew	
Jasmine	You've got this! Easy!

Was it hard to translate the paragraph form into dialogue? Some lines were probably more difficult than others. Keep in mind, when writing dialogue, the same principle that you've learned throughout this book: It's all about the action. Their words should reveal action and emotion. In Dayna's script below, you will notice that some of the actions from the paragraph form have made their way into the dialogue through stage directions (unspoken actions and descriptions that are in parentheses). These directions will be helpful for the actors who eventually play these roles in the finished product.

Andrew	(on the headset) We'll get that to you right away, Ms. Pritchard! Thanks for calling! Bye! (runs his hand through his hair, turns to Jasmine) I don't know if I'm ever going to be ready to fly solo.
Jasmine	(smiles) You'll be ready. You're great on the phone! I like how you used her name at the end. Great work! (leans back in her chair, unwraps a lollipop, and pops it in her mouth)
Andrew	(takes a breath) I'm okay with the phone stuff. It's the documentation and things in between each call that are so hard!
Jasmine	Yeah, it's tough sometimes to fit it all in under four minutes between calls, but you'll get it. Alright, time's ticking. What did the last customer need?
Andrew	A spreadsheet with the customer's billing information for the past six months.
Jasmine	(checks her smartphone) You remember how to pull up the information, right?
Andrew	(navigates with his mouse) Yep, like this?
Jasmine	(glances up) That's right. And how do you download it as an Excel spreadsheet?
Andrew	(still navigating with mouse) By . . . (sits upright, tense) oh yeah! Click this button and then . . . download!
Jasmine	(texting) Like magic! There it is.
Andrew	(staring at the computer) Hold up. There's more information in here than just the customer's.
Jasmine	(puts her phone down) Let me see. Oh, you're right. Good eye, Andrew. Must have been another customer with that same last name and first initial.
Andrew	What's the procedure for this? Do I need to start over?
Jasmine	Hm . . . We're about out of time. There's a fix for that. (leans forward and takes the mouse) Here, just hide the rows containing the info for the other customer, like this. And then save. It's ready to go! (let's Andrew take over)
Andrew	(navigating) OK, and then attach it to the email and send it? Are you sure that's it?
Jasmine	Yep!
Andrew	Well . . . (hesitant) Here goes. (clicks) There, it's on its way! (looks to Jasmine for approval)
Jasmine	See? (points at Andrew with lollipop) You've got this! Easy! You're ready for your next call!

Dayna has pulled from her previous work to further flesh out her characters' actions and motivations in this version. Jasmine's value of customer care seems limited to the person-to-person connection she makes with customers on the phone, but she loses interest when it comes to sending paperwork to the customer. Dayna also brings out Jasmine's love for social media and possibly online shopping, which may be part of the reason she sends the spreadsheet incorrectly. Andrew's character is also fleshed out more as we see him hesitate before sending the email, then look to Jasmine for approval. The contrast between Jasmine's laid-back attitude and Andrew's nervousness is nice too. Most importantly, Dayna has shown us the conflicting action and provided compelling motivations for the characters to take those actions.

The story you are writing for the Well Adjusted clinic opens up many possibilities for demonstrating the conflicting action through interpersonal conflict. Dialogue is great for this. Challenge yourself to write the story as pure dialogue.

Make It Concrete

Dialogue is a great way to make the scene more realistic. There's another element that can make the story live and breathe for the audience: specificity. Details will help the audience relate even more to the story. To unearth those details, ask yourself:

- What small actions or information can reveal more about the characters?
- What meaningful props can the characters interact with to make the setting more real?

For her cybersecurity scene, Dayna answers the above questions in this way:

- Steve could say more about Bryan that relates to his past. His son's birthday could be next week. Steve could lunge for the power cord.
- Steve could be drinking coffee. He could slam it down at the end of the story.

~~Steve sits at his desk~~. **Steve takes a big gulp of coffee**. He scans his inbox. "An email from Bryan **Schultz**?! I haven't heard from him **since our football days!**" He chuckles quietly, then reads it aloud. "'Hey Steven! **Are you still an engineer?** I came across this incredible sale on sports equipment. Thought you might be interested with your son's little league. The link is below. **Go Tigers!**' . . . Hm, that seems odd. Bryan never calls me *Steven*." Steve had been thinking of purchasing a ball return for his son's birthday **next week**. He shrugs. "Can't hurt to check it out." He clicks the link. His computer screen freezes. Steve frantically hits ESC. Nothing happens. **He slams his coffee mug on the desk.** Finally, in a moment of desperation, he **lunges toward the wall** and yanks the cord out of the socket. Steve groans miserably. "I shouldn't have clicked that link!"

It's a much richer story now. The opening line offers more about who Steve is (he's a coffee drinker). Bryan has a last name, which feels more credible. Bryan is someone Steve played football with, which strengthens Steve's motivation to trust the email. Bryan gives us more information about Steve (he's an engineer) and ends the email with a reference to his former football team. These are plausible details as scammers often consult social media sites to learn more about their targets. The addition of his son's birthday next week also adds to Steve's motivation to click the link. Time's running out to get him a present. Slamming the coffee mug on the desk seems a little over the top, but so do some of the other actions at the end. The next step in building your story can help you tone it down or build it up more gradually.

Eliminate Extraneous Words

Remember, your story is about action. It's important to avoid embellishing or overwriting your story. All that will do is slow it down, weakening the plot. Adjectives and adverbs are parts of speech that get in the way of the action. Scan the Steve story for adjectives and adverbs. Did you notice these five?

- *big* gulp
- chuckles *quietly*
- seems *odd*

- *frantically* hits
- groans *miserably.*

All of these adjectives and adverbs, except for the third (seems odd), can be eliminated.

> Steve takes a ~~big~~ gulp of coffee. He scans his inbox. "An email from Bryan Schultz?! I haven't heard from him since our football days!" He chuckles ~~quietly~~, then reads it aloud. "'Hey Steven! Are you still an engineer? I came across this incredible sale on sports equipment. Thought you might be interested with your son's little league. The link is below. Go Tigers!' . . . Hm, that seems odd. Bryan never calls me *Steven.*" Steve had been thinking of purchasing a ball return for his son's birthday next week. He shrugs. "Can't hurt to check it out." He clicks the link. His computer screen freezes. Steve ~~frantically~~ hits ESC. Nothing **happens**. He slams his coffee mug on the desk. **Finally, in a moment of desperation,** he lunges toward the wall and yanks the cord out of the socket. Steve groans ~~miserably~~. "I shouldn't have clicked that link!"

Dayna has a leaner, action-packed story. The adjectives and adverbs are out of the way. If there are excessive adjectives and adverbs in your story, there are probably weak actions. But when actions are strong, there is little use for lengthy descriptions. Dayna is showing us the action in her story, thus the adjectives and adverbs are not necessary.

Adjectives and adverbs aren't the only words that could be trimmed. Notice how the italicized words in her story above also seem to be slowing the plot down.

- nothing *happens*
- *finally, in a moment of desperation.*

Take out *happens* and hear how it sounds: "Steve hits ESC. Nothing. He slams his coffee mug." Nice, right? Cutting that word quickens the pace and moves the plot forward. It feels more urgent now. Next, *Finally, in a moment of desperation* contains a lot of descriptive words that just aren't needed. Dayna removes these and revises the ending.

> Steve takes a gulp of coffee. He scans his inbox. "An email from Bryan Schultz?! I haven't heard from him since our football

days!" He chuckles, then reads it aloud. "'Hey Steven! Are you still an engineer? I came across this incredible sale on sports equipment. Thought you might be interested with your son's little league. The link is below. Go Tigers!' . . . Hm, that seems odd. Bryan never calls me *Steven*." Steve had been thinking of purchasing a ball return for his son's birthday next week. He shrugs. "Can't hurt to check it out." He clicks the link. His computer screen freezes. Steve hits ESC. **Nothing. He slams his coffee mug on the desk, lunges toward the wall and yanks the cord out of the socket.** Steve groans. "I shouldn't have clicked that link!"

This version of his story allows Dayna's learners to experience the conflict through observation. It is unhindered by excessive descriptions and allows them to feel what Steve is feeling in the moment.

Let Your Audience Discover the Story Premise

Effective stories convey the story premise through the actions of the characters, and for the most part, Dayna has done a good job with that. Her story premise is "A story about Steve, an engineer, who struggles to protect the company's information from scammers." Her first story about Steve started off with, "This is a story about phishing and how to respond to an email containing attachments or links," which force feeds the audience the story premise and dilutes the learner's experience to discover it for themselves by observing the action. It leaves no room for the learner to think through what's going on in the story. Clues that your story may be giving the story premise away are:

- excessive descriptions rather than showing the action
- revealing the thoughts of characters rather than their actions
- describing how characters feel instead of showing it
- stating an action from the action list instead of demonstrating a conflict with it.

Where might Dayna be giving away the story premise?

Look to the last line of the story. *Steve groans, "I shouldn't have clicked that link!"* This may seem like a minor point, but remember, the purpose of the story is to build a desire for resolution. Let's let the learner sit with the conflict a little longer by switching Steve's last line with one of the options below. Which one creates the strongest desire for resolution?

- Steve groans and puts his head in his hands.
- Steve groans. "What have I done?"
- Steve groans. "That was so stupid."
- Steve groans. "I can't believe I fell for that!"
- Steve groans. "Thanks a lot, Bryan."

Really, any of these options is a stronger choice than "I shouldn't have clicked that link!" They don't spell out the instruction. They infer it. Why is this good? Because showing the story premise, rather than telling it, allows the plot to unfold like real life, nuanced and complex. Life is not black and white. By focusing on the action of the story, rather than the telling of it, you mirror life more closely. This becomes even more crucial when there are more characters and more actions.

The Completed Story

If you are writing a longer story for training, you can break it up into scenes. Read Dayna's final story about Steve and ask yourself these questions:

- Do I know these characters?
- Do I feel for them?
- Can I see the story unfolding in my mind?
- Do I want resolution?

> Steve takes a gulp of coffee. He scans his inbox. "An email from Bryan Schultz?! I haven't heard from him since our football days!" He chuckles, then reads it aloud. "'Hey Steven! Are you still an engineer? I came across this incredible sale on sports equipment. Thought you might be interested with your son's little league. The link is below. Go Tigers!' . . . Hm, that seems odd. Bryan never calls me *Steven*." Steve had been thinking of purchasing a ball return for his son's birthday next

week. He shrugs. "Can't hurt to check it out." He clicks the link. His computer screen freezes. Steve hits ESC. Nothing. He slams his coffee mug on the desk, lunges toward the wall and yanks the cord out of the socket. Steve groans. "I can't believe I fell for that!"

When you share your story with people to review, you should ask those four questions. It's a great way to gauge whether or not the story is complete. Once you are satisfied with the script, you'll get to develop the story as a finished product.

With practice, you'll be able to start writing a good story based on the character descriptions and action list right out of the gate. You consume and tell stories on a daily basis. Trust your gut. These tips will help you refine that story. When you're stuck, come back to these exercises to get you up and running again. Or make these exercises part of your process. Use the Build the Story worksheet in appendix 1 to keep your story aligned with objectives and formulate the story premise.

Figure 7-8. Build the Story Worksheet

Build the Story Worksheet

After you've worked through each of the steps, record the final story on the Instructional Story Design Plan.

Story Premise

Write the story premise for each character and their corresponding action, using the story premise formula:

A story about [character name and position] who struggles to [an action from the action list].

Map the Plot With Core Actions

Answer the core action questions for the story.

Core questions	Core actions
Where are they in the story?	
What are they doing?	
What do they encounter that gives them an opportunity to do the action from the story premise?	
What do they do that's in conflict with that action?	

String the core actions together in a short paragraph to start the story.

PRACTICE STORY DESIGN:
Build the Story

Walk through each step described in this chapter to build your stories for Well Adjusted, the chiropractic clinic, using your character descriptions from chapter 5 and the information you recorded in the Show the Action exercise in chapter 6. These will be a fictional story. Complete each exercise below for Story 1, then come back and complete the steps for Story 2.

Story Premise

Write the story premise for each character and their corresponding action using the story premise formula:

A story about [character name and position] who struggles to [an action from the action list].

Story premise 1	Story premise 2

Map the Plot With Core Actions

Answer the core action questions for each story.

	Story 1	Story 2
Where are they in the story?		
What are they doing?		
What do they encounter that gives them an opportunity to do the action from the story premise?		
What do they do that's in conflict with that action?		

String the core actions together in a short paragraph to start each story.

Story 1	Story 2

Connect With the Character

In the Show the Action table you completed in chapter 6, integrate at least one motivation for the character into the story. Imagine real people having a real interaction with others in the scene. When you read through the story, you should feel like there is a good reason for their behavior. You may not like what the character is doing, but you should be able to relate to them. Don't worry so much about making them perfect. You have space to refine them. Write your stories below.

Story 1	Story 2

Refine the Verbs

Look back at your stories and look closely at the verbs.

- Are they in present tense? If not, re-write it in present tense.
- Do they need helping verbs? If so, they might be too weak.
- Could they be strengthened by using a synonym?

Rewrite the stories using the three questions above as your guide.

Story 1	Story 2

Escalate the Conflict With Dialogue

Look for opportunities to insert dialogue. You were challenged earlier in the chapter to try making one of the stories purely dialogue. Whether it's narrative or dialogue, let your characters speak!

Story 1	Story 2

Make It Concrete

Go back to your character descriptions and Show the Action exercise. Are there attributes of your character that could be shown by adding detail?

- What small actions or information can reveal more about the characters?
- What meaningful props can the characters interact with to make the setting more real?

Rewrite the stories using the above questions as your guide.

Story 1	Story 2

Eliminate Extraneous Words

This step sounds easy, but sometimes it's hard to do. You've put a lot of effort into writing the story that includes these descriptive words but go ahead and remove them. If the story seems weaker, it's probably not because it's missing the adjectives and adverbs. It's most likely because the action is too weak to carry the story by itself. You need to strengthen the action. Also look for extraneous words and phrases and remove them or replace them with action.

Rewrite the stories, removing adjectives, adverbs, and extraneous descriptions.

Story 1	Story 2

Let Your Audience Discover the Story Premise

Your stories should be action-packed now. Do another read-through and make sure you're not giving the story premise away. If not, you're done! If so, take a moment to rewrite your final version below.

Story 1	Story 2

You may want to present your story to Dr. Kobal—or not, depending on how involved you feel he needs to be in this process. Regardless, read through the scenes one more time and ask yourself, your client, or someone you trust, these questions:

- Do I know these characters?
- Do I feel for them?
- Can I see the story unfolding in my mind?
- Do I want resolution?

If you answer yes to all four questions, you're ready to produce it! To see another finished story based on this same audience profile and action list, see the completed Instructional Story Design Plan in appendix 3.

PART III
Deliver

Produce and present your story using tools you already own

CHAPTER EIGHT

Produce and Present With Available Tools

"What am I supposed to do with this script?"

Dayna sits down at her desk and smiles. She looks at the papers in her hand. She's just come back from Susan's office, where she presented each of her revised stories. They talked through some minor changes, but Susan signed off on both of them. She feels like doing a victory lap around the floor. Dayna reads through the final versions of her two stories.

Steve takes a gulp of coffee. He scans his inbox. "An email from Bryan Schultz?! I haven't heard from him since our football days!" He chuckles, then reads it aloud. "'Hey Steven! Are you still an engineer? I came across this incredible sale on sports equipment. Thought you might be interested with your son's little league. The link is below. Go Tigers!' . . . Hm, that seems odd. Bryan never calls me Steven." Steve had been thinking of purchasing a ball return for his son's birthday next week. He shrugs. "Can't hurt to check it out." He clicks the link. His computer screen freezes. Steve hits ESC. Nothing. He slams his coffee mug on the desk, lunges toward the wall and yanks the cord out of the socket. Steve groans. "I can't believe I fell for that!"

Dayna nods. "Yeah, this does seem more immediate." She likes how Steve reads the email aloud and responds before clicking the attachment. She flips to the Jasmine story. Her day with James's drama club kids inspired her to try full out dialogue.

Andrew	(on the headset) We'll get that to you right away, Ms. Pritchard! Thanks for calling! Bye! (runs his hand through his hair, turns to Jasmine) I don't know if I'm ever going to be ready to fly solo.
Jasmine	(smiles) You'll be ready. You're great on the phone! I like how you used her name at the end. Great work! (leans back in her chair, unwraps a lollipop, and pops it in her mouth)
Andrew	(takes a breath) I'm OK with the phone stuff. It's the documentation and things in between each call that are so hard!
Jasmine	Yeah, it's tough sometimes to fit it all in under four minutes between calls, but you'll get it. Alright, time's ticking. What did the last customer need?
Andrew	A spreadsheet with the customer's billing information for the past six months.
Jasmine	(checks her smartphone) You remember how to pull up the information, right?
Andrew	(navigates with his mouse) Yep, like this?
Jasmine	(glances up) That's right. And how do you download it as an Excel spreadsheet?
Andrew	(still navigating with mouse) By . . . (sits upright, tense) Oh yeah! Click this button and then . . . download!
Jasmine	(texting) Like magic! There it is.
Andrew	(staring at the computer) Hold up. There's more information in here than just the customer's.
Jasmine	(puts her phone down) Let me see. Oh, you're right. Good eye, Andrew. Must have been another customer with that same last name and first initial.
Andrew	What's the procedure for this? Do I need to start over?
Jasmine	Hm . . . We're about out of time. There's a fix for that. (leans forward and takes the mouse) Here, just hide the rows containing the info for the other customer, like this. And then save. It's ready to go! (let's Andrew take over)
Andrew	(navigating) OK, and then attach it to the email and send it? Are you sure that's it?
Jasmine	Yep!
Andrew	Well . . . (hesitant) Here goes. (clicks) There, it's on its way! (looks to Jasmine for approval)
Jasmine	See? (points at Andrew with lollipop) You've got this! Easy! You're ready for your next call!

"Nice!" Dayna takes a deep breath. "Now . . . What am I supposed to do with these?"

What to Do With Your Script

Dayna, of course, is discovering Story Design principles along the way, but you can answer Dayna's question at the beginning of the design phase. How will the story be developed into a finished work that can be delivered to your audience? There are three factors that help define the final product of your story: the development tools available, the delivery method, and the story form. Throughout the rest of the chapter, Dayna's two stories will be the subject of development from concept to storyboarding to production. She opts for some simple methods, but in chapter 9, you'll explore more complex ways to produce the story.

Use What You Have

Though the form your story will eventually take can determine its effectiveness, the bigger impact is how you've designed the story. If you have taken the steps outlined in the preceding chapters, leading up to development, you're on solid ground. How you produce the story is not as important as how it's designed. In fact, there are some very simple ways to develop your story into a viable final product without purchasing any equipment or software. Start by taking a look at what you already have in-house. If you have two or three of any of the following tools (Figure 8-1), you're ready to develop a story.

Figure 8-1. Development Tools

- ❑ Your voice
- ❑ Word
- ❑ PowerPoint
- ❑ Camera
- ❑ Microphone (USB)
- ❑ Audio editing software
- ❑ Materials for sketching or painting
- ❑ Visual design tools
- ❑ Animation tools
- ❑ Video camera
- ❑ Video editing software
- ❑ E-Learning authoring tool

Already you can see a wide range of story development options, from a choose-your-own adventure in an e-learning authoring tool to telling a story in a live setting. Once, during a virtual session for managers I was leading, the webinar tool froze and I couldn't show the video that contained the story, so I had to tell the story. Do you think the results from that webinar significantly shifted because I couldn't show the video? No, the knowledge, skills, and attitudes of the audience were affected just as much without the video as with it. So, though it would have been nice, simply from a presentation perspective, to not have to talk and tell the story myself, the story was designed for a specific impact. It achieved that impact both through video, in one session, and through telling it in another.

Use Your Voice to Tell a Story Well

"But I'm not a good storyteller! I could never do that!" When you are delivering training in-person, you may not have the luxury of producing a video and stepping aside to let someone else tell the story. Or, the video may not work. Sometimes you have to tell it yourself. That can seem scary because telling a story requires a level of vulnerability. You are talking to your audience about relatable characters in strong conflict and hoping that the desire for resolution kicks in. Those thoughts can be distracting and affect your telling of the story. Here are some things you can do to deliver a story well:

- **Trust the design**: You have spent time on sound design of the story. It will have the desired effect you're hoping for.
- **Read in your own voice**: Even if you are reading dialogue, don't worry about trying to make up a voice for each character.
- **Indicate characters by where you look**: If there are three characters in conversation, when you read Character A, look above the audience to the right corner of the room. When you read Character B, look above the audience to the left corner of the room. When you read Character C, look directly above the audience in front of you. When you read the narrator, look at your audience directly. If you are delivering the story virtually, use your computer's camera and let the audience see you and make "eye

contact" with the camera. Speak to your audience as if they were right in front of you.

- **Hold the script and read from it**: Memorization is rarely a requirement for good storytelling in a training setting. It's OK to read from the script. Practice enough so that you can look at the audience occasionally, or to the character's "point of focus" (see the previous tip). If delivering the story virtually, read from a script on your computer's screen so you can scan the story and glance at the camera occasionally.

- **Stand still**: Your hands will probably be occupied with the script or the slide advancer, but your feet may have a tendency to roam or rock or shift from side to side. Occasional shifting is OK, even a step or two. But it's best to find a comfortable stance and stay there while you deliver the story. While on camera with a virtual audience, adjust yourself or the camera so you appear in the middle of the screen without distractions in the background. If you are sitting, be sure the chair doesn't squeak and avoid shifting your weight or looking off-screen. Gesture as you would in-person. Though it may not seem so as you look out onto your audience, your voice is transporting them to another time and place where your relatable character lives. Don't let your extraneous movement distract them.

Narrow Down the Options

Once you've identified the development tools you own, think of how the final product will be delivered with the training. There are three main delivery methods: in-person, virtual and asynchronously (at the learner's own pace, like in e-learning).

If you are delivering the training in-person, the story options are most flexible. You can tell the story live, ask them to role-play, post visuals on a flip chart to support the story, project the story on slides, show a video—there are few limitations. Those limitations increase with a virtual delivery method. The platform you use may not support video. Still, the range of options is very wide. Asynchronous storytelling may not have all of the in-person options, but it can do something that is more difficult to do in a live situation: It can personalize the experience to each individual learner with branching scenarios.

Figure 8-2 is a chart that maps basic story forms on a scale from simple development to complex, and the types of stories that are suited (but not limited to) those forms.

Figure 8-2. Basic Story Forms Chart

SIMPLE ←——————————————————→ COMPLEX				
Spoken	**Written**	**Static Visuals**	**Audio**	**Video**
Role-play				
		Wordless comics/photos		
	Choose your own adventure	Choose your own adventure	Choose your own adventure	Choose your own adventure
Live presentation supported by slides or drawings		Live presentation supported by slides or drawings		
	Comic strip	Comic strip		
	Graphics/ photos paired with text	Graphics/ photos paired with text		
		Graphics/ photos paired with audio	Graphics/ photos paired with audio	
			Radio drama	
	Interactive PDF	Interactive PDF		
			Animated video	Animated video

Develop Dayna's Stories

Dayna wants to determine the best development options for each of her stories. First, she looks at the tools she has at her disposal to actually develop these stories. Here is her list:

- PowerPoint
- access to a few stock photos each month

- a smart phone with a camera
- a USB mic that she got for $90
- free audio editing software that can handle basic editing and mixing
- an e-learning authoring tool with a few built-in characters.

You may have less than Dayna. You may have more. But look objectively at what you have and ask yourself, "How can I use these tools to produce a story?" Dayna knows that the stories for this course will be delivered in the e-learning authoring tool. The Steve story about cybersecurity is the one she tackles first. It seems the simplest, since there is only one character and there is more narration than spoken text. She decides to stay on the simpler side and present this story using text with just a few supporting visuals. The second story about Jasmine and Andrew is written like a play. She likes the idea of making this one a little more complex. She decides to use photographs of two co-workers and add speech bubbles for the dialogue.

Dayna's choices make sense. It's her first attempt at using stories in her training design, so choosing something on the simple side is a good start. Before developing either of these stories, however, Dayna needs to take the practical step of storyboarding so she knows how much time it will take her to produce them and what assets need to be created.

Storyboard the Action

Storyboarding takes little time on the front end of story development and saves a lot of time during and after development. Simply put, storyboarding helps you to begin thinking in terms of a finished product. What will the learner see, hear, or read? By capturing this information at the beginning, you save yourself the headache of having to go back and get visuals you missed or scrapping everything and starting over after realizing halfway through that the set of images you needed from a photoshoot would be impossible to create on your budget. Storyboarding should be done any time the final product contains visual or audio elements.

Your story has a plot with distinct actions. Consider each of those actions a "scene" in your story. Each scene should contain one main action that can be easily illustrated. Create a table within a Word document with three columns (as pictured below) and break up the script into scenes, one per row. In the far-right column, include the narration or dialogue: This is your story. Dayna divides her story into separate scenes in the storyboard. Figure 8-3 is what it looks like.

Figure 8-3. Steve Storyboard: Narration

Audio	Visual	Story/Dialogue/Narration
		Steve takes a gulp of coffee. He scans his inbox. "An email from Bryan Schultz?! I haven't heard from him since our football days!"
		He chuckles, then reads it aloud. "'Hey Steven! Are you still an engineer? I came across this incredible sale on sports equipment. Thought you might be interested with your son's little league. The link is below. Go Tigers!'
		Hm, that seems odd. Bryan never calls me *Steven*." Steve had been thinking of purchasing a ball return for his son's birthday next week.
		He shrugs. "Can't hurt to check it out." He clicks the link.
		His computer screen freezes. Steve hits ESC. Nothing.
		He slams his coffee mug on the desk, lunges toward the wall and yanks the cord out of the socket.
		Steve groans. "I can't believe I fell for that!"

Now she needs to visualize what will appear on the screen for each scene. Use the middle column to describe what one will see (the action of the story playing out visually). Picture the story unfolding in your mind and put it into words. You can jot down your ideas in the chart above before moving on. When you're ready, take a look at how Dayna completed this section of her storyboard (Figure 8-4).

Figure 8-4. Steve Storyboard: Visuals

Audio	Visual	Story/Dialogue/Narration
	Steve setting a mug of coffee down on his desk, smiling. A picture of Bryan in a circle with a line to Steve's screen. Text on screen.	Steve takes a gulp of coffee. He scans his inbox. "An email from Bryan Schultz?! I haven't heard from him since our football days!"
	Close-up of Steve's screen with the words of the email on it. "He chuckles, then reads it aloud" text on screen top left. The rest of the text is in the email.	He chuckles, then reads it aloud. "'Hey Steven! Are you still an engineer? I came across this incredible sale on sports equipment. Thought you might be interested with your son's little league. The link is below. Go Tigers!'
	Close-up of Steve, confused, wary, skeptical. Text on screen.	Hm, that seems odd. Bryan never calls me Steven." Steve had been thinking of purchasing a ball return for his son's birthday next week.
	Close-up of Steve's computer with mouse over the link to buy. Text on screen.	He shrugs. "Can't hurt to check it out." He clicks the link.
	Steve at his desk, frantic. Hitting ESC. Text on screen.	His computer screen freezes. Steve hits ESC. Nothing.
	Steve lunging for the plug Text on screen	He slams his coffee mug on the desk, lunges toward the ~~wall~~ power strip and yanks the cord out of the socket.
	Steve holding the power cord, head in hand. Text on screen.	Steve groans. "I can't believe I fell for that!"

In addition to the action taking place in the middle column, she also makes a note that each screen will contain the text of the story. The text is part of the visual that will be seen by the learner. The left column is for mediums, like video, where the story may include sound effects or music. Dayna decides to keep Steve's story simple. She's not using audio and leaves this column blank.

Dayna scans through the visuals she will need to pull this off. It may be a little more complex than she originally thought. But she's not required to use all of these visuals if she wants a simpler solution. She could choose just one or two of these visuals. If so, she should choose those visuals that will make the most emotional impact on his audience. Notice on the second-to-the last row, she replaces "wall" with "power strip." During storyboarding, you picture the scene unfolding. As Dayna does this, she realizes that the computers in her office are all plugged into power strips located underneath the desk. Steve lunging for the wall is impractical, so she makes the revision. Take note of these details and allow yourself the liberty to make these kinds of changes in the storyboard phase. It will save a lot of time in production.

A Finished Product

Dayna decides to focus the story on Steve and not worry about the computer screen. She asks a co-worker to pose at his desk with three different expressions that represent the three main events in the story: smiling, confused, and frantic. She takes the pictures on her phone and designs three slides that look like this (Figure 8-5).

Figure 8-5. Completed Steve Story: Photos and Text

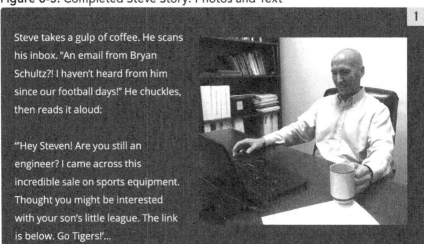

...Hm, that seems odd. Bryan never calls me *Steven.*"

Steve had been thinking of purchasing a ball return for his son's birthday next week. He shrugs.

"Can't hurt to check it out."

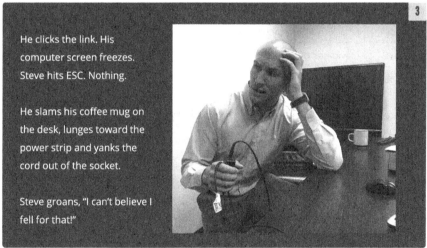

He clicks the link. His computer screen freezes. Steve hits ESC. Nothing.

He slams his coffee mug on the desk, lunges toward the power strip and yanks the cord out of the socket.

Steve groans, "I can't believe I fell for that!"

With the Steve story developed in a short amount of time, Dayna's ready to tackle something a little more challenging with the Jasmine story.

Storyboarding Jasmine's Story

Take a look at Jasmine's story. How would you divide this story into scenes? Look at the conversation. Where are the natural breaks? Where do the characters' intentions shift? Notice that Andrew begins on the phone. Where does the action shift to a conversation with Jasmine? Where does Jasmine shift the action to delivering on the last customer's request? Then, where does Andrew's action shift to looking up the information? Draw a horizontal line between each major action in the story that follows.

Figure 8-6. Jasmine Story: Division of Scenes

Andrew	(on the headset) We'll get that to you right away, Ms. Pritchard! Thanks for calling! Bye! (runs his hand through his hair, turns to Jasmine) I don't know if I'm ever going to be ready to fly solo.
Jasmine	(smiles) You'll be ready. You're great on the phone! I like how you used her name at the end. Great work! (leans back in her chair, unwraps a lollipop, and pops it in her mouth)
Andrew	(takes a breath) I'm OK with the phone stuff. It's the documentation and things in between each call that are so hard!
Jasmine	Yeah, it's tough sometimes to fit it all in under four minutes between calls, but you'll get it. Alright, time's ticking. What did the last customer need?
Andrew	A spreadsheet with the customer's billing information for the past six months.
Jasmine	(checks her smartphone) You remember how to pull up the information, right?
Andrew	(navigates with his mouse) Yep, like this?
Jasmine	(glances up) That's right. And how do you download it as an Excel spreadsheet?
Andrew	(still navigating with mouse) By . . . (sits upright, tense) Oh yeah! Click this button and then . . . download!
Jasmine	(texting) Like magic! There it is.
Andrew	(staring at the computer) Hold up. There's more information in here than just the customer's.
Jasmine	(puts her phone down) Let me see. Oh, you're right. Good eye, Andrew. Must have been another customer with that same last name and first initial.
Andrew	What's the procedure for this? Do I need to start over?
Jasmine	Hm . . . We're about out of time. There's a fix for that. (leans forward and takes the mouse) Here, just hide the rows containing the info for the other customer, like this. And then save. It's ready to go! (let's Andrew take over)
Andrew	(navigating) OK, and then attach it to the email and send it? Are you sure that's it?
Jasmine	Yep!
Andrew	Well (hesitant) . . . Here goes. (clicks) There, it's on its way! (looks to Jasmine for approval)
Jasmine	See? (points at Andrew with lollipop) You've got this! Easy! You're ready for your next call!

Dayna's division of scenes probably looks similar to your own ideas.

Once you've divided the action into scenes, think about the visuals needed to support each scene. What are the characters doing? Do they wear a certain expression? Remember, Dayna wants to stage and photograph employees doing these actions. The information in the visual column will help her to direct employees when he takes photos of them (Figure 8-7).

Figure 8-7. Jasmine Storyboard: Dialogue

Audio	Visual	Story/Dialogue/Narration
		Andrew: We'll get that to you right away, Ms. Pritchard! Thanks for calling! Bye!
		Andrew: I don't know if I'm ever going to be ready to fly solo. **Jasmine:** You'll be ready. You're great on the phone! I like how you used her name at the end. Great work! **Andrew:** I'm OK with the phone stuff. It's the documentation and things in between each call that are so hard! **Jasmine:** Yeah, it's tough sometimes to fit it all in under four minutes between calls, but you'll get it.
		Jasmine: Alright, time's ticking. What did the last customer need? **Andrew:** A spreadsheet with the customer's billing information for the past six months.
		Jasmine: You remember how to pull up the information, right? **Andrew:** Yep, like this? **Jasmine:** That's right. And how do you download it as an Excel spreadsheet? **Andrew:** By . . . Oh yeah! Click this button and then . . . download! **Jasmine:** Like magic! There it is.
		Andrew: Hold up. There's more information in here than just the customer's. **Jasmine:** Let me see. Oh, you're right. Must have been another customer with that same last name and first initial. **Andrew:** What's the procedure for this? Do I need to start over? **Jasmine:** Hm . . . We're about out of time.

Figure 8-7. Jasmine Storyboard: Dialogue (cont.)

Audio	Visual	Story/Dialogue/Narration
		Jasmine: There's a fix for that. Here, just hide the rows containing the info for the other customer, like this. And then save. It's ready to go!
		Andrew: OK, and then attach it to the email and send it? Are you sure that's it? **Jasmine:** Yep! **Andrew:** Well . . . Here goes . . . It's on its way! **Jasmine:** See? You're getting it! Easy!

Below is Dayna's storyboard with the visuals described in the middle column (Figure 8-8). Again, she chooses not to use music or sound effects, which would appear in the left column. The next chapter will explore more audio options. A storyboard template is available in appendix 1 and at needastory.com/book-resources.

Figure 8-8. Jasmine Storyboard: Visuals

Audio	Visual	Story/Dialogue/Narration
	Andrew at his desk and Jasmine to his left in a chair pulled up beside his. He's talking into the headset. Jasmine is listening in, smiling.	**Andrew:** We'll get that to you right away, Ms. Pritchard! Thanks for calling! Bye!
	Andrew is running his hand through his hair. Jasmine is holding a lollipop she's just unwrapped.	**Andrew:** I don't know if I'm ever going to be ready to fly solo. **Jasmine:** You'll be ready. You're great on the phone! I like how you used her name at the end. Great work! **Andrew:** I'm OK with the phone stuff. It's the documentation and things in between each call that are so hard! **Jasmine:** Yeah, it's tough sometimes to fit it all in under four minutes between calls, but you'll get it.

Audio	Visual	Story/Dialogue/Narration
	Jasmine is talking with the lollipop in her mouth. Andrew is looking at his notepad.	**Jasmine:** Alright, time's ticking. What did the last customer need? **Andrew:** A spreadsheet with the customer's billing information for the past six months.
	Jasmine is looking at her phone. Andrew is sitting upright, looking intensely at his computer screen. One hand on the mouse. One on the keyboard.	**Jasmine:** You remember how to pull up the information, right? **Andrew:** Yep, like this? **Jasmine:** That's right. And how do you download it as an Excel spreadsheet? **Andrew:** By . . . Oh yeah! Click this button and then . . . download! **Jasmine:** Like magic! There it is.
	Andrew is pointing to computer, still facing it. He looks worried. Jasmine leans forward, still holding her phone, looking at the screen.	**Andrew:** Hold up. There's more information in here than just the customer's. **Jasmine:** Let me see. Oh, you're right. Must have been another customer with that same last name and first initial.
	Close-up of Andrew facing Jasmine.	**Andrew:** What's the procedure for this? Do I need to start over?
	Close up of Jasmine with one hand on mouth, the other holding her lollipop. She's navigating.	**Jasmine:** Hm . . . We're about out of time. There's a fix for that. Here, just hide the rows containing the info for the other customer, like this. And then save. It's ready to go!
	Andrew in the foreground. Jasmine in the background. He's navigating. He looks worried.	**Andrew:** OK, and then attach it to the email and send it? Are you sure that's it? **Jasmine:** Yep! **Andrew:** Well . . . Here goes . . . It's on its way! **Jasmine:** See? You're getting it! Easy!

Another Finished Product

The storyboard took her less than an hour to create, and she's optimistic it will take even less time in future projects now that she's familiar with the process. Dayna now knows that she needs eight unique photographs for the scenes. She recruits two more volunteer employees. She's already pictured, in her mind, what will be needed for the set and what each actor will need to do to make the scene work. Instead of plain text with images, this time, she pairs the pictures with speech bubbles.

Figure 8-9. Completed Jasmine Story: Photos and Speech Bubbles

Figure 8-9. Completed Jasmine Story: Photos and Speech Bubbles (cont.)

The storyboard template is in appendix 1 and at needastory.com/ book-resources. After you've completed the practice section, check out the completed template in appendix 3 for another example.

PRACTICE STORY DESIGN:
Storyboard

With your written stories for the Well Adjusted staff training, it's time to develop them. Start off by assessing the tools at your disposal and the story form you'd like to use.

Development Tools
- ❏ Your voice
- ❏ Word
- ❏ PowerPoint
- ❏ Camera
- ❏ Microphone (USB)
- ❏ Audio editing software
- ❏ Materials for sketching or painting
- ❏ Visual design tools
- ❏ Animation tools
- ❏ Video camera
- ❏ Video editing software
- ❏ E-Learning authoring tool

Story Form

Consider how complex you want the story to be, then circle the possible story forms you want to try. Then move on to the storyboarding exercise.

SIMPLE ←				→ COMPLEX
Spoken	**Written**	**Static Visuals**	**Audio**	**Video**
Role-play				
		Wordless comics/photos		
	Choose your own adventure	Choose your own adventure	Choose your own adventure	Choose your own adventure
Live presentation supported by slides or drawings		Live presentation supported by slides or drawings		
	Comic strip	Comic strip		
	Graphics/ photos paired with text	Graphics/ photos paired with text		
		Graphics/ photos paired with audio	Graphics/ photos paired with audio	
			Radio drama	
	Interactive PDF	Interactive PDF		
			Animated video	Animated video

Storyboard

Complete the storyboard table below. Break up your story into main scenes. You're looking for main actions. It doesn't need to switch scenes with every single line of the story or dialogue. Then complete the middle column. Picture the action unfolding and describe it in this column. What will the learner see as they watch the story? If you include music or sound effects as part of the production of the story, indicate that in the left column.

Audio	Visual	Story/Dialogue/Narration

CHAPTER NINE

Develop at a Deeper Level

True Test

Dayna runs through the Steve and Jasmine–Andrew story slides one more time on her laptop, making small adjustments. "I think this is as good as it's going get." She bites her lip and leans back in her chair. "I need to show these to somebody." Fayette is out of the office. Susan? She shakes her head. "I don't want to bother Susan yet." She puts her hand on her cheek. Who would look at these stories with a critical eye? She takes a quick breath and sits upright. Dayna picks up the phone and dials. "Hey, this is Dayna from learning and development. Do you have a minute for me to show you something for the compliance course? OK, I'll be right over." She hangs up, closes her laptop, and heads down the hall. She's going to put her stories to the test with Randall.

Moments later, Dayna watches Randall as he reviews the stories on her laptop. A small nod. That's good. Was that almost a smile? It's hard to tell what he thinks of the stories. When he finishes reviewing, he turns to Dayna and says, "That'll work."

She feels relieved, but asks, "Do you feel like you know the characters?"

"I know the guy who did Andrew's part."

"No, what I mean is, do you feel like they are realistic characters?"

"Sure," he replies.

She remembers about not asking yes-or-no questions. "How do you feel when you watch these stories?" It didn't come out like Dayna wanted it to, but Randall answers the question anyway.

"It felt like they were doing something that was going to cause me a lot of work." Dayna grins. Randall continues, "But I can see why they did it."

"What do you mean?" asks Dana.

"The email to Steve seemed pretty legit."

Dana prompts him with, "And what about the Jasmine and Andrew story?"

Randall says matter-of-factly, "Yeah, I can see why Jasmine's in a rush. She's mentoring Andrew. She probably has a lot of work to do herself. Plus, Andrew's only got four minutes. That's a lot of pressure."

"You made my day, Randall." Dayna stands and picks up her laptop. "Thank you."

She's walking away when Randall stops her. "Hey . . . " Dayna turns to face him. "How do the stories end?"

Dayna could jump up and down, but instead she grins wryly and says, "You'll have to take the course to find out."

The Power of Simple

Dayna has succeeded in producing two stories that even Randall approves of. He felt like he knew the characters. He felt something for them. And he expressed a desire for resolution. She accomplished this using basic tools and applications. Your story can have a similarly powerful impact on your audience because it is well designed. Producing that story can be as simple or as complex as the need calls for, but never discount the power of simple.

In this chapter, you'll explore some different, sometimes more complex, techniques of producing your story using text, graphics, audio, animation, and video. Examples of each technique are displayed in the book. Examples containing audio, animation, or video can found at needastory.com/book-resources (referred to as "the book resources page online" in this chapter).

Text

People still enjoy reading stories. There are some great ways to delivery your text-only story:

- printed copies that learners read (out loud or to themselves) at a live training session
- pre- or post-reading

- a series of slides in e-learning with only text that can help the learner slow down and take in the story.

You've read most of the stories in this book—no illustrations. No audio. Despite the claims that humans have the attention span of a goldfish, people only pay attention to videos, and other fallacies, there is always time for a story, even if it has to be read. Apply basic readability principles and your audience will stay with you:

- Keep the paragraphs short.
- Line break every time someone new speaks during dialogue.
- Ask a grammar expert (copy editor) to review the text.
- Read it out loud. Is it conversational? It's easy to lapse into corporate speak or industry jargon when text is the only avenue of telling the story.

This method of delivering a story is particularly effective when training senior leaders, board members, or audiences who are accustomed to reviewing written reports. Text-only is also a good venue for audiences who may perceive being "told" a story off-putting (such as being read aloud to during an in-person training or watching a video). This audience would rather be in control of the pace at which they consume the story.

Dayna could produce the Steve story using text only. It may look something like this (Figure 9-1).

Figure 9-1. Steve Story: Text Only

Cybersecurity Course

STEVE'S STORY

Steve takes a gulp of coffee. He scans his inbox. **"An email from Bryan Schultz?! I haven't heard from him since our football days!"** He chuckles, then reads it aloud:

"'Hey Steven! Are you still an engineer? I came across this incredible sale on sports equipment. Thought you might be interested with your son's little league. The link is below. Go Tigers!'

...Hm, that seems odd. Bryan never calls me *Steven*."

Steve had been thinking of purchasing a ball return for his son's birthday next week. He shrugs. **"Can't hurt to check it out."**

Figure 9-1. Steve Story: Text Only (cont.)

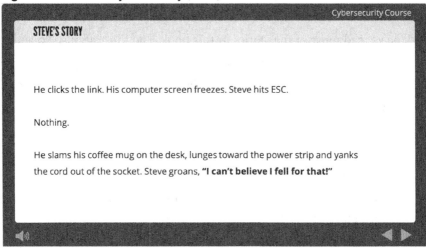

It's powerful because it is designed to be so. The fact that it is text-only doesn't diminish its power. And in some cases, it may be more powerful to let your audience create what the character looks like and sounds like in their minds rather than to display that character on a screen.

Text can still be a creative means of delivering a story. The first time I saw a video produced by The Girl Effect, a nonprofit that empowers girls in Africa and Asia to change their lives, my audio was off, so I didn't hear the powerful music that accompanies the text-only story. Though the story isn't designed for training, it is designed to prompt a new behavior: to donate to their organization. Words and phrases appear on the screen in quick succession, building momentum and deepening the emotional connection to the main character, a girl, and stirring you to do something to help her. It is a masterfully designed marketing video. There's no reason why a text-only video similar to this couldn't be used for training.

Graphics

Whether you have access to graphics tools or not, nearly everyone has access to PowerPoint or another similar presentation creation option, which is surprisingly good for creating graphics. Figure 9-2 is a version of the Steve story using graphics that were created on PowerPoint using shapes.

Figure 9-2. Steve Story: Graphics

STEVE'S STORY

Steve takes a gulp of coffee. He scans his inbox. "An email from Bryan Schultz?! I haven't heard from him since our football days!" He chuckles, then reads it aloud:

TO: Steve
FROM: Bryan

Hey Steven!

Are you still an engineer? I came across this incredible sale on sports equipment. Thought you might be interested with your son's little league. The link is below. Go Tigers!

Get your discount!

...Hm, that seems odd. Bryan never calls me *Steven*."

Steve had been thinking of purchasing a baseball return for his son's birthday next week. He shrugs.

"Can't hurt to check it out."

He clicks the link. His computer screen freezes. Steve hits ESC.

Nothing.

He slams his coffee mug on the desk, lunges toward the power strip and yanks the cord out of the socket.

Steve groans, "I can't believe I fell for that!"

Graphics of objects, like the ones used in Steve's story, create a stylized look and feel that can create a sense of mystery or an incomplete picture, which increases curiosity and the desire for resolution. If you feel intimidated by making your own graphics in PowerPoint, visit needastory.com/book-resources and download the PowerPoint practice deck to master the basic skills and get started.

Audio

Even older than written stories are audio-driven stories. Turns out people still enjoy listening to stories, whether in person or remotely! If the story can't be delivered in person, you will need the help of audio tools to make that happen. Fortunately, audio recording and editing has become so much easier with USB mics that can record audio straight into free recording and editing software on your computer or handheld devices. The cost to record audio is minimal. It's possible to set up an effective recording studio for under $200.

Audio can be combined with other foundational elements of production, like photos, graphics, or animated video to add vocal variety and a good dose of reality to the story. For instance, in Figure 9-3, imagine Jasmine and Andrew having the same exchange as the story with speech bubbles. But this time, audio is added to the scene. Listening to Jasmine and Andrew speak in their own voices makes the conversation much more like reality. Visit needastory.com/book-resources for recommendations on tools and tips for recording your stories. You can also listen to an audio sample of Steve and Jasmine's stories and watch a sample video.

If this book were printed in color, you'd notice in Figure 9-3, when Jasmine speaks, her character is in color, while the rest of the photo is in black and white. When Andrew speaks, his character is in color. The video of this story was created in PowerPoint, using the "Remove Background" picture feature to isolate the image of the speaking character in the color photograph, which was placed on top of the full picture in black and white. Audio was added to the deck and the slides were timed to the dialogue. The entire deck was converted to an MP4 video file, which is a PowerPoint feature as well. This same effect can be produced using more robust editing tools, but it's nice to know that you have this capability in a tool you probably already own.

Figure 9-3. Jasmine Story: Photos and Audio

Audio can also be paired with Steve's story. In this case, instead of dialogue, Steve's story is told by a third person narrator. Notice the addition of music and sound effects, which accentuate a sense of mystery (Figure 9-4).

Figure 9-4. Steve Story: Graphics and Audio

For notes on how to set up photo shoot or audio recording with volunteer employees at your company, download the Guide for Directing Amateur Actors at needastory.com/book-resources.

Music and Sound Effects

Music

Music can take the emotional connection with your audience up several notches but use it sparingly in your story. A story over-saturated with music loses its effectiveness. Below are listed the basic uses for music in your story, listed in order from most common to least common. Start with just one of these instances and build music into the story gradually. A simple intro may be all that you need.

- **Intro**: To set the mood for the scene, insert a brief musical introduction that fades as dialogue or narration begins.
- **Outro**: End the story with a brief musical outro that fades in as dialogue or narration comes to a close. Or start the outro right after the last line of the story. Choose a piece of music that evokes the emotion you want to leave with your audience as the story ends. If you want a consistent emotion throughout, start with an intro of music, then use another portion of that same music to use as the outro. If the emotional tone of the scene changes significantly from beginning to end, you may want to choose two different pieces, but in a similar style.
- **Underscore**: Establish an underlying tone for the entire scene with music that plays underneath the dialogue or narration. Choose carefully! Underscore should be consciously unnoticed. The purpose is to create a subtle emotional connection, not draw attention to itself. Underscore music then is usually free of dynamic shifts in tempo or volume. Think of the music as a wash of steady emotion: a predictable rhythm and consistent instrumentation that matches the emotion of the scene.
- **Key moments**: Punctuate actions that are key moments of conflict, twists in the plot, decision points for the characters or notable humor with appropriate music. This music has a much higher emotional punch than underscore. Choose music that fits

the emotion of the moment.

Expand music options beyond your personal preference. Find inspiration in the music your audience listens to. Most importantly, music is there to support your design. Choose it well and your audience will be thrilled! Visit needastory.com/book-resources for an example of how music has been used to enhance the Steve story.

Sound Effects

Sound effects are not usually necessary for a story to be effective, but they can be fun! They help bring the audience into the scene. There are two basic sound effects:

- Realistic sound effects imitate real life, like crumpling paper, turning a socket wrench, typing on a laptop, or writing on a whiteboard. Human sounds, like sighing, laughing, cheering, or clapping are considered sound effects. There are so many resources for free and pay-to-use sound effects. Even so, depending on how customized your sound effects need to be, you may find yourself in your recording closet with everyday objects, slamming a phone into its cradle, clapping two pieces of wood together, or pouring a cup of water to record your own sound effects. What if you need the ambient sound of a train yard, or the sound of a woman walking in high heels, getting into a pick-up, and driving off? Sound effects can take you places.

- Unrealistic sound effects, like boings and pops and synthesized sounds, are less common and more stylized but may also help create the right emotion for a story. For instance, in Steve's story with the graphics, an echo effect was applied to the click of the mouse to create an unrealistic sound that accentuated the conflict. These kinds of effects create drama out of real life. It's fascinating how these unrealistic sound effects are received by your audience. Once, I designed audio-driven course on fraud. The entire story was told through very simple graphics of individual objects from the story, like a set of keys, a phone or a car, accompanied by short musical punctuations. The only sound effects included in the course were unrealistic ones—poinks, drips, and cracks that I

> made with my own recorded voice. But when I received feedback
> from my audience, they commented on how they liked hearing the
> jingle of the keys, the footsteps of the character, and the sounds of
> the hospital room.
>
> I issue the same caution with sound effects as with music. Be
> selective! Don't try to provide a sound effect for every single action in
> the scene. Start with an important action and build it out from there.
> You don't want to create expectations for your audience that you can't
> maintain throughout all of the scenes.

Use your audio editing tool to layer the music and sound effects with the
dialogue or narration. If you haven't used such a tool, start with a free one.
The learning curve is not as steep as you may think. The waveforms for each
audio track that appear on the screen can be copied and pasted like you would
copy and paste text. The volume for each track can be adjusted and the entire
project can be exported as an MP3 file, ready to be embedded into your story.

Animated Video

Creating animated video has become a lot more accessible with online tools
that allow you to customize characters and upload audio files and visual assets.
Characters can be easily programmed to lip sync to the dialogue. Sophisticated camera movement gives the story movie appeal. Depending on your
audience and budget, animated video is a great option. Your animated characters can be in practically any scenario doing anything that your actors can do,
and more (Figure 9-5). Consult the Audio Recording portion of the Guide
for Directing Amateur Actors and watch an animated version of Jasmine and
Andrew's story on the book resources page.

You may encounter some resistance to animated video from stakeholders
who feel that their content is too serious for animation or that the audience
is too senior to present an animated video to. But, when done well, animated
video can be appropriate for any audience and any topic. You'll receive some
valuable resources for overcoming barriers like this in chapter 12.

Figure 9-5. Jasmine Story: Animated

Video

Video can be fantastic if you have the means to hire a professional film crew and actors (or if you are a professional videographer yourself). If you are shooting your own video footage, there are some distinct challenges to consider:

- Capturing quality audio is complicated for video. Video on a phone or tablet may produce a decent image, but likely the audio is not going to be great. Even with a professional camera, additional investment will be needed for quality audio.
- Video editing is complex and time-consuming as it involves editing for visual as well as audio and syncing the two.
- Using amateur actors for video is hard. Doing a photo shoot and an audio recording session with volunteer employees is more attainable, because the actors only have to focus on one thing at a time: posing for a photograph or speaking the lines. For video, actors have to

focus on both, plus they have to memorize their lines! Bring out the video camera and watch amateur actors freeze.

- People are critical of acting, even when it's not acting. Think of the times you've watched a senior leader on a talking head video and thought, "Man, he needs to loosen up." "I can totally see her eyes reading the teleprompter!" "Can he be any more monotone?" Show the series of Andrew–Jasmine photographs synced to audio and people will say, "Hey, that's cool. They did a great job!" Take those same two actors and put them in front of a camera, and no matter how well they do, people will have something critical to say about their acting. That's not a great position to put your volunteer actors in.

- Videos are outdated quickly. Because of the investment, you'll want to get long use out of your video story, which means the course you are developing is also going to stick around for a while. Let's say you plan to keep the video story for five years. If something significant changes to the content of the course, it may also affect the video, which may require reshooting some of the content. Then there's the clothing. Styles and fads change quickly. It may not be a deal breaker, but it's definitely worth considering if video is your choice. Besides trendy clothes or hair styles, you'll want to avoid references to pop culture that may not be relevant in five years.

If you want to start self-producing videos with amateur actors, consider producing only part of the story with video (Figure 9-6). Start with short scripts that can be easily memorized or even improvised by the actor. Watch an example of this kind of video from the Steve story and the Jasmine story on the book resources page online.

Video may be your best solution. If it is, you can go into it with your eyes wide open to ensure your video remains fresh for as long as possible. If video is out of reach, there are many other options at your disposal.

Figure 9-6. Jasmine and Andrew Story: Video

Constraints Produce Creativity

The number of tools that are available to create compelling stories is growing. But start simple. Embrace your constraints. And let creativity spring out of those constraints. Do you have a camera? A device that can record audio or video? What about PowerPoint? You have something you can use to develop your story. Start with that. You'll be surprised how creative you can be using what you have.

PRACTICE STORY DESIGN:
Produce the Story

You think about Dr. Kobal's staff. You picture them in the therapy bay, ready to receive training. You look around the room. There's a mix of expressions on each face. One of the back-office workers is texting. The doctor in the back looks like she's ready to bolt. Three therapists are huddled together whispering and occasionally bursting out into laughter. Janine, from the front, is sitting alone. She offers an encouraging smile. Dr. Kobal strolls up to the front and says, "I'd like to thank you all for gathering today. We have a very exciting guest. I'd like for you to take notes." You look around the room. No one has a pen. Good thing you brought some just in case. "I think you're going to enjoy it!" He looks at you. "It's all yours!"

Are you picturing it? Now imagine the story unfolding before them. Are you telling the story with visual support from PowerPoint? Are you showing an animated video? Are you ready to make it happen!? Review your decisions from the practice session in chapter 8, give yourself a deadline for completion, and go for it!

CHAPTER TEN

Train With Stories

Showcase

"Get out!" James sets his drink down on the table. "You made this in PowerPoint?!"

Dayna grins. "Yep!" She feels excited to show James her work. She asked James to meet her at the Question Mark Grill so she could show him her finished stories. "So . . . am I up for a Pulitzer?"

"And an Emmy!" They laugh. "Seriously, Dayna, I'm very impressed. I mean, I would have never thought to put photographs with speech bubbles. It works! It feels kind of like a video!"

"Thanks! I think my co-workers did a pretty good job acting." Dayna closes her laptop.

"They had a good director!"

"You taught me everything I know. It's about action, right?"

"Right! I won't take it to heart that I didn't get the lead role," James says.

Dayna laughs. "What about the Steve story? Did you like that one?"

"It's perfect. I totally get why he clicked on that invite. I might have done the same thing!" Dayna smiles. James continues, "What does the compliance director think?"

"She signed off on it this afternoon. She likes it a lot."

"Yeah, but what did she say?" James prods. "Come on, did she say it was brilliant?"

"Well." Dayna blushes. "Something like that."

"Ingenious?" Dayna shakes her head. "A masterpiece?"

Dayna rolls her eyes. "She said it was intelligent and engaging."

"Sounds like compliance-speak for *brilliant* to me!" James says. "So what's next?"

"That's what I wanted to talk with you about," says Dayna.

"Oh good! I wouldn't mind playing Steve in the musical version!" They laugh.

"Well, after the musical, I've got to deliver training."

"Oh yeah," says James. "So what's the plan?"

Dayna takes a drink. "I was thinking that each training module would start with the story to, you know, set the context and the problem. Then, it could go right into demonstrating the right way to do things."

James clarifies, "You mean, just leave Steve and Andrew and Jasmine in the dust and jump right into training?"

"Well, not exactly," Dayna explains. "See, the story is the hook that draws them in. But the training is, well, still just compliance training."

"But what happens to your characters?" James asks.

"I'm not sure," Dayna admits.

James pushes, "You've produced this great need for resolution. It'd be a shame to leave the characters behind like that. Isn't there some way to include their story in the training?"

Dayna thinks it through. "Well, their story is in the training . . . but I see what you mean. Maybe I could follow their story through somehow and show what happens?"

"What makes the stories relevant to the learner?" James asks.

"Everything," says Dayna, "The characters are in conflict with the actions we want employees to take."

James nods. "Okay, so after reading the Jasmine story, I'm not sure I know what actions you want me to take. I mean, I kind of know, but I don't know that I could put it into words. Shouldn't the story have some kind of impact on the training?"

"Yeah." Dayna and James sit quietly for a minute. Finally Dayna speaks, thinking out loud, "Learners need to do something." She pauses. "A lot of training is telling, then testing, right?" James nods. Dayna continues, "But if we begin with these stories, it's kind of like immersing the learner in the situation right up front. It's not *telling* the learner . . . it's *showing* them. In a way, it's like throwing them into the scene to figure things out."

"Totally." James agrees.

"So, what if we left some room after the story to give the learner some space to think?" Dayna looks at James for his opinion.

"Think during a compliance course? That sounds radical. Go on."

"Alright." Dayna leans forward. "The story ends. On the next slide, we ask the learner to identify what was wrong in the scenario, without telling them anything. You know, let them figure it out?"

"Give me an example. What about the Steve story?"

"Right. Steve's story ends with him in a panic. The next slide gives the learner a question and some options."

"Multiple choice?" asks James.

"Yes."

James nods. "What's the question and what are the options?"

"Let's see, it could be something like, 'What has Steve just done?' And the options are 'Introduced a virus into his computer,' 'Given access to an unauthorized individual,' or 'Exposed the company to a security risk.'"

"Isn't it all of those things?" asks James.

"Well, oh yeah, I guess it'd be 'All of the above!'"

James groans. "No! Too easy! Come on! There's got to be something better than that!"

Dayna smiles. "Coming up with multiple choice questions on the fly isn't easy, you know."

"Hold on," says James, "You created these stories based on an audience profile and a list of actions, right?"

Dayna nods. "That's right."

"So shouldn't your multiple choice question be about . . . "

Dayna gets it and interrupts, " . . . the action! Yes! Not identifying the problem but doing something about it. That would help them to think things through and figure it out for themselves."

James is right there with her. "The story helps them to assess their skills in a real-world situation right at the top!"

"I like the way you put that," says Dayna.

"So what's your new multiple choice question?"

Dayna opens her laptop and pulls up the cyber security action list.

Figure 10-1. Cybersecurity Action List

> - Scan emails for common phishing clues using the Phishing Clues job aid.
> - Forward suspicious emails to the help desk without clicking links or opening attachments.
> - Report suspected breaches in security.
>   - Call cybersecurity office.
>   - Notify your supervisor.

"According to the action list, the step that Steve should take now is report the suspected breach in security."

James looks at the screen. "OK, yeah, I see that. It's too late for him to take steps 1 or 2. He's already up to step 3."

"I think these are the choices I can use," says Dayna. "They're all things that Steve was in conflict with in the story, and they're all related to cybersecurity. None of them are distractors, necessarily. It would help the learner assess where they are in the story."

James spells it out. "So the question is, 'What should Steve do right now?'"

Dayna nods. "Yes, and the choices are 'Scan the email for phishing clues,' 'Forward the email to the help desk,' or 'Report it to cybersecurity.'"

James looks at the action list on Dayna's screen. "So, they'd have to know these steps to answer correctly? It seems kind of unfair to ask them this question if they don't know that process."

Dayna sits up straight. "I know! I could link to the online job aid right here on the slide."

"But, isn't that giving away the answer?"

"It's not giving away the answer!" Dayna says. "It's part of figuring things out, like in the real world, right?"

"Like in the real world," James repeats. "Because in the real world, they have this job aid, so why not give it to them in the course so they can practice using it?"

"I couldn't have said it better!" Dayna grins. "What do you think?"

James grins. "It's brilliant."

Stories Center Stage in Training

The Story Design model connects the story to action. The last connecting piece of the model is training (Figure 10-2).

Figure 10-2. Training in the Story Design Model

Once you've spent time and resources designing and developing a story for training, you want to maximize its power throughout the rest of the course; you want to keep the story center stage. As James mentioned, you don't want to leave the characters in the dust once the training begins. Imagine a training experience that begins with "At the end of the course, you will be able to protect our systems from security breaches," compared to one that begins with a story, like Steve's, where you are thrust into the action immediately and need to make a choice. The first appeals to the intellect only. But the second engages the intellect and the emotions. The rider and the elephant, mentioned in chapter 1, are fully on board! Action is the focus of the Story Design process in discovery, design, and delivery. The action that learners must take to impact the business outcome is realized through training, supercharged by the story.

Story Design's profound impact on the learning experience can be strengthened using some simple training techniques for e-learning, instructor-led training, and virtual solutions. Invite your audience to continue to interact with the characters as learners seek to resolve their conflict. The following techniques will help guide your audience through training, keeping the story central to the experience. As you move through each technique, remember that the goal is to move learners up the design continuum toward practice (Figure 10-3).

Figure 10-3. Design Continuum

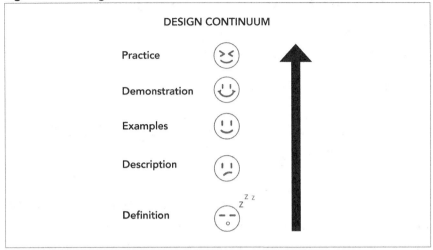

Reflection

Dayna's first instinct to give her audience time to think was a good one. Reflection can be as simple as assessing one's emotional state or identifying the missteps of the character. Allow the learner to think through the story and make their own observations. Figure 10-4 shows two examples of reflection.

Figure 10-4. Reflection Questions

![Privacy Course slide: A woman pointing at a computer screen with a speech bubble reading "Oh no! We've got to spend time doing disclosure tracking now!" Next to it: "How do you think Jasmine feels?" with options: Guilty, for telling Andrew to send the attachment with hidden rows; Frustrated, spending time on the tedious process of tracking; Worried that Andrew may have lost trust in her; Stressed, taking time away from production]

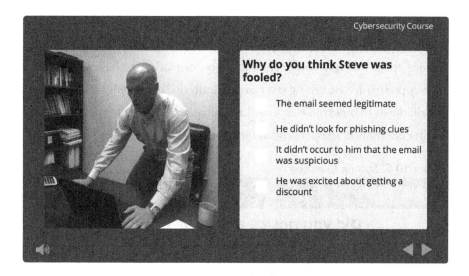

Notice that for each reflection, a character or image from the story appears along with the question. For e-learning there may not be a correct choice for a reflection question. If you are presenting to a live audience, prepare more questions that prompt participants to offer deeper insights that lead to identifying the root problem. A reflection question is especially effective when training an audience on interpersonal or leadership skills but can be used for any type of training.

Solving

The next natural step to reflection is figuring out the right course of action. Solving questions will differ for each course and for each delivery mode, but contain the same elements:

- The question asks learners to do something.
- The choices are plausible.
- Access to the same resources that are available to them on the job.

Ask Learners to Do Something

It's the learner's turn to take action. A solving question will prompt the learner to make a choice that aligns with the action list. Because you have refined the action list to observable actions, it will make it much easier for you to develop these choices. Think back to some of Dayna's early action lists that contained objectives like "understand the privacy policy." Now include this as one of the options for a multiple-choice question. You can't, right? Understanding the privacy policy isn't something you can physically do. That's why it's so important to drill down to observable actions. Live audiences benefit from being asked a solving question as an open-ended question, such as the ones in Figure 10-5.

Figure 10-5. Solving Questions

If, in an instructor-led or virtual course, learners offer solutions to a solving question like, "Steve should have known better," or "The leader should have been there for them," or "They should be familiar with the manual," keep asking them to explain until they offer an observable action, like "Steve needs to let his supervisor know about it right away," or "The leader needs to schedule one-on-ones with each of her employees," or "The manual says you should turn off the machine before doing the repair." When solutions that learners offer start aligning with the action list, you know you've designed your story well and your audience is ready for training.

Design Plausible Choices

Open-ended questions are not as effective for e-learning. When designing multiple-choice options, make sure the options are plausible. Dayna and James created a question for e-learning that draws upon the action list, with plausible choices and real-world guidance as a follow-up to the Steve story, like the slide in Figure 10-6.

Figure 10-6. Steve Story: Real Choices

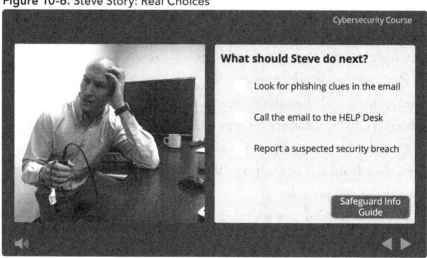

Each of the choices is a correct step of the process, but the learners must know the process in order to choose correctly. Creating options that appear in a process may not always be possible. The question may need distractor options. Distractors are plausible options that have a negative or less than optimal outcome. During discovery, you unearth some of the actions employees are taking to contribute to the root problem. Include those actions as distractor options.

Give Them Access to the Resources

Usually, it is appropriate to give learners access to the same resources in the course that are available to them on the job, unless the content must be memorized. In most jobs, employees have access to manuals, policies, and job aids to do their work effectively. They may not always use those resources, but the training can help them with that by giving them practice using those resources in solving questions, even during the assessment. Unless the training is embedded in their work flow, the course itself should not be considered their sole resource. Forcing learners to recall information that only exists in the course may test short-term memory but does little for knowledge transfer. There are exceptions, of course, when learners need to memorize something to make important decisions at a moment's notice. But even in these cases, they likely will have access to documented protocol back on the job. Giving the learner no access to on-the-job resources should be a conscious decision, not an oversight.

Providing real-world resources also has an advantage when training your audience on brand new content. Learners may have no idea what the process is or what the character should do next. But, if they are given access to a job aid, they can compare the situation in the story with the guidance from the job aid and figure it out. The story, paired with real-world guidance, makes this possible.

For instructor-led courses, bring the job aid into the room, or let the audience use their devices to access the resources. For virtual audiences, provide a link to the job aid in the chat or email them the resource in advance. In the e-learning examples above, each slide contains a button that links learners to the applicable resource.

Feedback

Up until now in the training, the learner has been active, reflecting, thinking through, figuring out, and making choices. Once learners make a choice, follow it up with immediate feedback that demonstrates its benefits or consequences. Let them feel the weight of that choice. Feedback affirms the learner's action or redirects it.

The instructor or subject matter experts can provide this feedback in live or virtual training. For e-learning, design feedback similar to that in Figures 10-7 and 10-8.

Figure 10-7. Steve Story: Feedback

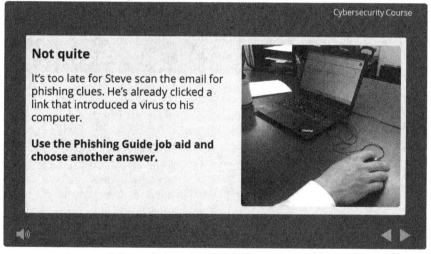

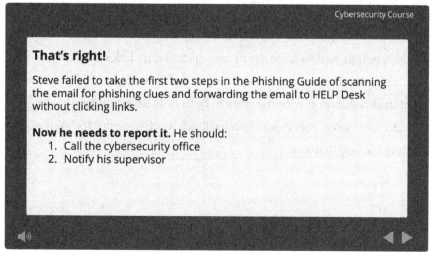

Figure 10-8. Jasmine Story: Feedback With Additional Questions

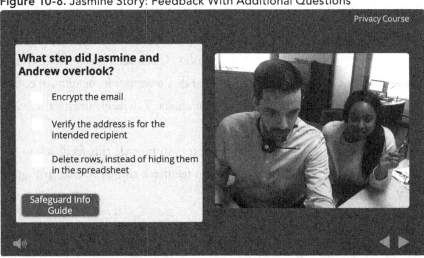

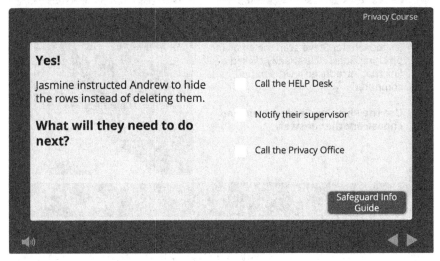

Notice that feedback for the privacy question includes a follow-up question. This can continue until the entire process is complete. Also notice the emotional connection with the story in both of these examples.

Here are some other possible feedback or follow-up techniques that support learning transfer.

Examples

Demonstrate the desired behavior. Show why the behavior is appropriate (Figure 10-9).

Figure 10-9. Training With Examples

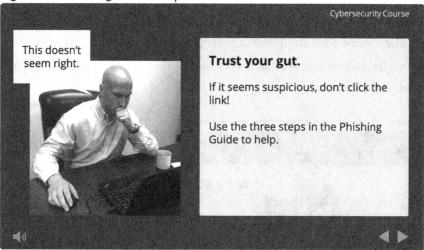

Nonexamples

The story itself is a demonstration of a nonexample. Bring it back and contrast it to the example. Show why it's inappropriate behavior. Nonexamples help make the appropriate behavior crystal clear (Figure 10-10).

The core technique of story–reflection–solving–feedback breaks the tell-then-test cycle. It can be repeated as often as needed to train the audience on every objective. This technique gives learners a chance to think things through, make meaningful choices, and remember them for a long time after training is over. It enables adoption of new behaviors, so the learner grows and the business meets its goals.

The Story–Reflection–Solving–Feedback worksheet is contained in appendix 1. You can also access an electronic version at needastory.com/book-resources.

Figure 10-10. Training With Non-Examples

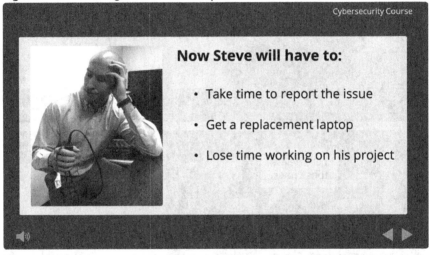

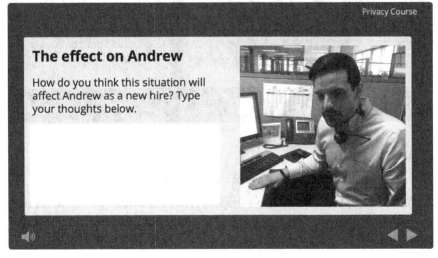

Figure 10-11. Story-Reflection-Solving-Feedback Worksheet

**Story–Reflection–Solving–Feedback
Worksheet for Training**

Use this worksheet like a design document for instruction.

Story

You've developed your story. What actions from the action list are you training on?

Reflection

Give your audience a chance to reflect on the story. Design a reflection question that allows them to relive the story in their minds and feel what the characters were feeling. Your reflection question can be similar to one of these questions:

- How would you feel if ... ?
- Why do you think ... ?
- What did you observe ... ?

Write some possible reflection questions below.

PRACTICE STORY DESIGN:
Use the Story to Train

Dr. Kobal is counting on you to make a significant impact on his staff at Well Adjusted. You're going to deliver that impact through effective training that is supercharged with Story Design. Use the story–reflection–solving–feedback steps below to design the instruction portion of the training.

Story

You've developed your stories. They're ready to go. You may want to note the two actions you decided to focus on below as a reference.

Reflection

Give your audience a chance to reflect on the story. Let them discover the action you are training them on. Design a reflection question that allows them to relive the story in their minds and feel what the characters were feeling. Your reflection question can be similar to one of these:

- How would you feel if you were the patient?
- Why do you think the patient feels this way?
- What did the staff do to make the patient feel this way?

Notice that the first two questions are more intuitive and trigger emotional recall. The last question focuses on observable actions. If you are designing for e-learning, you may need to provide multiple choice options for each of these questions. Write some possible reflection questions below.

Solving

You've presented the problem through story. Now, give the learner an opportunity to solve it. You could do so with a series of questions that progress from general to specific. If you are presenting this to a live audience, you can piggyback on their answers to ask for even more specific actions. If you are limited to e-learning, you may need a predetermined series of questions or a set of branching questions that leads the learner closer and closer to practice on the design continuum. However you deliver the training, the questions could progress similar to these:

- What about this seems wrong?
- What did the doctor say that seemed disrespectful?
- What about this situation made the therapist's behavior even more serious?
- What could the staff members do to fix this situation?
- How should they communicate so this doesn't happen again?
- If the doctor does disrespect the therapist again in the future, how should he respond?
- What should the therapist do in the future to make sure he demonstrates respect toward the doctor?
- How would you respond if someone came to you and said something similar?

Write a few solving questions and possible options that lead the learner toward practice on the design continuum.

Feedback

Look at your questions above. What kind of feedback will you offer for each of the options you've provided? Remember, feedback affirms the learner's action or redirects it.

PART IV
Overcome Barriers

Convince stakeholders of story's power and design
a storytelling landscape with no boundaries

CHAPTER ELEVEN

Stories for Every Audience: Case Studies

Numbers Tell the Story

"Wow, these are great numbers, Dayna! Knowledge and skills are way up!" Fayette, Dayna's manager, is reviewing the results of the compliance training she designed for cybersecurity. Dayna had been keeping her eye on the survey ever since the course was released a month and a half ago. Employees still had another week to complete the course, but most had taken the course and she wanted to share the preliminary numbers with Fayette. She scans her copy of the results.

Figure 11-1. Survey Results

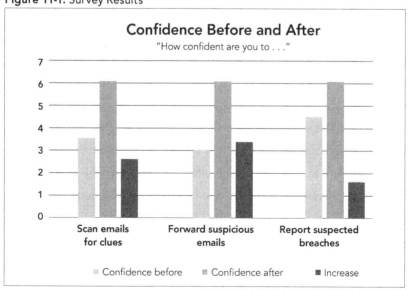

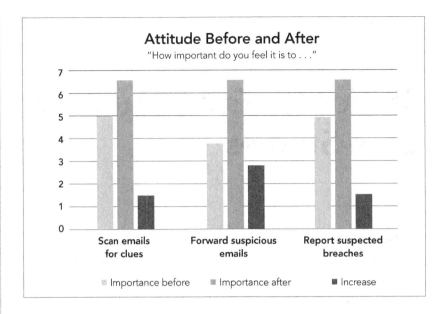

The Before Training and After Training numbers show an increase in confidence to perform (knowledge and skills) for all three actions, especially numbers one and two: "Scan emails for common phishing clues" and "Forward suspicious emails to the help desk." Importance (attitude) also increased, but by less of a margin.

"Thanks!" Dayna is proud of the metrics. "I contacted cybersecurity this morning. It's probably too early to tell, but I asked them about the number of reported phishing emails they received in the past three weeks."

"Oh?" Fayette raises her eyebrows. "What did they say?"

"Usually, they handle about 24 phishing email reports in a month. But in the past three weeks, they've handled 50."

"OK, that's a big increase. Can it be attributed to training?"

"I think so. There's been no other intervention in the past two months."

"Impressive, Dayna." Fayette looks back at the page of results. "Why do you think 'Report suspected breaches in security' has less of an increase than the other two objectives?"

Dayna leans back in her chair. "I've been thinking about that. I believe it's because of the story."

"I really liked that story," says Fayette. "It was a creative way to frame the content."

Dayna nods. "Thanks, but I can't take the credit for that one."

"Oh?"

"Yeah, that was actually Susan's idea," she says.

"The director of compliance asked for a story?"

Dayna laughs. "Yes, she told me that she wanted the training to be engaging and that one thing that engaged her was stories." Dayna flips through the papers in her file folder. "I actually have her note on the original action list somewhere." She pulls out the well-worn paper and hands it to Fayette and points to the yellow sticky note. "There on the bottom of the page."

Fayette reads out loud the words Susan scribbled. "I love a good story." She keeps looking at the paper. "Hm, so do I." She looks back up. "So what makes you think the increase in the first two objectives is a result of the story?"

Dayna sits on the edge of her chair. "Well, I think the story affected the results of all three, but the reason it affects the first two more is because of the conflict."

Fayette isn't following. "The conflict in the story?"

"Exactly! It's about the conflict in the story! Steve's actions in the story were in conflict with the first two objectives. For action number one, he didn't scan the email for phishing clues. See"—Dayna holds up her copy and points to the first action's results. "That's a nice leap in KSA." Fayette nods and she continues, "The highest increase in KSA, though, is *Forward suspicious emails to the help desk without clicking links or opening attachments.* In the story, Steve actively did something in conflict with this. He clicked a link and that's where the virus was introduced to his computer."

"I see. So what about the third objective?"

"Well, I think . . . I really think that this objective showed less of an increase for two reasons. First, Steve was never in conflict with this action." Dayna pauses.

"Wasn't he?" asks Fayette. "I don't remember him ever reporting the issue."

"Right, but you know why, right?" Dayna pauses.

Fayette responds almost immediately. "Wait, he *did* report the issue. I remember in the feedback of one of the questions later in the course. He was on the phone reporting to the help desk."

"Right, but during the story at the beginning of the course—" Dayna says.

"The story ends with Steve holding a cord in his hand—before we know what he does about it! I remember!" Fayette leans back in her chair, thinking. "So, because the learners never saw Steve in direct conflict with reporting?" She looks at Dayna.

"They have less of a connection with that action."

Fayette is curious now. "And how might the story be revised to make that connection?

"Well," says Dayna, "Even though Steve does yank the cord out of the socket, I think we'd have to see Steve ignoring the issue over a longer period of time to really connect with the reporting action."

Fayette agrees. "That makes sense."

"But if you look at the numbers, the action to report was already higher than the other two before training. People generally already know they should call the help desk. It's the preventive steps they aren't as familiar with. I think that the story is good as it is and the increase in the number of reports is proof for that. But there's another number I want to share with you."

Fayette puts her glasses on the desk. "OK."

"I also asked cybersecurity about the number of actual incidents from the past three weeks. In the months leading up to this training, there was a spike in that number. Cybersecurity was handling at least six incidents a week."

"Yes, I remember Susan telling me that when she asked me for training support," says Fayette.

"In the past three weeks, guess how many incidents have occurred?" Dayna smiles. "Zero."

"You're kidding."

"Actually, there have been two incidents. But get this. I sent a list of the employees who hadn't taken training yet to my contact in cybersecurity and asked if either of the two incidents involved one of those employees."

Fayette chuckles. "So? What did he say?"

"Both of them were on the list!"

"Well, Dayna, you're on a roll." Fayette smiles.

"You know, it's actually been fun. I didn't think I had it in me to write a story."

Fayette opens her notebook. "Maybe you'll have a chance to write another one. I got a call today from a VP in sales. He wants systems training for his sales reps on how to enter information in their CRM system."

Dayna doesn't hesitate. "Great! Did he give you an action list?"

She cocks her head. "You keep using the word *action* instead of *performance* objective. What's that all about?"

"Oh yeah"—she blushes—"It's just easier for subject matter experts to understand what we're asking employees to do. Know what I mean? It's all about the action."

"It's all about the action," Fayette repeats out loud. "I like it!"

Dayna smiles. She can't take credit for that one either.

Proof Positive

Dayna is convinced that storytelling has increased the knowledge, skills, and attitudes associated with her training. She feels ready to take on any training with her newfound storytelling chops. And she should. She's confident that she can make storytelling work for any course. But her next stakeholder is about to give her a run for her money. You'll hear more about that in chapter 12.

Stories With No Boundaries

In chapter 1, you learned that Story Design is a core skill for instructional design. Master it and you can apply it to any training program for any audience. No matter who your audience is, no matter what you are training them to do, Story Design can be applied to motivate learners to take action on new knowledge, new skills, and new attitudes using story's power to connect with your audience emotionally.

The power of your story has no limits, but its design and delivery does. You are likely already familiar with the constraints of time, tools, and technology. But there's another constraint: people. Not everyone is receptive to the idea of stories for training. This chapter and the next equip you to combat resistance to Story Design. In this chapter, you'll explore how five real-world companies have brought stories center stage to their training programs:

- leadership program at Pizza Hut
- compliance training at Southwest Airlines
- sales program at PepsiCo
- new hire onboarding at a large service organization
- systems training at a global electronics distributor.

Think of these examples as inspiration for your own programs and as proof to skeptical stakeholders that stories work. If your next project is related to one of these, take note of how to structure your approach so the characters in conflict have maximum impact. Specific technologies used in these design solutions may or may not be at your disposal. But remember, constraints are the catalyst for creativity.

Leadership Training at Pizza Hut, LLC (Blended Learning)

The incredibly talented design team at Pizza Hut's Center of Restaurant Excellence created a curriculum for shift leaders that integrates relatable characters in strong conflict in almost every aspect of the learning experience. Story Design is the heartbeat of this program. It's a great example of leadership training that contains all the right ingredients.

Like Television Episodes

Imagine you are a team member at a Pizza Hut restaurant. You're doing great work and your manager talks with you about becoming a shift leader. That means you would transition from being a team member to a team leader—a leader of your peers. And some of them have been there longer than you. If you agree to explore this possible promotion, you'll be introduced to a series of stories and training that unfold like television episodes. The online courses are displayed in a Netflix-like learning portal. Each season, or set of learning modules, within the portal contains a playlist of leadership skills that are more difficult to master than the season before. It's brilliantly designed for this specific audience to address not only the key leadership skills important to leading in the Pizza Hut culture but also the emotions new leaders experience coming into the role.

Stories saturate every aspect of the training experience, which is a mix of online training, on-the-job-challenges, self-reflection, coaching, and workshops. The learner records their observations in a journal that also guides them through the entire experience, so they know exactly where they are in the process. Sometimes that experience is facilitated by their manager. Sometimes it is guided by the online stories. And near the program's end, they attend a workshop to further practice and refine their skills. At the center of those stories is a young man named Zack.

The Zack Attack

By design, Zack is relatable. Like most of the learners, his character is doing great work at a Pizza Hut restaurant and is asked if he would like to become a shift leader. He's likeable and upbeat, with lots of leadership potential. At times, he's kind of scared about taking on this leadership role. As Zack's story unfolds, learners watch him face strong conflict with performances from the action list and help him figure out what steps to take based on the training they've received through Zack's manager.

Zack is the hero of the story, but so are the learners. They learn alongside Zack. They grow with him. Learners complete exercises in their journals to solidify what they've learned through Zack's story. But the training doesn't stop there. Learners talk through the story and the exercises with their manager. The story provides a common language for both mentor and mentee: "Remember when Zack acknowledged the contributions of a team member? How do you feel about doing this yourself?" Thanks to the story, the learner and their manager can communicate efficiently and with a full understanding of the context. The training also includes on-the-job assignments to practice the new skills. Their manager coaches them how to improve those skills. In the story, learners have already seen Zack struggle to perform. They've learned through his mistakes and through their own choices and feedback. They are mentally prepared to execute on the action in real life.

Periodically, in the online training, Zack reveals what he's feeling about performing certain tasks through a short video where he talks directly to the learner. These glimpses into what Zack is feeling are called Zack Attacks. In these brief videos, he comments on the conflict he's experiencing at the restaurant and talks about his own internal conflict. In a way, it's a story within a larger story. This is another great use of storytelling that connects with learners emotionally.

Assessing Through Storytelling

Each season in the online training begins with a dilemma, a realistic scenario in which Zack and the team face a challenge that a shift leader would encounter on any given day. Through the dilemma, they meet several characters who teach them how to use the tools to handle the situation. Then they have the opportunity to help Zack solve the dilemma. The designers wanted to give the learners a space to practice and fail safely. So at the end of each season, the learner faces another series of challenges. This time, they are placed inside a virtual Pizza Hut, where they apply their newly acquired knowledge and skills. Every choice they make is rated.

Story Design has made its way into every aspect of this training for shift leaders: improved knowledge transfer. Quicker skill-building. Lasting results.

Takeaways

Discover. Pizza Hut, LLC started the process of discovering stories by bringing all of the right people to the table, particularly those who were closer to the learners and their managers. The design team met for hours with subject matter experts and franchisees to refine characters and conflict so stories were real to life. The result was a well-rounded experience for the learner that was supported by the franchise community.

Design. The Story Design model of placing relatable characters in conflict is practiced in so many ways that translate beautifully to the learner. The pattern of story–reflection–solving–feedback is repeated using the online course, the journal, and coaching by the learner's manager. The dilemmas put the learner in the middle of a shift, filled with lots of conflict that they need to resolve. Zack's story (and his Zack Attacks) give the learner the opportunity to observe, feel, and make choices on his behalf. The journal offers time for reflection. Both the online course and the learner's manager provide feedback on the learner's performance. Pizza Hut maximized Story Design from the course's introduction all the way through to the assessment.

Deliver. There are some sophisticated components of Pizza Hut's delivery of the training, such as the customized learning portal constructed like a Netflix playlist and the gamified opening and closing dilemmas. But there are also some simple solutions. For instance, they originally brought the actor playing Zack into a studio for his Zack Attack videos. But the results seemed over-produced and a little contrived. The actor suggested that he film it himself using the video app on his phone. It worked even better! The main Zack stories did not use video at all. Photographs of the actors speaking, paired with audio, was all that was needed to develop them. It's interesting to also note that the journal is a printed, bound book that not only guides the learner through the training experience and prompts reflection, but also contains the resources that serve as a reference for their tenure as a leader with Pizza Hut.

Compliance Training at Southwest Airlines (Instructor-Led)

I had the privilege of sitting in on an award-winning, story-based compliance course for leaders at Southwest Airlines that models the technique of story–reflection–solving–feedback. Formerly, the course had been a full day of lecture. Now, it's a half day of instructor-led storytelling and real-world decision making. The experience simulates real-life situations drawn from case studies.

The Stories Unfold

Leaders sit at tables in groups of four or five. Every leader has a workbook that guides them through an assigned compliance-related story. The facilitator welcomes everyone and gives each table an iPad. The session begins and each table works at their own pace. The stories unfold through video, audio recordings, images of emails, letters, and text messages. The stories contain emotionally charged, tough situations for leaders to deal with. Periodically, the workbook instructs leaders to stop and reflect on the story and record their own thoughts before discussing the facts as a group and making decisions from a list of options. They also record their reasons for the decisions they make. After each decision point, the story continues and more facts unfold. The process repeats itself until the story ends. But the story isn't over. It isn't solved. The desire for resolution among participants is very real.

During this first half of the session, they are completely engaged in discussion, wrestling with some of their decisions and referring to the policies that are conveniently located in the back of the workbook or on the intranet. Time flies by. The design of the training is impressive, but it gets better.

Feedback From Subject Matter Experts

Up to this point in the session, participants have experienced story, reflection, and solving, but they haven't yet received any feedback regarding their choices. Their next assignment is to present their stories and the decisions they made to their peers in the presence of subject matter experts. This is their moment of truth. Stakeholders from HR and legal provide immediate feedback on their choices, share additional relevant case studies, and offer compelling evidence for why the choices they made were good ones (or not). Leaders often ask additional questions based on the feedback of the subject matter experts. This leads to more discussion, more thinking, more figuring out, more learning.

From "Sit and Get" to Action

Leaders leave the experience having practiced making choices based on real-world stories, using real-world guidance and hearing from the actual people they will interact with should such a situation arise on their job. In total, they have heard five compliance stories, plus the stories told by subject matter experts and the stories told by their peers. All this makes it more likely they will remember what to do than from sitting in an eight-hour lecture.

Southwest Airlines's complete transformation of compliance training from an all-day "sit and get" to an action-packed learning experience owes its success to well-designed stories. The efficiency of stories to cover a lot of ground in a short time contributes to cutting the training time in half. There is no question that stories are the reason why everyone in the room is focused and participating.

There's another reason why this compliance course is so successful. Remember in chapter 1, I described a story for training called The Coffeeshop? One of the biggest benefits of that experience was that it left room for self-discovery. Employees came up with their own solutions for a problem that existed in the story. That's what goes on in this room of leaders at Southwest Airlines as they interact with the stories for compliance. Discovering a truth for oneself is always more effective than being told.

Takeaways

Discover. The stakeholders for this course from HR and legal provided the case studies that the narratives were built around. The fact that they also participated in the implementation of training is a testimony to the trust they have in the design team to deliver a valuable learning experience. Good relationships with stakeholders and subject matter experts made it easy for the design team to discover relevant stories. Analysis of these real-life stories offered insights into who the characters should be and how the conflict aligned with performance objectives.

Design. Compliance training designed to check a box is not fun. Sometimes it even feels disrespectful, like a waste of time. Southwest Airlines elevated compliance training beyond a checked box to practical application. Also, as leaders discussed the stories, the company's core values and people-focused culture rose to the surface again and again. Applying Story Design to required training equipped learners to think critically about the action they needed to perform and how to perform it. Storytelling for compliance is a respectful choice that makes good use of learners' time and strengthens the company's ethical culture.

Deliver. The facilitator of the class started with an effective metaphor right out of the gate and asked for participants to respond with their observations. She set the tone for active participation, which was necessary because most of the content was delivered by the media elements and the participants themselves. Videos, letters, emails, and voicemails were uploaded to each table's iPad. Professional actors played the characters, which was a good choice given the complexity of the roles. In addition to the workbook, there were two other assets worth noting that helped the learners present their conclusions seamlessly during the second half of the course. Learners were given a card that contained the content of what each person at the table needed to share with the group during their presentation. The card contained a short pre-scripted paragraph and included blanks to fill in page number references and the table's conclusions—a thoughtful touch for those who may not be as comfortable winging a presentation. Subject matter experts had similar cards that helped them keep track of the choices each team made for the story so they could speak to those points in their feedback. The course was delivered with respect for these leaders' knowledge and time. Yes, it checked the boxes, but it did so much more. The learners in this class are ready to handle challenging compliance issues with confidence.

Sales Training at PepsiCo (Blended: E-Learning, Instructor-Led, Role Play)

The design team of PepsiCo's Key Account Academy prepares their sales force for the real world by immersing them in a story that plays out in the most interesting way. Their spot-on character descriptions and their step-by-step process yields a rich training experience that mimics reality. The story begins online, which prepares them for an intense in-person session.

Character Analysis

The main character of this story is Cathy, a sales account manager, who is tasked with preparing for a complex sale to a fictitious company. Her instructor, Mr. Torres, is speaking to the camera as if he's speaking to Cathy, so we don't see what she looks like until later. Essentially, the learner is in Cathy's seat, making choices throughout the online course on her behalf. Led by Mr. Torres through a series of questions, learners complete a job aid that they will take with them to the instructor-led portion of the experience. With each question, the learner explores a bulletin board that contains scraps of intelligence—excerpts from emails, sticky notes, magazine clippings—about five key players in the fictitious company. They learn about their influence, personalities, position in the company, and other factors that affect the sales approach. Yes, there is a lot missing information, just like in real life, but by the end of the online course, they have studied each character from so many angles that they have enough information about them to create an action plan. Now is when the fun starts.

Based on What You Know

One of the best things about the course is its ambiguity. Sales people don't always know everything they should about the people they are selling to. The designers brought this ambiguity into the learner's experience to provide practice dealing with unknowns. And the best way to resolve an unknown is, as you have learned in this book, to ask the right questions. Learners gather for an in-person session a week or so after they have taken the online course. They have their step-by-step job aid. They know who the key players are. They have their action plan. Each table discusses their observations and action plans to decide as a group which key player they need to speak with first. Then they plan for that meeting. Using flip charts, they draft a list of questions they need to ask. It becomes apparent through their discussions that they don't know who the decision maker is in the fictitious company. They need to find that out.

Cathy's Blunder

After some brainstorming, the learners take a break to watch a video. In the story, Cathy, the sales account manager, meets with one of the key players, Jim, who is the most vocally opposed to the deal. Cathy does a few things well, but then the meeting takes a turn. Instead of building credibility with Jim, she tries to sell him the promotion of the month. Jim is not impressed. The phone rings. He cuts the meeting short. Cathy leaves frustrated. Learners have the opportunity after watching the video to share their insights. What did Cathy do well? What could she have done better? Where did she deviate from the sales principles? How could she have connected with Jim on a personal level? After participants share their insights, they watch another video.

Behind the Scenes

The second video is unique. It's as if the cameras kept rolling after Cathy left the room. Carolyn, another key player, comes into Jim's office and asks how the sales call went with PepsiCo. Jim complains that Cathy doesn't understand their company's goals. Carolyn, who's fairly new to the company, questions Jim on the company's goals and ends up having a revealing dialogue that provides new insights into the company and into Jim. It's the conversation Cathy should have had. Participants review the types of questions that should be asked and tweak their action plans. But they still don't know who the decision maker is.

Winning Moment

The Cathy story wraps up with two final scenes. Cathy gets another meeting with Jim. Just before she walks in, Jim is on the phone with his assistant. "Call me in 10 minutes," he says. This time, Cathy makes a personal connection with Jim and builds credibility. In the middle of the meeting, Jim's phone rings. Participants smile and make the connection. The last time the phone rang, it was a set-up, just like this time. But this time, Jim ignores the call and by the end of the meeting becomes an advocate for Cathy, who asks to meet with Carolyn. He agrees to set up the meeting. Cathy leaves, but, again, the cameras keep rolling. Jim stops Carolyn and asks her to meet with Cathy. She's hesitant, but Jim insists, "You need to be there. You're the one who makes decisions on this kind of thing." Ah! Finally, it's revealed who the decision maker is.

In Real Life

The story about the fictious company is over. But not the experience. The design team took it one more brilliant step further: practice. Each participant receives a card describing the customer they must sell a product to. They have 30-45 minutes to use the job aid and prepare their questions. Then they engage in an eight to 10 minute sales call with a certified instructor who tests their questioning and listening abilities. They receive a final score and feedback. The deep experience of analyzing the players, planning their sales approach, and learning from Cathy is made possible through story design principles.

Takeaways

Discover. The design team at PepsiCo recognized several years ago that top-down training wasn't enough to prepare their sales staff. In their rapidly changing business, they needed to flip the training model and give their sales staff hands-on experience as soon as possible when they came on board. To create experiential training, the design team spent hours researching. They interviewed sales staff in the field. They interviewed leadership teams. They even interviewed current customers to get a better understanding of what takes place in the key players' minds. Through these interviews, they discovered a storehouse of potential characters, plots, and storylines that account managers can quickly relate to—because they are real. In this case, there are two audience profiles—the sales staff and the customer—that make the training credible and complete. That takes time to create. If you are designing for an immersive training experience, block out plenty of time for discovery.

Design. A heavy emphasis for this project is character descriptions. Everything centers on finding out who the key players of the fictitious company are and how to sell them a product. Learners ascertain certain characteristics of each key player to complete the job aid in the online course. The job aid itself serves as a bridge from the analysis in the online course to planning in the live session. Notice also that throughout the experience, the many unknowns about these characters fuel the desire for resolution for a prolonged time. Slowly, participants fill in the gaps with more information, but there are no pat solutions for their challenges. The method of story–reflection–solving–feedback is repeated several times throughout the training experience, especially after the videos, where Cathy, the main character, acts in conflict with the principles from training. Brainstorming and planning with peers keeps account managers actively involved in their own learning. And the practice session tests their new skills in the most realistic method possible. To summarize the team's design choices: They recreated real-world sales challenges and gave account managers plenty of room to discover and practice solutions with immediate feedback from the experts.

Deliver. There are two primary delivery modes for the training: computer-based training and instructor-led training. In the online course, participants complete a job aid with the help of an online instructor, a professional actor on video who talks to the camera. The character descriptions are artfully laid out on the bulletin board. The pictures of each of the characters are actually silhouettes, which add to the mystery of the unknown. The newspaper, email clippings, and sticky notes are arranged around them. In the classroom setting, participants focus on their work around flip charts as they collaborate with their peers for solutions. The videos of Cathy, Jim, and Carolyn were filmed with the help of a vendor. And the practice role play is facilitated by an instructor. One of the greatest testimonies to the course's effectiveness is when their account managers go into the real world and they recognize it as something that they've experienced in training.

Orientation for New Managers at a Service Industry Corporation (Virtual)

Newly hired and newly promoted managers at this company are required to attend an hour-long webinar with staff from the ethics and compliance department. The first half of the hour trains managers how to practically promote an open-door policy, which is supported by a story about Maggie, a newly promoted manager, who struggles in doing so. Here's how the experience plays out.

Maggie's Story

"I'd like to tell you story about Maggie," says the facilitator. "She's recently been promoted to management. She has always exceeded expectations for delivering quality work on time. When she was promoted to management, her team was excited . . . but lately, she's noticed that they are not as enthusiastic. Some of their deadlines have started to slip too. She decides to talk about it with them at her next staff meeting."

The story continues, showing whiteboard illustrations of Maggie meeting with her team. She's generally met with awkward silence and doesn't know what to make of it, until one of her employees meets with her afterwards to tell her what's really going on. Maggie is shocked. One employee has a side business. The other is watching YouTube all day. Another team member seems distant. Two of her employees feel like they're making up for all the work their co-workers aren't doing. But what surprises her the most is that her employees feel like she doesn't care about those things as long as the work is getting done. The story ends with, "This was not what she expected management to be like."

Chat Box on Fire

After the story, the facilitator asks managers on the webinar to answer a question: "What's the problem on Maggie's team?" The chat box is on fire! Managers on the call are anxious to share their opinions and insights. Another question: "What should Maggie do now to prevent this from continuing?" Again, great insights are shared. Many of those insights align with the action list. The facilitator then walks them through four practical actions managers can take to encourage employees to speak up about workplace concerns. Everything is related back to Maggie's story.

Afterward, managers are asked to share one thing they are going to do with their team to make sure their employees know that they have an open-door policy. The facilitator waits as they think. It takes some time, but eventually, the gold nuggets start popping up in chat. It's apparent from the comments that they've got it.

Powerful Effect

This training, like others in this chapter, follows the technique of story–reflection–solving–feedback. The facilitator tells them the story, with the aid of illustrations. Managers are asked to think through what just happened in the story and assess the potential problems. They offer their suggestions for how to fix those problems and receive immediate feedback from the facilitator. It is a powerful first impression on managers to maintain this company's ethical culture, made possible through storytelling.

Takeaways

Discover. The design team of this company are in touch with their audience. They have a network of managers throughout the enterprise who serve as ambassadors for compliance. These ambassadors also help keep the department in touch with what's happening in the operational areas of the company. At least once every two years, the compliance staff visits each of the company's regional locations to meet with employees and hold a special forum with management. Their knowledge of the audience helped create a character that new managers could relate to. The action list was derived from a larger master training plan for managers. The webinar is one of many pieces designed to support manager expectations for ethical behavior.

Design. Maggie's character was specifically designed to reflect the character of the audience. After analyzing the audience, it was apparent that managers were not intentionally discouraging employees from coming to them with a concern. It was appropriate then for Maggie to exhibit the more common behavior of not saying enough about being available to her employees if they had a concern, a message the design team felt couldn't be overcommunicated.

Deliver. The story itself was developed in PowerPoint as a series of simple illustrations narrated by the facilitator. If you fear the technical difficulties of showing videos during virtual training, this is a great solution. The webinar itself also opens up an opportunity that is unique to a virtual delivery: chat! Multiple people can express their ideas simultaneously. As participants entered their thoughts in chat, the facilitator reads most of them out loud and either asks a follow-up question to dig deeper or affirms why their answer is spot on. Participants are also welcomed to unmute themselves to respond or explain an answer further. To collect data on the course's effectiveness, time is built in to the hour for learners to respond to a survey that is accessed through a link in chat. Almost every participant completes the survey, which consistently indicates a significant increase in knowledge, skills, and attitudes. It's clear from learner comments that their favorite parts of the webinar are the story and the chance to share their own insights and learn from others.

Systems Training at a Texas-Based Global Electronics Distributor (E-Learning)

When the company's design team was approached by supply planners about a problem with their supply planning system, they followed the Story Design model to develop an e-learning course that fixed the root problem and achieved the business outcome. It's a powerful example of discovering the story through analysis.

Gianna Has a Problem

The course begins with a story. Gianna receives an email from the sales department complaining that a customer did not receive the product they needed. She's surprised. "I know I set up the system to automatically order that supply," she thinks. She checks the system. She had switched the product from auto to manual planning and changed the minimum field to "1." She thought it would automatically send a purchase request when the minimum was reached. Then she checks the amount available. Zero. OK. No product was ordered. And there's no way to get it quickly. Now she's panicked.

Learning the Math

Many supply planners taking the course know exactly how Gianna feels. Gianna thought she was helping the business by keeping the system from ordering excess inventory. The unintentional outcome is that many product lines were depleted. Not coincidentally, this is exactly what was happening on the job. The good intentions of supply planners to keep inventory at a more manageable number resulted in no inventory at all, which started affecting the business, and more importantly, affecting their customers who were upset and taking their business elsewhere. The emotional connection with Gianna is real.

After learners experience Gianna's crisis, they're ready to learn how to fix the problem. They dive into a series of exercises that walk them through every step to successfully set up manual planning in their supply planning system. Along the way, they see what Gianna did to mess things up and learn what to do instead. They are instructed how to complete every computer screen in the system and every switch that needs to be flipped in order to set up manual planning without depleting product lines. They even learn a complex math formula. The assessment tests all of these skills.

Measurable Results

What's most impressive about this course is the results of the training. Before training, there were significant problems with the way manual planning was set up. Since the training, there have been no major problems with this issue. The training completely fixed the root problem. On occasion, when someone does set up manual planning in the wrong way, management assigns them this course. That's something to be proud of.

Takeaways

Discover. The planning system was new for the company. When the product lines started to become depleted, supply planners thought it had something to do with switching from auto to manual planning, but they weren't exactly sure where the root problem existed. Fortunately, the design team asked good questions to unearth the cause of the problem. A common question they asked to understand how the system worked was "What would happen if ..." As they kept drilling down, they discovered that indeed, this was not a problem with the system itself, but with how the system was being operated. Thus, the ideal solution was skills training. The business outcome was evident: no more depleted product lines. Through the discovery stage, they learned what was being done incorrectly and developed an action list of logically and sequentially ordered steps supply planners needed to take.

Design. A member of the company's design team had attended a Story Design workshop and used the Story Design model to create Gianna, a supply planner who struggled to set up manual planning correctly (the story premise). She placed Gianna in conflict with the action list, which produced a desire for resolution within the learner. The training following the story completed the connection between the story and action. Gianna's mistakes were referenced throughout instruction, which kept the emotional connection to the story alive. The design team chose to bring Gianna back to bookend the training. She saw what she did wrong and fixed it so that future products are ordered in a timely manner. This can be a good choice when training needs to be reinforced or it feels like the story could use closure. The parallel process of Story Design with instructional design resulted in a powerful online learning experience that made a huge business impact, saving money and customer loyalty.

242 • Chapter Eleven

Deliver. The entire course was developed in an authoring tool the company already owned. The story was built using the authoring tool's built-in comic characters, and it was told by a narrator—an audio file embedded into the course. Though the story was referenced throughout the course, the story itself was told on two slides (one at the beginning and one at the end of the course). This simple solution magnified the instructional impact to achieve the business results.

PRACTICE STORY DESIGN:
Learn From Others

Jot down some of the ideas you learned from these five case studies that you'd like to try in your own training programs. If you don't have a specific project in mind, apply them to your Well Adjusted example project.

How might you use these case studies to support a Story Design approach to training? Do you have resistant leaders? Stakeholders? Team members that need a little convincing? In chapter 12, you'll be equipped with more tools and tips to make a case for stories for learning. If you saw a case study in this chapter that relates to an upcoming project, how might you use it to convince your own organization to give Story Design a chance?

CHAPTER TWELVE

Win Over Stakeholders to Storytelling

Resistance

Dayna reviews her action list and audience profile before heading into the office of Ivan, the divisional VP of sales. Last month, when Ivan received a message from a client complaining that she was receiving sales calls from his staff, he set up a meeting with the sales managers.

"I got a message from GrelCorp yesterday complaining that we were placing sales calls. We've already got their business! What's going on?"

The sales managers look around the room. Some of them shrug. Grace speaks up, "That was me. I had one of my sales reps call GrelCorp."

"Why? Were you trying to upsell them?" Ivan wants an answer.

Grace is calm. "No. According to the CRM, they're still a prospect."

"What?" Jeremy speaks up. "I sold them two weeks ago!"

"I guess you should have updated the CRM," Grace says matter-of-factly.

"I did update it!" Jeremy replies defensively.

Ivan steps in. "Has anyone else experienced this issue? Any calls to prospectives who turned out to be clients?" Ten hands go up. Ivan takes a deep breath. "We have an issue."

Jeremy speaks up. "It's not me. I can tell you that. There's probably a problem with the system!"

Immediately after the meeting, Ivan asks his assistant to run a report. Twenty-two clients were incorrectly marked as prospective clients. And it isn't just Jeremy's clients. It is a wide-spread problem.

That's when he called Fayette to ask for training.

Dayna had already met with Ivan, when she asked many questions to identify the root problem and the business outcome. Training appeared to be a good solution. The company had recently upgraded their LMS to support mobile. And as the sales team was often travelling, mobile learning seemed like the best approach.

She had also met with Grace, who had a good grasp on how to operate the CRM. Grace showed her the steps to transfer a potential client to an actual client in the system. It wasn't quite as easy as checking a box. There were about ten steps in the process, including mandatory notes to record the details of the sale. During her conversation with Grace, she discovered other things about the sales staff. Apparently, many of the seasoned sales staff were some of the least reliable in updating the CRM. Grace felt like it wasn't because they didn't know how to do it, but they didn't know how important it was to the process. Also, the work life of salespeople was back-to-back meetings, phone calls, and travel. It was difficult for some of them to find time for updating the system. They tried to put it off until the end of the week when business slowed down some, but often forgot.

Earlier that morning, Dayna emailed Ivan the action list and a brief description of the audience for his approval. She also included a short story about Mason, a sales person who struggles to update the CRM when potential clients signed on as clients.

She smiles. "Looks like I'll get to produce another story." Ivan's door opens. One of his sales managers walks out. Dayna peeks in. Ivan is typing. Dayna knocks. "Is this still a good time to talk about the training?"

Ivan looks at his watch. "Oh! Yeah, sorry. Of course, come on in! Let's see, you sent me something." Ivan looks through the papers on his desk. "Please go ahead and have a seat. I glanced at it this morning." Ivan turns back to his computer. He opens Dayna's email and the attachment. "Here it is! Yes." He scans through the email. "It all looks good." He's still reading. "Yep, that's definitely the problem! When can the training be done?"

Dayna says, "I can get started right away. I confirmed the action list with Grace and even tried it out on the system. We made a few tweaks. I think it's ready to go."

"Very good!" Ivan looks at his watch again.

"When I talked with Grace about the sales staff, she mentioned some issues that I think the story will help with."

"Excuse me?" Ivan looks at Dayna blankly.

Dayna points to Ivan's computer screen. "The story there . . . about Mason? Did you read that part?"

Ivan seems confused. "Story? What are you talking about? This is a training course."

Dayna leans forward. "Right, but it starts with a story."

"The course? The course starts with a story?" Ivan raises one eyebrow.

"Yes, before the training, there's a story about this sales guy who . . . "

"No, no, no. We don't need story time. We need training."

"Well . . . " Dayna is not sure what to say. "I don't think the training will be complete without the story. I mean, I don't think it will address all of the reasons why people aren't taking the action you want them to take without the story."

Ivan looks at Dayna. "And just how is this story going to play out?"

Dayna looks down at her notes. "I . . . I'm not sure. I haven't written it yet."

Ivan shakes his head. "Just make the course as short as possible." He looks at his watch again. "As short as possible, OK?" Ivan stands.

Dayna picks up her notes. She stands and shakes Ivan's hand. "OK."

"Stories Are Fluff!"

Dayna has come head-to-head with a common objection to (and misperception of) storytelling for training. On the surface, it appears that Ivan's objection is a time issue. He believes that a story will rob his staff of valuable time. This is understandable, considering the pace sales staff keep at work. Underneath his comment is the thought that the content should be enough by itself. The story is fluff. This is a reasonable, though misguided, response. It's not an uncommon perception in the business world that stories are for entertainment, not serious work. Though that idea is slowly turning, resistance to storytelling for training exists and you will undoubtedly encounter it, sometimes from within your own ranks.

Other forms of resistance may sound like, "Oh, this is training for the board of directors. They don't want stories." Or "My content is too serious for stories!" Often stakeholders will say something akin to Ivan's objection, "We don't have time for stories." Or they may simply say, "No!" It's important to identify the source of their resistance, but there is hope for countering even the most skeptical stakeholder. Deep down, they are wired for stories.

The resources in this chapter will help you build a strategy for approaching stakeholders who may resist the idea of storytelling for training. Your strategy will depend on the level of trust that stakeholders have in the design team. Think of advocacy for storytelling as a way to educate those who resist. Keep the design continuum in mind. The design continuum is actually a great tool to figure out where you need to start the conversation (Figure 12-1).

Figure 12-1. Design Continuum for Stakeholders

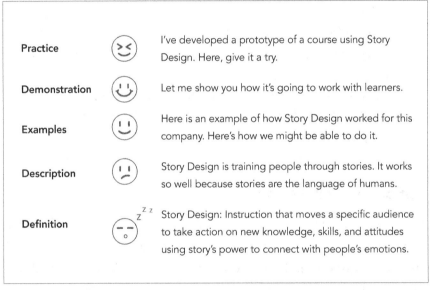

Practice		I've developed a prototype of a course using Story Design. Here, give it a try.
Demonstration		Let me show you how it's going to work with learners.
Examples		Here is an example of how Story Design worked for this company. Here's how we might be able to do it.
Description		Story Design is training people through stories. It works so well because stories are the language of humans.
Definition		Story Design: Instruction that moves a specific audience to take action on new knowledge, skills, and attitudes using story's power to connect with people's emotions.

Is this a brand-new concept for your stakeholders? Start with a definition. Tell them what you mean by storytelling, using Story Design principles that draw from sound instructional design. Then work your way up the design continuum, providing a description, examples, and a demonstration of how it works and give them practice with the concept by producing a prototype.

To make the road smoother for you and your stakeholders, consider the small steps you can take to introduce storytelling to the training. Bite off the amount of storytelling your team and your stakeholders can handle.

If you encounter resistance, consider some of the following techniques to overcome it:

- Appeal to their intellect.
- Appeal to their emotions.
- Involve them in story creation.
- Start slow and steady.
- Share quantitative and qualitative feedback.

Appeal to Their Intellect (Rider)

Though there may be a lack of resources for practical know-how when it comes to storytelling for training, there is no shortage of research that proves storytelling's power for learning. Equip yourself with evidence to show stakeholders that storytelling works. You can use some of the research quoted in this book to show stakeholders how storytelling affects memory, prepares learners for action, and stirs them emotionally. Some stakeholders may appreciate a baseline knowledge of why our brains are wired for storytelling. Paul J. Zak's article "Why Your Brain Loves Good Storytelling" in *Harvard Business Review* (2014) can succinctly satisfy that need.

"My experiments show that character-driven stories with emotional content result in a better understanding of the key points a speaker wishes to make and enable better recall of these points weeks later," Zak, a neuroeconomist, writes. "In terms of making impact, this blows the standard PowerPoint presentation to bits."

Zak describes the consistent release of oxytocin (a chemical that enhances our ability to empathize with and experience someone else's emotions) in response to videotaped, character-driven stories. His research shows a direct correlation between the release of oxytocin and the increase in behavior change based on that emotional connection with the character. His application of neurobiology to business presentations is completely relevant to the goal of training: to move your audience to do something different than what they are doing now.

Paul Zak is one of many researchers who present a compelling justification for storytelling that will appeal to your stakeholder's intellect.

Appeal to Their Emotions (Elephant)

Approach your conversation with wary stakeholders as you approach story-based training itself: Appeal to their emotions by telling them a story. Your goal is to convince them to use Story Design in an upcoming project. That's the primary action on your action list. Draft a short audience profile on your stakeholders. What are their values? What are their current circumstances and how are they reacting to them? What do they fear? What do they like to do in their spare time?

What story can you share with your stakeholder that will connect with them emotionally? A case study from this book is a starting point. A success story you have from another project is even more compelling. Dayna could share the design and results from her compliance course.

As you plan for the conversation, think in terms of helping the stakeholder to "cross the threshold." In the hero's journey, your stakeholder is the hero that can make training a meaningful experience through storytelling. You are the mentor that can guide them out of the mundane ordinary world of clicking *Next* into a special world where Story Design transforms the training experience. Likely, their resistance stems from an aversion to change or inconvenience. But you're there to help guide them through the journey.

There's an effective way to introduce productive conflict in your presentation of Story Design to the stakeholder. To help them commit to a storytelling approach in training, contrast *what is* and *what could be*. In her book *Resonate* (2010), Nancy Duarte says, "Let's remember that there is one indisputable attribute of a good story: There must be some kind of conflict or imbalance perceived by the audience that your presentation resolves. This sense of discord is what persuades them to care enough to jump in. In a presentation, you create imbalance by consciously juxtaposing *what is* with *what could be*."

Show the stakeholder a sample of the training that exists now. Contrast it with an example of what you are proposing. Show the stakeholder how learners are responding to the existing training. Contrast it with how learners will respond to story-based training. Let them feel the difference. Tell them, "You have the opportunity to make this a powerful learning experience for employees." Give them a chance to own the decision and jump in. Reinforce their decision by referring to the project as "bringing their vision for story-based training to life." Make it incredibly clear that they are the hero.

Involve Stakeholders in Creating the Story

Convincing stakeholders to adopt Story Design for their learning solution is a great way to practice it. You can do this by involving stakeholders in creating the story. Dayna had an open door to use this technique with Ivan. Had she taken advantage of it, her conversation may have gone something like this:

Ivan	And just how is this story going to play out?
Dayna	Well, let's say that you have a staff member who's been updating the CRM incorrectly or not at all. Why do you think he or she might do that?
Ivan	I don't know.
Dayna	OK, well would it be reasonable that the sales person had another appointment and didn't have time to update the system properly?
Ivan	Yes. They have pretty packed days. But that doesn't mean they couldn't do it later that day.
Dayna	When would that be?
Ivan	When they had a break. Maybe at dinner.
Dayna	For a typical day on the road, would a sales person have the opportunity to stop for a break?
Ivan	Mm. That's a good question.
Dayna	Could they be having dinner with a client?
Ivan	Yes. Actually, yes. Dinner with a client or a potential client isn't unusual. Or they could be in the car travelling to another city in the area.

Dayna	Alright, let's pretend that a sales person—we'll call him Mason—is going to meet with several existing and potential clients on this one trip. In the morning, he meets with a potential client and they sign on. He doesn't have time to enter that information into the CRM yet because he has to drive to the next city to meet another potential client. He gets there just in time to grab some lunch, sign on, and start the process of updating the client in the system, but has to stop halfway through because it's time to meet with the next prospective. Does that sound plausible?
Ivan	That seems pretty typical. Yeah, I'd say it's spot on.
Dayna	What might happen next that keeps Mason from updating the first client in the system?
Ivan	Well, he might sign on another client that day. He might have to drive to another city. He might have dinner with an existing client.
Dayna	And by the time he finally checks into his hotel at 10 p.m. . . . .
Ivan	He's exhausted.
Dayna	So that's the story! It's short. It acknowledges a plausible reason why your staff may not be following through with updating the CRM. We can end the story with another sales staff calling the same client he just signed on, which would be an embarrassment.
Ivan	It *is* an embarrassment! That's why we need this training!
Dayna	By including the story, it will help your staff understand why completing the process is a big deal. They'll get it. They'll pay more attention. And they'll relate to it because it's actually happening.
Ivan	That's good. But I think we have another problem.
Dayna	What's that?
Ivan	We need a way for the CRM to be updated immediately. I don't think our current process is sustainable. I need to rethink how we're approaching this.

Notice that Dayna fields some possibilities of how the story might unfold. She gives the sales person a name and begins the story with the knowledge she already has of the situation. She leaves room for Ivan to give his own input, correct the story, and drive it forward. By the end, Ivan has, in a sense, experienced the story for himself and realizes how valuable it can be for training. He also realizes, by playing out this fictious story, that he may need to fix the process. Don't be surprised when this happens if you try this technique with stakeholders.

Storytelling forces us to think in terms of time and space, rather than theories or ideals. As a result, storytelling has a great way of uncovering gaps in our reasoning. Thinking in storytelling terms puts the stakeholders and SMEs in the place of the learner and unearths inconsistencies in the action list. It's the quintessence of design thinking.

Start Slow and Steady

Unless your stakeholders (and others involved) are completely supportive of Story Design, it is likely that you will need to start slow and gradually build story's influence into your training. Here are some ways to get started and build momentum.

Build Context at the Beginning

Presenting the story as a means of providing context and motivation is a good place to start. You may need to leave the content of the course relatively untouched, depending on how protective stakeholders (or the legal department) are of their language. So rather than completely redesigning the course, choose the higher-level actions on the action list and focus on creating relatable characters in strong conflict in a story at the beginning. Ending the story at the climax of conflict creates a desire for resolution, because they care about the characters and want their problems to be fixed. That's where training steps in and spans the gap between the story and learning.

Bring the Story Back at the End

If stakeholders agree to an opening story, it may be easy to convince them to close out the course with a story. Pick up where the story left off and ask learners to identify the best solution. This could be in the form of an assessment. Or demonstrate how the characters resolve the conflict for their own story as a recap of what they've just learned.

Refer to the Story Throughout the Training

This requires a bit more trust with stakeholders, because now you are *messing with* their content more directly. But rather than jumping to "Let me make your content more conversational," approach this as a *rearrangement* of content. Implement an abbreviated version of the story–reflection–solving–feedback technique. Summarize a portion of the story that was told at the beginning. Build in a brief reflection based on the story. Give learners a chance to solve a problem. Then put their original content (untouched) into the feedback. Take an hour or so to build four to five slides that demonstrate this technique. Present it to your stakeholders. Dayna could build a prototype that looks this (Figure 12-2).

Figure 12-2. Dayna's Prototype

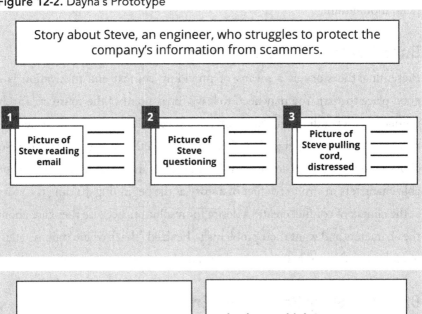

Picture of Steve holding cord	**What should Steve do next?** ☐ Look for phishing clues in the email ☐ Call the email to the HELP Desk ☐ Report a suspected security breach <div align="right">**Link to Phishing Guide job aid**</div>

Correct feedback

Steve failed to take the first two steps in the Phishing Guide of scanning the email for phishing clues and forwarding the email to HELP Desk without clicking links.

Now he needs to report it. He should:
1. Call the cybersecurity office
2. Notify his supervisor

Start Short and Small

Choosing a short course that has a limited audience is a great way to get started with Story Design. Stakeholders may be more comfortable trying a new design method if the impact involves less people. Perhaps you have a series of short courses for a smaller audience. Choose one of them to apply Story Design to. A limited audience gives you the opportunity to create a robust audience profile and create relatable characters. Since the course is short, the conflict is laser-focused on one or two actions. A short and small project makes follow-up and tracking more manageable as well.

Share Quantitative and Qualitative Feedback

Don't neglect to gather data supporting the success of your storytelling pilots. It's difficult for stakeholders to deny reliable metrics. If you take on a short and small project, as described above, share the quantitative and qualitative feedback with stakeholders. Show the results of the short module that included storytelling in comparison with the other modules where Story Design was not applied. There are two appeals of data to your stakeholders: numbers and internal credibility.

Numbers

Hard data are indispensable in winning over stakeholders, especially those in senior leadership. Sharing data that support your initiatives demonstrates that you can speak the same language as the stakeholders. By tracking metrics before your program went into effect and after, you'll be equipped to prove the value Story Design can have on the business.

Dayna already had some compelling evidence from her previous project that she could share with Ivan. Here is a suggestion for measuring the change in knowledge, skills, and attitude of any training (Figure 12-3). Confidence is a measure of knowledge and skills. Importance measures attitude. After the course has been taken, learners complete the survey and rate their confidence and importance before training and after training. Compare the difference between before and after training to measure if there was a significant impact upon knowledge, skills, and attitudes.

Figure 12-3. Survey Sample for Measuring Effectiveness

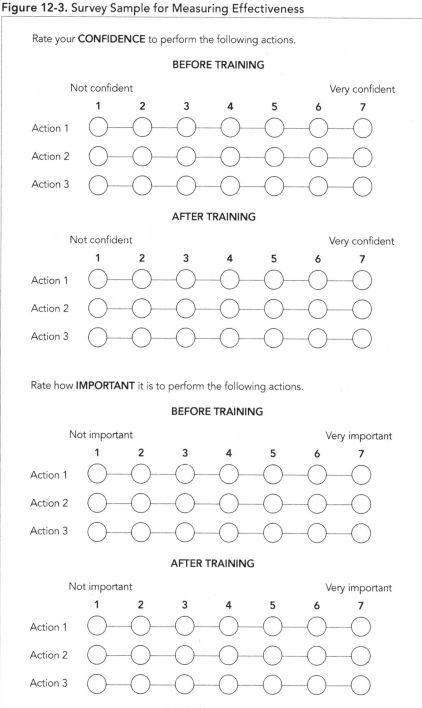

Dayna also has some convincing metrics regarding a change in business outcomes: a decrease in the number of employees who inadvertently introduced a virus to the system from clicking on a link with a phishing email. If you have results from previous un-storied training solutions, compare those results with those where Story Design was applied. Showing a side-by-side comparison of the two types of training and their associated metrics quickly captures the story's power to make a difference in the workplace.

One company I worked with wanted to isolate the effectiveness of stories on their training. So, they designed a survey that asked participants to rank the effectiveness of each story to increase their confidence to perform a specific action and their belief in the importance of performing that action. Links to each of the stories were provided within the survey. Not surprisingly, the results showed that the stories had a significant influence on performance. There is already a body of work that proves this in research, but this company now has tangible evidence specific to their training that substantiates their storytelling strategy.

Internal Credibility

Metrics are an objective, outside source of credibility. But you also want to make the metrics a matter of internal credibility. In other words, you want the stakeholder to personally believe in the effectiveness of storytelling for training. If you provide only statistics from a credible source, but the stakeholder still does not believe in Story Design's effectiveness for themselves, they will remain a skeptic no matter how much research you throw at them.

While I was designing a course with multiple stakeholders from three different departments, it became evident that two of the stakeholders were more comfortable with the idea of storytelling in their portion of the course. The third stakeholder expressed resistance: "Our content is too serious." I provided research from credible sources to show the validity of storytelling in training, but the third stakeholder still didn't budge. To respect each stakeholders' comfort level, I decided to make stories the centerpiece of training for the two departments that were comfortable with Story Design. The training was viewed in a positive light by employees, who actually started talking about the stories from the course. For the third stakeholder, I kept storytelling to a minimum.

The following year, when these same three stakeholders gathered to plan for another course, there were many metrics to share. I presented the numbers that showed effectiveness and shared qualitative feedback that pointed to the positive contributions of storytelling. But the two stakeholders who embraced storytelling for their content had more to share. They were so enthused about the stories for their content that they started using the stories as standalone assets on their department webpages and developed a communications campaign to advertise them. They had ideas for more stories for the next course. In short, they believed in the power of Story Design. Their belief was contagious. After that conversation, the third stakeholder changed their belief. Maybe it was the numbers. Maybe it was the enthusiasm of the other two stakeholders. Whatever it was, their skepticism turned into full-on support. If you find yourself hitting a brick wall with a stakeholder, respect their comfort level. Internal credibility may take some time to kick in.

Pace and Traction

Above all, the best way to overcome barriers to Story Design is to produce quality work. Give yourself time and space to practice using the techniques in the book. Designing a story-based multi-course curriculum as your first project may not be the best choice. Set reasonable goals, and start with one salient, well-designed story. Pace yourself. Leave room for how much time and resources you can afford to put into it. Gauge the comfort level of your stakeholders and subject matter experts. Once you've successfully implemented Story Design for one project, document it. Hold on to that story. It's the first of many to come. Soon, you will have a library of stories to show stakeholders as examples. If you work with stakeholders more than once, use the traction you've gained to further Story Design's impact on the learning experience.

Remember, constraints force creativity. Stakeholders and subject matter experts set some of those constraints. As mentioned in chapter 3, the boundary lines of constraints are an invitation for creativity. Respect those boundaries and create an amazing story your stakeholders are comfortable with. As those constraints loosen, you can expand your storytelling repertoire. Master PRIMED questions for interviewing stakeholders to discover better stories. Develop more interesting plots that grab the focus of your learners. Explore new delivery methods using available technology.

Once you've mastered one Story Design project, you'll be eager to find the story in other training programs. And so will your stakeholders!

PRACTICE STORY DESIGN:
Overcome Barriers

Besides the case studies from chapter 11, how might you approach wary stakeholders to adopt Story Design for their training programs? Use the space below to reflect on the tips from this chapter and create a persuasive strategy. If you need an example training to work from, apply these strategies to your Well Adjusted program.

- Appeal to their intellect.
- Appeal to their emotions.
- Involve stakeholders in creating the story.
- Insert the story at the beginning or end.
- Limit Story Design to a small project and build from there.
- Share data from former projects.
- Offer feedback from stakeholders you've already won over.

Your strategy:

CHAPTER THIRTEEN

Your Future As a Story Designer

The Mission

"James!" Dayna waves at her friend from across the crowded lobby of the theater. He sees her and weaves his way through the crowd.

"Hey, thanks for coming!" He gives her a hug.

"I'm glad I got to see you! You were really amazing!"

"Thanks! I'm exhausted . . . and starved!"

"Dinner's on me. Come on!" They make their way outside. "I don't think I've ever seen you in a musical before. Have you always known how to tap dance?"

"Nope. Had to pick that up for this show." James adds in his best Cockney accent, "The trick, me lady, is to smile real big so people look at your face . . . and don't see how bad you step in time!" He strikes a pose.

Dayna laughs. "You fooled me."

"Dancing with a big chimney broom is a nice distractor too."

"I thought you looked like a pro. You must be a quick study," Dayna says. "Where do you want to eat?"

"Are you good with Thai?"

"Never had it, but I'll try it!"

James motions. "It's a few blocks this way. Not a far walk."

They start walking and Dayna asks, "So now that your show is almost done, what's next for you?"

"Honestly, I haven't thought that far ahead. I've been buried in rehearsals. I haven't even had time to audition for anything else."

"Maybe I'll offer you a part in my new story. I'm looking for a corporate tap dancer," Dayna quips.

James slaps his head. "With all the time I've been putting into the show, I haven't heard the latest about your training stories! How's it going?"

"Good. Actually, really good. Writing stories has changed how I think about training. It's like, as soon as I sit down with the stakeholder the first thing I'm thinking of is, 'Where's the story here?' Can you believe that? Me?"

"You've come a long way, Dayna. That's awesome!"

Dana shakes her head. "Remember the first story I ever wrote about *the employee*?"

"How could I forget? Riveting stuff," James teases.

"Thanks for everything you did," she says. "I'd still be staring at that sticky note from the compliance director wondering how to write a story if you hadn't helped me."

"So what's the next project?" asks James. They stop at a crosswalk.

Dayna turns to James. "Well, I've been looking into some gaming ideas for an upcoming training project for customer service."

James presses the crosswalk button. "Gaming? No story?"

"Oh, absolutely there will be a story! It's about Brenda, a customer advocate. She struggles to input customer requests into the system within a certain timeframe and still maintain a conversational tone with the client. That's the story part."

"She's already got a name!"

"Yeah, I already had an audience profile for customer service from the compliance project, so creating a character was pretty easy. And after meeting with the subject matter expert, it was apparent that the actions fell into two categories: systems skills and interpersonal skills." The light turns green and they walk on. "This is the cool part," Dayna exclaims. "When I looked at the external pressures employees are facing, the one that rose to the top was time constraints. So, that's when I started thinking: It's got all the makings of a game."

James nods. "I think I see where you're going with this. You've got to get a lot done in a short amount of time and keep the customer happy. Like . . . waiting tables?"

"That's a great comparison!"

"Ooo, too many of those jobs. I can feel the stress already!"

"And that's the point!" Dayna punctuates, "Customer service can be stressful! In the course, the customer advocate gets a simple request. It's easy to fulfill within the timeframe. Then the learner levels up and gets a more complex request. But the time limit remains the same."

"Let's turn here. The Thai place is just around the corner." James prompts, "And the story? How does the story fit in with the game?"

"The story is the set up for the game. The learner sits in Brenda's seat, literally, to help her overcome her struggles. They can feel the conflict and start thinking of ways to resolve it before the game even begins."

James turns to Dayna and points with both hands. "Unbelievable! I want to take that course!" They stop in front of the restaurant.

Dayna smiles. "Yeah, I guess that's my mission."

"What?"

"To connect to my audience. If I can do that, I don't think there's anything I can't train people to do."

James high fives her. "That's what I'm talking about!" He opens the door to the restaurant and waves Dayna in. "Ladies and gents, instructional designer extraordinaire!"

Dayna walks in. "I prefer to think of myself as a storyteller."

An Exciting Future

Are you ready to flex your storytelling skills and connect with your audience? Are you convinced that designers are in the best position to tell the right story for their audience? Are you ready to convince resistant stakeholders and peers that stories make a measurable impact on business outcomes? If so, you're on the edge of an exciting future.

Keeping Pace With Technology

The pursuit for more engaging, immersive training leads us to explore technology as a means of making that happen. One walk down the expo hall of any talent development conference is proof enough that the industry has grown exponentially. The advances in technology in the field continue to open new doors of opportunity for designers and developers of training to create amazing experiences for learners. As always, the technology itself is never the solution for a well-designed course. Just as a social media tool doesn't ensure that a company collaborates, there isn't a story-creation tool out there that can automatically make a good story for your audience. At the baseline, there has to be thoughtful design. Just as a culture of collaboration must be consciously built, a well-told story for training must be designed. And once it's designed, bring on the technology.

Story Design is a competency that grows with you. Following are training delivery options that are made possible by technology. You are in a position to supercharge each of these delivery options with Story Design. Here's how to use stories for:

- branching scenarios
- blended learning
- microlearning
- games
- immersive technologies.

Stories for Branching Scenarios

Branching scenarios are made possible by authoring tools that give the learner an experience in which the story unfolds according to the choices of the learner. The learner proceeds down the path of their choice, receives immediate feedback, then the story continues. Branching can be fairly simple, but if there are many decision points and several choices for each of those decision points, the storyboard can quickly become complex. This is choose-your-own-adventure for learning. If your e-learning design solution calls for a series of branching scenarios, you need to know Cathy Moore, internationally recognized training designer. She offers extensive insights into branching scenarios on her blog and in her book *Map It* (2017). Here is a summary of her process for creating the mechanics of branching scenarios:

1. Analyze (particularly in order to list observable actions).
2. Prototype one decision point (after working with the SME to make sure the decision point is real to life).
3. Test the prototype (on the SME, the client, or a group of learners).
4. Add more branches (by beginning with all the possible endings and then mapping what decision points are needed to reach all of those endings).

This is a great method for building the framework, but branching scenarios need a story. You can draw upon the strengths of Story Design to lead learners through each of those decision points that align with actions from the action list. Use chapter 4 to help unearth those actions during SME interviews. Create relatable characters using the guideposts from chapter 5. I recommend using a fictious character based on the learner profile as your main character rather than casting the learner in this role. Consult chapter 7 to map the plot from decision point to decision point and build a cohesive story with several endings, depending on the decision made. Story Design inside the framework of branching scenarios is a powerful learning experience.

Stories for Blended Learning

Blended learning allows for multiple delivery options, preferably housed in one central location, like an LMS or a webpage. It uses the diversity of technology to deliver the right solution for the right content.

In chapter 11 you read a case study about orientation for new managers. This webinar is one piece of a master training plan, which includes toolkits that support key behaviors. The toolkit for one behavior contains a video, an e-learning course, a webinar, a job aid, and a PowerPoint deck. You can design blended resources to support specific knowledge, skills, and attitudes, weaving them together with a story. Common characters and plot lines help managers connect the dots between all of the resources.

Pizza Hut's leadership training also uses blended learning, with a combination of video, e-learning, coaching, a workshop, and even a journal for learners to keep track of their reflections on training. Stories permeated each of the delivery methods.

Technology makes all of these delivery modes accessible. If your ideal solution involves blended learning, make sure your action list is in good order. Then determine how to best support those actions. To affect attitude, a video or written story may meet that need. Certain skills may require in-person or virtual support. Organize the training according to sequence or complexity. Use Story Design to build a series of stories that relate to one another. Tap into the emotional connection you've made for one delivery method to feed into another one to create a truly blended learning experience.

Stories for Microlearning

Microlearning (learning one or two actions from the action list in a short amount of time) is not a new concept. But technology has increased access to short tutorials on everything from how to replace the door of a dishwasher to how to do an HTTP request in HTML. People can now find quick answers to their questions in online forums, videos, brief articles, and diagrams.

Microlearning is ideal for situations where the learner has limited time, and the knowledge and skills can reasonably be gained quickly. It is a flexible solution that can adapt to the learner's specific needs. It can also be inserted in the process of the workflow, which can mean, when someone needs to learn—or refresh—a specific skill, the training is easy to find. However, the misconception that the attention span of humans is shrinking is never a good reason for designing microlearning.

Microlearning has some pitfalls. I participated in a concurrent session with Karl Kapp at a conference (read more about him in Stories for Games). I took notes as Karl outlined four pitfalls of microlearning. If a curriculum contains a series of microlearning modules, participation may suffer when learners:

- Forget about completing all the modules.
- Get bored with it.
- Feel disconnected from the big picture.
- Get lost.

As he spoke, I wrote in the margin of my notes, "Stories can help tie this together." Then he added, "Games can help tie this together."

Games are discussed next, but here's how Story Design can help tie together microlearning. Take a look at your action list. Can these actions be learned independently from one another? Do they build upon one another in sequence? Are the actions trainable in a short amount of time? If so, micro-learning may be a good solution. If the actions are more dependent upon one another or the time it takes to reasonably train someone to do them is more than fifteen minutes, a different solution, like blended learning, may better serve your learners.

Since microlearning is short and concentrated, focus on one to three actions from the list and plan on an abbreviated time for training. Ask time-specific questions during stakeholder and SME interviews to build an audience profile that includes how long learners may have to interact with a microlearning course or asset. Microlearning may be ideal for an audience who works in production, or an audience of executives who have little time outside of meetings, or for audiences that have a wide range of knowledge and skills and want to pick which module will meet their needs.

So, if microlearning is short, do you have time to tell a story? Yes. There is always time for a well-designed story. Remember, stories are efficient. They can cover a lot of ground in a short amount of time. A two-minute story can cover eight or more of the actions on your list, plus it can demonstrate the nuances of human interaction. You may design one overarching story for the entire curriculum and keep referring back to the story in each of the microle-arning modules. Or divide the story according to the action and interject the story at the beginning of a new series of actions. Or create mini stories within each module.

Like blended learning, microlearning can take any form: an e-learning course, a video, a short check-in with a mentor, a standalone quiz, a job aid, a chat bot, or an in-application tutorial. Technology helps make all of these solutions trackable. Flex microlearning's adaptability to meet learners right where they are. Hold all the pieces together with Story Design.

Stories for Games

One of my family's rituals almost every evening, even on school nights, is playing a game. Cards, dominoes, board games, dice games, word games, it doesn't matter. Games are fun! Part of what makes games so fun, and challenging, is the common constraints that everyone must adhere to and respect. You have to think. There's strategy involved. There are tactics. There's luck. And, of course, the thrill of a well-played queen of spades in the game of Hearts.

Many games are not guided by an internal story, but no one around that table would deny that something unexpected is unfolding with every round, similar to the plot of a story. No one knows what their opponent has in their head or in their hand. You make educated guesses. During play, you are constantly making choices and receiving immediate feedback on those choices (just like during a well-designed learning course). You hold your breath, hoping you don't get sent to jail. You rejoice when you roll doubles. You moan when you land on Boardwalk, which is already owned by an opponent, along with Park Place and two houses. The plot thickens. Emotions run high.

For all these reasons, games, instruction, and stories are perfect companions. If you are considering gamification for your learning solution, there are some great books, like *Play to Learn* by Karl Kapp and Sharon Boller (2017), that will guide you through the steps of designing a game for learning.

The complexity of gamification may vary greatly depending on the centrality of the game to the learning experience. Technology might be available to easily add interactions within a course that includes common game elements, like point systems, badges, and timers. But these game mechanics on their own do not equal gamification—or good instructional design. There must be a solid design behind the game. Gamified learning, similar to instructional design, brings the learner to decision points where the learner can practice a skill, based on knowledge they've gained from playing the game. They receive immediate feedback. They learn from their mistakes. They tackle another problem. They level up. They compete against themselves or others or the clock. They easily track their progress on the leaderboard or by how far they've advanced in the game.

Karl Kapp is an expert on the convergence of learning, technology, and business with a focus on game-thinking, games, and gamification for learning. He says in his book *The Gamification of Learning and Instruction* (2012), "storytelling is an essential part of the gamification of learning and instruction. The element of 'story' provides relevance and meaning to the experience. It provides context for the application of tasks." It's interesting that Dr. Kapp points out *relevance, meaning,* and *context* as the storytelling elements that influence gamification. Let's look at each of these attributes.

Relevance implies that the characters in the game are relatable. They are also in similar situations as the audience's work environment or an environment that serves as an equivalent metaphor of their workplace. Use the audience profile questionnaire (chapter 3) to formulate characters that mirror the feelings and circumstances of your audience. Pay special attention to external pressures, like deadlines, interpersonal conflict, high turnover, or burdensome duties like fulfilling requests for an external audit. External pressures at work will inform the constraints of the game.

Another attribute of stories as applied to gamification is that stories provide *meaning*. It's imperative that the decision points in the game align to actions from the action list and that all of the choices are plausible. Distinguishing with the SME what *should* be done and what *is* being done will help create meaningful decision moments.

Lastly, *context*. A story boosts the emotional connection with the audience in a gamified learning experience. If designed well, the story triggers similar emotions that the audience feels at work. The story also unites the independent tasks in the game. As learners complete the tasks, the story unfolds to show how their actions affect the bigger picture. Consult "Start with the story premise" in chapter 7 for guidance on how to construct the story premise—fiction, nonfiction, or metaphor—that will provide the best context.

Gamified learning is powerful. Story-based gamified learning is relevant, meaningful, and contextual. In other words, awesome!

Stories for Immersive Technologies

I remember the first time I put on a virtual reality (VR) headset. Instantly, I was standing on top of a building. I slowly turned around and took in the scene. I could see the sky above, the streets below, the tops of other buildings around me. I looked down at myself. I was wearing work boots and jeans. My mission was to inspect the roof for possible safety hazards and fix them. With the help of a clicker, I put on a safety harness, climbed a tower, used a wrench, took notes on a clipboard. I learned what to look for. I discovered the process for how to fix a leak in the air conditioning unit. I felt what it was like to do this job—to be on top of a roof—without ever stepping foot outside.

The experience had story elements. I was the main character and there were problems that I needed to fix. I tried and failed sometimes. Ultimately, I succeeded in my mission. Thanks to VR, I was transported to a setting that mirrored reality. There's no doubt that it was a powerful learning moment. It was a physical and intellectual experience. But what if Story Design was applied to this scenario? What if there was an emotional component? Clearly, I was role-playing, but other than the fact that my character was a roof inspector, I didn't know much else about him. What are the current circumstances at work? How has he reacted to those current circumstances? What does he fear? What's at stake if he doesn't perform correctly? And what are the external pressures associated with this job? What if, before he goes to the roof, his boss chews him out for botching the last job? What if he has a narrow window of time to complete the inspection before an approaching thunderstorm hits? What if the building is a hospital out of power? The effectiveness of this VR experience would increase exponentially.

Many companies have started to use stories in their VR training. They craft relatable characters and put them in strong conflict. A retail store prepares their cashiers for the holiday rush by recreating the scene in VR. A corporate leadership course places leaders in a virtual reality meeting to confront an employee for misconduct. Another retail company prepares their employees for armed robberies. The employee must make choices at gun point. Talk about strong conflict.

Similar to VR is augmented reality (AR). AR's ability to superimpose three-dimensional images on top of real-world scenes is widely adopted by talent development for training in healthcare, science, space, military, manufacturing, and onboarding programs. Its usefulness for hands-on practice, especially in situations where safety is a concern, increases learning transfer. AR is similar to microlearning in that many times each individual AR component is a self-contained task, while a series of AR learning moments can benefit from a story that connects the pieces with the whole. The story can also propel the learner to the next interaction and keep the learner focused on completing and absorbing all of the content. See the Stories for Microlearning section in this chapter for more on the benefits of Story Design for situations like this one.

Technology is rapidly pushing the limits of how we can learn, but storytelling has no problem keeping pace. Developers of AR, VR, and future immersive technologies who apply Story Design will give their audience a full experience—mind, body, and emotions.

Your Future With Story Design

The world of work is always changing. New skills need to be learned. From artificial intelligence to machine learning to data analytics and the Internet of Things, the future of learning is for those who embrace their role as storytellers. No matter how digitally disrupted our world becomes, or how technologically advanced our training resources are, there's always time for a well-designed story.

You've heard a lot about action in this book. Now that you've made it through, experienced Story Design for yourself, and completed the exercises, it's time for you to take action and make it a reality for your audience. Join the growing community of designers who are transforming their company's training one story at a time through Story Design.

PRACTICE STORY DESIGN:
The Future

Think of the stories you created for Well Adjusted, the chiropractic clinic. Would they benefit from a training method represented in this chapter? Can you imagine it as part of a blended learning or microlearning program? Can you picture the story as the plot for a game or an immersive learning experience through VR or AR? Stories have a wonderful attribute: flexibility. They will serve you no matter what technology is used to create the course. Take a moment to write down ideas you have in mind that exercise the power of stories for the future of learning technologies.

You, the Story Designer

A seasoned leader in instructional technology attended one of my Story Design workshops. Afterward, she said, "Story Design completely reframed my approach to instructional design." How she phrased that has stuck with me. Story Design doesn't replace instructional design, but if you can write a story—flesh and blood characters that learners can relate to and strong conflict that aligns with the action your audience needs to take—your training will have a distinct advantage. You have a new frame for analysis, design, development, implementation, and evaluation (ADDIE). Your deep knowledge of the audience and ability to clearly articulate what your audience needs to do to meet business outcomes and deal with root problems places you in a position of influence to affect the future of training.

Stories reframe training for learners too. They are mentally and emotionally present in the training itself. They feel respected because the designer took time to get to know them. They are challenged to think critically and make difficult choices. They are more prepared to take action and more likely to remember what they need to do in the future because they remember the story. Their recall of the content can be reinforced after training is done too. Let the story bleed into job aids and post-training communications. Post the story as a standalone video, PowerPoint deck, or comic on the company's website. Link to stories in company-wide communications. Soon, the frame around training starts to look a lot more attractive and meaningful to learners. You have the power to change the culture of training within your organization through storytelling.

You are embarking on a fulfilling journey of creating training that makes a lasting and motivating impact on your learners through storytelling. If you need encouragement along the way, connect with me on LinkedIn or attend a Story Design workshop to help put these principles into action. Most of all, share your successes with our Story Design community at needastory.com. Your contributions are needed. Before you close this book, I'd like to leave you with one last story.

An Open Door

I was a little nervous as I took the elevator up to the third floor. "This instructional design job sounds exciting," I thought. "But I'm not sure they'll want my experience." My resume looked, well, interesting. Education: BA in acting, MFA in choreography. Experience: Actor, dancer, director, banker's assistant, full-time minister, insurance analyst. A circuitous path to say the least. I thought back to the recitation classes I had taught in graduate school. I had students up on their feet, recreating history. I thought of the plays I'd written and directed. And the way I taught the youth at the church in New York City: through stories. I thought of my own children. Every night they wanted a new adventure told by me, not one from a book. All my life, I've relied on stories to lead, to teach, to entertain, and to create experiences for people. Experiences that I hoped they'd remember for a long time.

The elevator door opened. I took a deep breath. But it wasn't the interview I expected. You know, with the weird questions like "Tell us about a time when you failed miserably." Instead, they picked things from my resume that they appreciated. I found it easy to connect my varied education and experience with the skills they were looking for in a designer, though I'd never had an official talent development position ever in my life. I was surprised by their openness and curiosity about me and what I could bring to their program. But what surprised me the most came at the very end of the conversation. "We're looking for someone who can tell a good story for our training."

I smiled. "I can do that," I said.

These two managers opened up a door for me. Today, they know how grateful I am for giving me a shot.

Talent development benefits from the expertise of those who have spent their lives studying instructional design. But our industry needs people from diverse backgrounds too. Whether you are a seasoned instructional designer or you are coming to this industry from education or finance or the military, you have a unique story and special skills to offer the rest of us. I've given you mine in this book.

Use it as your guide and write a story they'll never forget.

Acknowledgments

Storytelling has been used to transfer knowledge and skills for time immemorial. As we face wave after wave of digital disruption in our industry, it's easy to forget the story behind what we're training people to do. But throughout talent development history, there have been advocates of storytelling who keep the human connection alive. As I've journeyed to create a methodology for making this connection more attainable, certain people have crossed my path and encouraged me to keep going. I'd like to thank some of them here.

Attendees of every Story Design workshop: Thank you for joining me on this journey. Your application of the principles and practices in this book convinced me that documenting Story Design for a larger audience was needed. You've paved the way for all the others who will implement Story Design in their own organizations.

The wonderful people at ATD Press: Jack Harlow, Eliza Blanchard, Hannah Sternberg, and Rose Richey, thank you for your support along the publishing path. I so appreciate each of your gifts.

Brian French, the producer for every online Story Design workshop and one of the most talented people I know. Amy Jones, my analysis hero, who has taught me so much about the importance and power of data.

Karl Kapp, thank you for all that you invest in the present and in the future of talent development, and for your generous spirit of support for this book. Julie Dirksen, thank you for your encouragement and for your advice on publishing. Kevin Thorn, thanks for raising the storytelling banner with me.

The organizational leaders, champions of storytelling, that I've had the honor to work with, including those whose training examples are in this book. Thank you for sharing your stories!

Jason Smith, Andraya Goodwin-Bhuyan, and Jacob Payne, who made Steve, Jasmine, and Andrew's stories come to life.

My parents, Dick and Prudy Greene, for supporting my insatiable drive for making stories and for participating in many of them!

Phineas and Leanora Greene, the number 1 fans of my stories. I love y'all!

Tricia Greene, for carefully reading every line (multiple times) and offering thoughtful—and always spot on—feedback. For your love. For your prayers. I could not have done this without you.

God, the creator of the greatest story ever told. Thank you for the inspiration and creativity to discover, design, and deliver!

Guides and Worksheets

The collection of guides and worksheets you've encountered and used throughout the book are compiled in this appendix for quick reference. You may also download them at needastory.com/book-resources. You can use the worksheets as a space to do iterative work and record the outcomes on the Instructional Story Design Plan in appendix 2.

Story Design Model

The Story Design Model is an easy way to remember what you are looking for as you discover, design, and deliver stories for training.

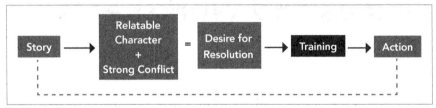

PRIMED for Learning

Use PRIMED for Learning to unearth the business outcome, the root problem, and the ideal solution. Record these on the Instructional Story Design Plan in appendix 2.

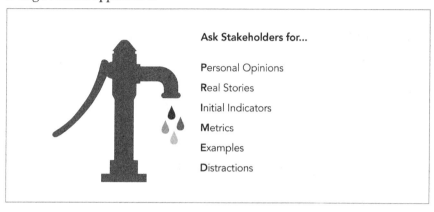

Ask Stakeholders for...

Personal Opinions

Real Stories

Initial Indicators

Metrics

Examples

Distractions

Audience Profile Questionnaire

The information you gather about your audience will provide valuable intelligence for creating relatable characters. Once you've gathered this information, record a summary on the Instructional Story Design Plan in appendix 2.

Personal Information

Look for interesting details that provide motivation for your characters.

What is their primary language?	
What is their education and background?	
What is their job or role?	
How long have they been with the company?	
What industry is the company in?	
How long have they been in this field of work?	
Where does the learner live?	
What types of music do they listen to?	
What types of games do they like to play?	
What types of movies do they like to see?	
What type of humor do they appreciate?	
What types of sports do they like?	
What forms of entertainment do they enjoy?	
What are the demographics of the company?	

What They Already Know

Look for opportunities to move the learner up the design continuum from definition to practice, using stories as examples to allow for self-discovery.

What is the learner's pre-existing knowledge of the material being presented?	

Values and Motivation

Look for drivers behind why characters do what they do.

What do they value most about their job?	
What do they value most in life?	
What motivates them at work?	
What do they do in their spare time?	
What will motivate them to take the training?	
What will motivate them to act on the training?	

Circumstances at Work and Reaction to Circumstances

Mirror circumstances in real life within your story. Look for emotional reactions that can accentuate strong conflict.

Describe their current circumstances at work.	
How are they currently reacting to circumstances at work?	
What challenges them most at work?	
Has anything happened recently in the organization that may make them feel vulnerable?	
Who or what has influence over them?	
Who do they have influence over?	
Will this training or message create a shift in power?	
How are they likely to respond to this training in light of their circumstances at work?	

Fears, Risk, Comfort Zone, and Commitment

Look for sources of internal or external conflict that may prevent learners from taking action on the training. Weave these sources of conflict within the story.

What might they misunderstand about the message?	
Why might they believe the change doesn't make sense for them or their organization?	

What would they sacrifice if they acted upon your idea or training?	
What is the perceived risk?	
What are the physical or emotional risks they will need to take?	
How will this stretch them?	
Who or what might they have to confront as a result of this training?	

What is their tolerance level for change?	
How far out of their comfort zone are you asking them to go?	
Are you asking them to unlearn something? What?	

Are they willing to commit time to take the training?	
Are they willing to commit to acting upon the training?	
What preconceptions do they have regarding the training?	

Benefits

As characters behave in conflict with the action list, look for opportunities to show the fallout (the ways they will miss out on the benefits listed here).

How will they personally benefit from the training and taking action? What's in it for them?	
How will training help their sphere of influence?	
How will the company benefit?	
How will the client benefit?	

Technology and Logistics

What is their experience with e-learning? Mobile learning? Gamification? Social media?	
Where will they take the training?	
Describe the environment where they will take this training.	
Will the learner be able to hear or play audio when taking the training?	
What types of mobile devices do they own?	

Action List Template

Use the reminders at the bottom of the template to structure the action list. Record your final action list in the Instructional Story Design Plan in appendix 2.

Main action	
Sub-action 1	
Sub-sub action A	
Sub-sub action B	
Sub-sub action C	
Sub-action 2	
Sub-sub action A	
Sub-sub action B	
Sub-sub action C	
Sub-action 3	
Sub-sub action A	
Sub-sub action B	
Sub-sub action C	
Sub-action 4	
Sub-sub action A	
Sub-sub action B	
Sub-sub action C	

Use Strong, Positive Action Verbs

- Write the actions as if you are speaking directly to the learner.
- Write observable actions.
- Avoid *avoid*. It's hard sometimes, but keep verbs focused on performance, rather than non-performance!
- Dig deeper when verbs like *understand* or *be aware* creep up. What actions should take place as a result of understanding or being aware?

Put Actions in a Logical Order

- If you are building an action list for a process, the main action should appear at the top and the steps to accomplish that action fall underneath it in a logical order from top to bottom. The same is true for sub-actions and sub-sub-actions.
- If you are building an action list for skills that are not a sequential process, you may choose to order it from easy to difficult, from familiar to not familiar, or from tasks that affect individuals to tasks that affect the entire department.
- As you share with your stakeholders, ask them to sign off on the action list to validate its completeness and accuracy. Since they already have a familiarity with outlines, it will be easier for them to review using this format.

Character Description Worksheet

Use the guideposts to compile the final character description, which you can record on the Instructional Story Design Plan in appendix 2.

Guidepost	Character description
Position At work, in life	
Conflict Which action are they in conflict with? What nouns and adjectives come to mind?	
Peers How does their personality contrast with other characters in the story?	
Appearance Physical attributes can be helpful in creating the story, even if the final portrayal isn't an exact match.	
Personal information Look to the audience profile for this information.	
Values Look to the audience profile for this information.	
Reaction to current circumstances Look to the audience profile for this information.	
Fears Look to the audience profile for this information.	
Backstory Details about their history that may affect the action of the story, true to audience profile.	
Name Read through the above description. What name comes to mind?	

Show the Action Worksheet

This worksheet will help with the completion of the next worksheet, Build the Story.

Identify the actions and the conflict for your story. Each of the characters for the story you are creating is in conflict with one or more of the actions from the action list. To begin thinking in terms of action and conflict, ask yourself these three questions and complete the worksheet.

1. Is the character doing realistic things?

First, imagine the character in conflict with their corresponding action. What are they doing in the scene? Describe some of the actions you might see them do.

Are these actions observable? Are they in keeping with the character description? Weed out any that don't fit these two requirements.

2. Is the action conflict?

Next, narrow the actions down to the ones that are in direct conflict with their corresponding action from the action list and write that action in the second column next to their name. Is the conflicting action directly related to the action from the action list?

Character name	Conflicting action	Why the character does this

3. Is the character motivated to do these actions?

Complete the table by writing some reasons in the last column of why the character might take the conflicting action. Consult their character descriptions and look for external and internal pressures that influence their decisions.

Build the Story Worksheet

After you've worked through each of the steps, record the final story on the Instructional Story Design Plan.

Story Premise

Write the story premise for each character and their corresponding action, using the story premise formula:

A story about [character name and position] who struggles to [an action from the action list].

Map the Plot With Core Actions

Answer the core action questions for the story.

Core questions	Core actions
Where are they in the story?	
What are they doing?	
What do they encounter that gives them an opportunity to do the action from the story premise?	
What do they do that's in conflict with that action?	

String the core actions together in a short paragraph to start the story.

Connect With the Character

From the Show the Action worksheet, integrate at least one motivation for the character into the story. Write your story below.

Refine the Verbs

Look back at your story and look closely at the verbs.

- Are they in present tense? If not, rewrite it in present tense.
- Do they need helping verbs? If so, they might be too weak.
- Could they be strengthened by using a synonym?

Rewrite the story using these three questions as your guide.

Escalate the Conflict With Dialogue

Look for opportunities to insert dialogue. Let us hear the character speak!

Make It Concrete

Go back to your character descriptions and Show the Action exercise. Are there attributes of your character that could be shown by adding detail?

- What small actions or information can reveal more about the characters?
- What meaningful props can the characters interact with to make the setting more real?

Rewrite the story using these questions as your guide.

Eliminate Adjectives and Adverbs

Rewrite the story eliminating adjectives and adverbs. If the story seems weaker, it's probably not because it's missing the adjectives and adverbs. It's most likely because the action is too weak to carry the story by itself. You need to strengthen the action. Also look for extraneous words and phrases to trim.

Let Your Audience Discover the Story Premise

Your stories should be action-packed now. Do another read-through and make sure you're not giving the story premise away. If you are, rewrite the story and give the audience room to discover the story themselves.

Assess Your Story

Ask yourself these questions. If you (and the stakeholder) can answer yes to all four, your story is done! Record the final version in the Instructional Story Design Plan.

- Do I know these characters?
- Do I feel for them?
- Can I see the story unfolding in my mind?
- Do I want resolution?

Storyboard Template

On the Instructional Story Design Plan, work through which story form is most suitable, given your audience and the development tools at your disposal. If the story form involves visual or audio components, use a storyboard template to record those elements. Break up the story into scenes by row and imagine the story unfolding. Record what you see and hear in the storyboard.

Audio (Music and sound effects)	Visual (Appears on the screen)	Dialogue and narration (Story broken into scenes per row)

Story–Reflection–Solving–Feedback Worksheet for Training

Use this worksheet like a design document for instruction.

Story

You've developed your story. What actions from the action list are you training on?

Reflection

Give your audience a chance to reflect on the story. Design a reflection question that allows them to relive the story in their minds and feel what the characters were feeling. Your reflection question can be similar to one of these questions:

- How would you feel if ...?
- Why do you think ...?
- What did you observe ...?

Write some possible reflection questions below.

Solving

You've presented the problem through story. Now, give the learner an opportunity to solve it. Write a few solving questions and possible options that lead the learner toward practice on the design continuum.

Feedback

Look at your possible questions above. What kind of feedback will you offer for each of the options you've provided? Remember, feedback affirms the learner's action or redirects it.

Instructional Story Design Plan

The Instructional Story Design Plan collects the information you've unearthed from using the worksheets in appendix 1. Editable versions of these worksheets and this plan are also available at needastory.com/book-resources.

Goal of Training

Use the PRIMED for Learning questions in appendix 1 to unearth the business outcome, the root problem, and the ideal solution. Record your answers below.

Business outcome (measurable)	
Root problem (changeable)	
Training solution (knowledge, skills, or attitude)	

Use the answers you recorded above to write the goal for this training, like this:

Eliminate the root problem + to achieve the business outcome
+ by implementing the training solution

Write your goal for training in the space below.

Audience Profile Summary

Use the Audience Profile Questionnaire in appendix 1 and summarize based on the following categories.

Personal information	
What they already know	
Values and motivation	
Circumstances at work and reactions to circumstances	
Fears	
Benefits	
Technology and logistics	

Action List

Record the final action list below. See appendix 1 for the Action List Template tips.

Main action	
Sub-action 1	
Sub-sub action A	
Sub-sub action B	
Sub-sub action C	
Sub-action 2	
Sub-sub action A	
Sub-sub action B	
Sub-sub action C	

Sub-action 3	
Sub-sub action A	
Sub-sub action B	
Sub-sub action C	
Sub-action 4	
Sub-sub action A	
Sub-sub action B	
Sub-sub action C	

Character Descriptions

Compile the character attributes from the Character Description Worksheet in appendix 1 and write a summary description of each character.

Character name	Character description

Write Your Story

Use the Show the Action and the Build the Story worksheets to formulate your story. Record the final version below.

Produce Your Story

Choose a story form that is most appropriate for your audience.

SIMPLE ←				→ COMPLEX
Spoken	**Written**	**Static Visuals**	**Audio**	**Video**
Role-play				
		Wordless comics/photos		
	Choose your own adventure	Choose your own adventure	Choose your own adventure	Choose your own adventure
Live presentation supported by slides or drawings		Live presentation supported by slides or drawings		
	Comic strip	Comic strip		
	Graphics/ photos paired with text	Graphics/ photos paired with text		
		Graphics/ photos paired with audio	Graphics/ photos paired with audio	
			Radio drama	
	Interactive PDF	Interactive PDF		
			Animated video	Animated video

What development tools and applications are at your disposal to produce the story?

Audio equipment	
Audio editing	
Video equipment	
Video editing	
Animation tools	
Camera	
Graphics creation tools	
E-Learning authoring tools	
Webinar applications	
Live presentation tools	

If the final product of your story includes audio and visuals, use the Storyboard Template in appendix 1 to plan for development. Then use the Story-Reflection-Solving-Feedback worksheet as a design document for training.

APPENDIX 3
Completed Instructional Story Design Plan

Throughout the book, you've put Story Design principles into practice, developing a story for the staff at Well Adjusted Chiropractic. I've completed this plan as one example of how the assignment could be fulfilled. Many of the answers to the questions in the plan have come from participants in Story Design workshops over the years. Your plan is just as valid, and your story can be just as strong if you've followed the steps outlined in each chapter.

Goal of Training

Use the PRIMED for Learning questions in appendix 1 to unearth the business outcome, the root problem, and the ideal solution. Record your answers below.

Business outcome (measurable)	Increase loyalty of client base; decrease turnover of staff and doctors.
Root problem (changeable)	Trust, internally and among clients, has deteriorated as a result of poor communication among the staff and with clients.
Training solution (knowledge, skills, or attitude)	Staff members master open communication between peers and clients.

Use the answers you recorded above to write the goal for this training, like this:

Eliminate the root problem + to achieve the business outcome

+ by implementing the training solution

Write your goal for training in the space below.

Build trust among peers and client base to increase loyalty of client base and decrease turnover of staff and doctors as staff members master open communication between their peers and clients.

Audience Profile Summary

Use the Audience Profile Questionnaire in appendix 1 and summarize based on the following categories.

Personal information	*Front desk and therapy bay are young. Shop, go to movies, spend time with their kids, go to the gym.*
What they already know	*The entire office seems to have little awareness of how their lack of communication affects others in the office.*
Values and motivation	*Productivity; some value customer service.*
Circumstances at work and reactions to circumstances	*Productivity is suffering, clients are not returning, very high turnover, constantly training new people, overwhelmed by paperwork from regulations. Generally, they are cordial to one another, but sometimes are oblivious to clients, trying to get them through the system as quickly as possible. Frustrated with inefficient processes, buckling down to complete paperwork.*
Fears	*That they will lose too many clients.*
Benefits	*Mutual respect. Clarity on expectations. Engaged with one another and with the business.*
Technology and logistics	*Seems to be an in-person opportunity for training rather than e-learning. Do they have a projector? How will the story or training be delivered?*

Action List

Record the final action list below. See appendix 1 for the Action List Template tips.

Build strong client trust.
Promote open communication between staff members.
Inform staff members in other areas of important information concerning clients.
Respect other staff members as you want to be respected in the presence of clients.
Focus conversation around the client, not personal issues.
Protect the client's privacy in the presence of other clients.

Character Descriptions

Compile the character attributes from the Character Description Worksheet in appendix 1 and write a summary description of each character.

Character name	Character description
Dr. Leona Strate	A doctor in a chiropractic clinic. Meticulous, human bulldozer, hair always tied up in a bun, ironed white lab coat, pristine appearance, values quality work and timeliness, just trying to get clients through the system at the clinic, expects staff to follow strict protocol, Ivy Leaguer, enjoys shopping with her daughter.
Julius Trumble	A therapist in a chiropractic clinic. Easy-going athlete, helpful, in-shape, wide smile, disheveled hair, values relationships, frustrated with inefficient processes that keep him from focusing on the client, adjusts therapy to the client's needs without consulting with doctors, works out three times a week and goes to the movies with his girlfriend every Friday, employed at the clinic for five years.

Write Your Story

Use the Show the Action and the Build the Story worksheets to formulate your story. Record the final version below.

| Story 1 | Julius gives his physical therapy patient, Ms. Coney, a high five and congratulates her on finishing her third level of the physical rehab program. Her progress after the car accident is slow but steady. Ms. Coney thanks Julius for modifying the original program Dr. Strate prescribed and leaves. Julius smiles and reviews Dr. Strate's recommended program on Ms. Coney's chart. "Yeah, she definitely needs a slower pace than this," he says to himself. He looks at the stack of paperwork he has left over from yesterday. He sighs and tosses Ms. Coney's chart into the out box. He has two more patients waiting for him. Later, Millie, from the front desk, picks up Ms. Coney's chart. She asks Julius if there are any changes to her treatment. Julius looks over his shoulder, "Nope, it's ready to go!" |

Story 2	Dr. Strate storms into the therapy bay. "Where's Julius?" she mutters under her breath. She sees him, takes a deep breath, and walks over to him.
	Julius is helping a patient with shoulder exercises on a floor mat. He looks up. "Oh, hi, Dr. Strate! How are you?"
	Dr. Strate steps between Julius and his patient and thrusts a file in his face. "You changed this client's prescribed rehabilitation plan without telling me," she says flatly.
	Julius looks at Dr. Strate, then glances at the patient. "Uh . . . can we discuss this later?"
	Dr. Strate's eyes narrow. "We can discuss your qualifications as a therapist in this clinic. You can't even follow simple instructions!"
	"I can explain about Ms. Coney, but I don't think this is the best place to . . . "
	She interrupts him. "What do you think you're doing to my patients, Julius? I expect precise therapy for them, but obviously you aren't interested in that!"

Produce Your Story

I've produced these stories in several ways for Story Design workshops over the years. Some simple, some complex. Visit needastory.com/book-resources to view Dayna's fully produced Steve and Jasmine/Andrew stories. These techniques can be used for your stories for training too!

Note that these two stories could be told in sequence, stopping in between to provide time for reflection, solving, and feedback. Julius's actions in the first story impact Dr. Strate's actions in the second story.

References

Dirksen, J. 2011. *Design For How People Learn*. Indianapolis: New Riders.

Duarte, N. 2010. *Resonate*. Hoboken, NJ: Wiley.

Haidt, J. 2006. *The Happiness Hypothesis*. New York: Basic Books.

Heath, C., and D. Heath. 2007. *Made to Stick*. New York: Penguin Random House.

Kapp, K. 2012. *The Gamification of Learning and Instruction*. Hoboken, NJ: Wiley.

Kapp, K., and S. Boller. 2017. *Play to Learn*. Alexandria, VA: ATD Press.

Moore, C. 2017. *Map It*. Montesa Press.

Zak, P. 2014. "Why Your Brain Loves Good Storytelling." *Harvard Business Review*, October 28.

Index

Page numbers followed by *f* refer to figures.

storyboards as, 171–178, 172f–183f, 179-180, 183, 185
text-only stories, 188–190, 189f–190f
video, 197–199, 197f, 199f
your voice, 168–169
training
for attitude, 37
goal of, 8, 31–33
training with stories, 201–217
and feedback, 211–214, 211f–215f, 217
and reflection, 206, 206f–207f, 207, 215–216
and solving, 207–210, 208f, 209f, 216–217
in Story Design Model, 205, 205f

U

underscoring, with music, 195
untouchable audience, 61
USB mics, 192

V

values
in Audience Profile Questionnaire, 281
of your audience, 54–55
of your characters, 96–97
verbs, building the story with, 144–146, 160, 284, 289
video
animated, 197, 197f
using, 198–199, 199f
virtual orientation case study (service industry corporation), 237–239
virtual reality (VR), 268–269
visuals, building the story with, 178f–179f
voice, using your, 168–169

W

"Why Your Brain Loves Good Storytelling" (Zak), 247
winning over stakeholders, 243–258
by appealing to their emotions, 248–249
by appealing to their intellect, 247–248
by involving them in creating the story, 249–251
by setting a realistic pace, 257–258
by sharing feedback, 254, 255f, 256–257
by starting slow and steady, 251–253, 252f–253f
by using metrics, 254, 255f, 256–257
who think stories are "fluff," 245–247
words, building the story by eliminating extraneous, 153–155, 161
work circumstances

of your audience, 55–56
of your characters, 97, 97f–98f, 98
worksheets
Build the Story Worksheet, 288-290, 297–299, 303–304
Character Description Worksheet, 105, 105f, 106, 116f, 286, 297, 303
Show the Action Worksheet, 123, 124, 124f, 287, 297–299, 303–304
Story–Reflection–Solving–Feedback worksheet, 214, 215f, 292–293
Story Worksheet, 157, 157f

Z

Zak, Paul J., 247–248

About the Author

Photo Credit: Jonathan Crawford

Rance Greene consults companies who need business solutions that harness the power of stories to connect with people emotionally and equip them for action. He designs stories to communicate value propositions, manage change, and teach new skills. His training solutions have been recognized by ATD, The eLearning Guild, *Training* magazine, and the Telly Awards. Follow Rance at needastory.com or connect with him on LinkedIn to stay in touch with the latest on Story Design. He'd love to hear how you've used the principles in this book to connect with your audience and achieve greater business outcomes.